The Parasite

MICHEL SERRES is professor of the history of science at Paris I Sorbonne. He is the author of Hermes: Literature, Science, Philosophy, *also from Johns Hopkins.*

LAWRENCE R. SCHEHR teaches French at the University of South Alabama.

The Parasite

Michel Serres

Translated, with notes, by
Lawrence R. Schehr

THE JOHNS HOPKINS UNIVERSITY PRESS
Baltimore and London

The Johns Hopkins University Press, Baltimore, Maryland 21218
The Johns Hopkins Press Ltd., London

Library of Congress Cataloging in Publication Data

Serres, Michel.
    The parasite.

    Translation of: Le parasite.
    I. Schehr, Lawrence R.   II. Title
PQ2679.E679P313   7848'.91407   81–19277
ISBN 0–8018–2456–7   AACR2

Contents

Translator's Preface

Michel Serres, the polymath, presents his translator with an extremely arduous task. A difficult style, multilingual puns, a wealth of knowledge and references—all combine to make the text not at all easy to elucidate.

Two words merit brief mention in this preface. The first is the title, *parasite*. In French, the word has three meanings: a biological parasite, a social parasite, and static. The English *parasite* corresponds only to the first two meanings in French. Thus the reader should always be aware of this additional resonance in the French that is not translatable into English. The second word is *hôte,* which corresponds to both *host* and *guest* in English. I have used *guest* and *host* in English where one of the two meanings was implied more than the other, but the other word is always implicitly present. At times, I have used the two together to reinforce the double meaning.

I should like to thank Michel Serres for his help with certain passages.

Translator's Introduction

Verne, Leibniz, Carpaccio, Musil, Lucretius, Turner, and now La Fontaine: a heterogeneous list united only by the fact that they have all been objects of Michel Serres's acute observations. Fueled by his varied background, his capacious knowledge of many disciplines, and his perceptive insights, these studies, along with many others, have been widely greeted as seminal, if not to say revolutionary, works. A selection of his earlier works has recently been translated and published as Michel Serres, *Hermes: Literature, Science, Philosophy,* edited by Josué V. Harari and David F. Bell (Baltimore: The Johns Hopkins University Press, 1981). Most of these essays deal with communication in a general sense: with the translation or interference (inter-reference) of two seemingly distinct fields. Serres analyzes the fundamental systems at work in a text as well as how these systems are analogous to those of another text from a different discipline: Turner and Carnot, or Zola and the theory of thermodynamics. For Serres, the human sciences, notably literature, painting, and philosophy, are not as far removed from the hard sciences, especially physics and mathematics, as the practitioners in one or the other of these disciplines might believe.

With the publication of *Hermès IV: La Distribution* and *La Naissance de la physique dans le texte de Lucrèce* in 1977, Serres enters a new and more radical phase in his work. Radical: the root, the beginning, the origin; radical: the revolutionary. In *La Distribution* he begins to ask questions and give answers about origins and roots—of language, of time, and of space. *La Naissance de la physique* is ostensibly a text on the beginning of atomist theory in Lucretius's *De natura rerum*. Serres shows modern science, that is to say, physics and its theories, to be older than had been thought; its roots are not in the Renaissance but in Rome. But in one long text in this book on Lucretius, in a chapter entitled "Violence et contrat" (included in the collection of translated essays), Serres goes even further back in his speculations and investigations. He begins to examine the threshold of culture, its origin, inception, root, and direction. It is an origin grounded in violence and polarization, in inclusion and exclusion. And this chapter is also a first sketch for Serres of his theory of human relations, a theory that takes shape in this book, *The Parasite*.

The Parasite starts with an author, as do many of Serres's other works; in this case it is Jean de La Fontaine, the author of the *Fables*. Serres develops his theory of human relations, the theory of the parasite—be it noise, guest, leech, or all three—with the support of a series of texts including La Fontaine, Rousseau, Molière, and the Acts of the Apostles. For Serres, the parasite is the primordial, one-way, and irreversible relation that is the base of human institutions and disciplines: society, economy, and work; human sciences and hard sciences; religion and history. All of these have the parasitic relation as their basic and fundamental component. Serres demonstrates this for each with equal facility and equal virtuosity, speaking the language of each of these fields and in the many-tongued, pentecostal language that for him is capable of discussing all these disciplines and institutions: the language of philosophy.

The parasite is a microbe, an insidious infection that takes without giving and weakens without killing. The parasite is also a guest, who exchanges his talk, praise, and flattery for food. The parasite is noise as well, the static in a system or the interference in a channel. These seemingly dissimilar activities are, according to Michel Serres, not merely coincidentally expressed by the same word (in French). Rather, they are intrinsically related and, in fact, they have the same basic function in a system. Whether it produces a fever or just hot air, the parasite is a thermal exciter. And as such, it is both the atom of a relation and the production of a change in this relation. Through a careful and cogent analysis of these various threads, Michel Serres produces an elegant theory of human relations and institutions, all of which have the same common factor: the parasite.

Part One

Interrupted Meals

Logics

Rats' Meals ———————————————————

————————————————— Cascades

The city rat invites the country rat onto the Persian rug. They gnaw and chew leftover bits of ortolan. Scraps, bits and pieces, leftovers: their royal feast is only a meal after a meal among the dirty dishes of a table that has not been cleared. The city rat has produced nothing and his dinner invitation costs him almost nothing. Boursault says this in his *Fables d'Esope,* where the city rat lives in the house of a big tax farmer. Oil, butter, ham, bacon, cheese—everything is available. It is easy to invite the country cousin and to regale oneself at the expense of another.

The tax farmer produced neither oil nor ham nor cheese; in fact, he produced nothing. But using power or the law, he can profit from these products. Likewise for the city rat who takes the farmer's leftovers. And the last to profit is the country rat. But we know that the feast is cut short. The two companions scurry off when they hear a noise at the door. It was only a noise, but it was also a message, a bit of information producing panic: an interruption, a corruption, a rupture of information. Was the noise really a message? Wasn't it, rather, static, a parasite? A parasite who has the last word, who produces disorder and who generates a different order. Let's go to the country where we eat only soup, but quietly and without interruption.

The tax farmer is a parasite, living off the fat of the land: a royal feast, ortolans, Persian rugs. The first rat is a parasite; for him, leftovers, the same Persian rug. Nothing is missing, says La Fontaine. At the table of the first, the table of the farmer, the second rat is a parasite. He permits himself to be entertained in such a fashion, never missing a bite. But strictly speaking, they all interrupt: the custom house officer makes

3

life hard for the working man, the rat taxes the farmer, the guest exploits his host. But I can no longer write; the noise, the ultimate parasite, through its interruption, wins the game. In the parasitic chain, the last to come tries to supplant his predecessor. The noise chases the country rat; the city rat remains, for he wants to finish the roast. A given parasite seeks to eject the parasite on the level immediately superior to his own. The following shows the cascade, which collapses when $P_1 = P_4$.

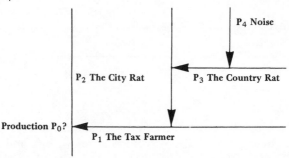

I leave it to you to think about this loud noise: the sounds of the street which would make the tax farmer give in; the creaking of the floor-boards, the cracking of the beams, which would chase the rats from the building.

Let's draw up the balance. In the beginning is production: the oil crusher, the butter churn, the smokehouse, the cheesemaker's hut. Yet I would still like to know what *produce* means. Those who call production reproduction make the job easy. Our world is full of copiers and repeaters, all highly rewarded with money and glory. It is better to interpret than to compose; it is better to have an opinion on a decision that has already been made than to make one's own. The modern illness is the engulfing of the new in the *duplicata,* the engulfing of intelligence in the pleasure [*jouissance*] of the homogeneous. Real production is undoubtedly rare, for it attracts parasites that immediately make it something common and banal. Real production is unexpected and improbable; it overflows with information and is always immediately parasited.

It attracts the farmer, whom I catch in the act of stealing (away). If he is a peasant, he raises cows and calves, pigs and poultry, living on butter and ham, eating at a table furnished with other foodstuffs; sometimes he sleeps in the barn, in the manure, among the livestock; he does not destroy nonrenewable resources, like a vulgar industrialist, but lives off the newborn. Industry pillages and plunders. Such a farmer is part of a matrix. Is he a parasite? If he is a tax-collector (an interrupter), he takes part of the products of others for his own profit or for the profit of the state to whom he respectfully defers. He is a veritable impostor.* His table abounds with cheeses, ham, bacon, butter, all produced by the first farmer. The situation repeats itself throughout history, for history has never lacked for political parasites. History is full of them, or maybe is made solely of them. Dinner is served among the parasites.

The rats are attracted to the table. One invites the other. It wouldn't occur to Bertrand or to Raton to eat, quite simply, something like chestnuts. They march Indian file, the monkey behind the cat, the country bumpkin behind the city slicker. Hence, the chain of my decisions, unitary in nature. The guest, though a rat, is a parasite for anthropology, a guest at an interrupted banquet, like that of Don Juan's Stone Guest, like the Last Supper.† The parasite of a meal, the parasite of satire and comedy, of Molière, Plautus, and Xenophon, of the history of religion. The host is not a parasite in this sense, but in order to live in the house of the tax farmer, within his walls, in his larder, he is a parasite in the biological sense, like a common louse, a tapeworm, like mistletoe, an epiphyte. I am broadening the matter; I shall come back to it. If the "guest" is a tax-collector, in the broadest sense, I consider him to be a parasite in the political sense, in that a human group is organized with one-way relations, where one eats the other and where the second cannot benefit at all from the first. The exchange is neither principal nor original nor fundamental; I do not know how to put it: the relation denoted by a single arrow is irreversible, just takes its place in the world. Man is a louse for other men. Thus man is a host for other men. The flow goes one way, never the other. I call this semiconduction, this valve, this single arrow, this relation without a reversal of direction, "parasitic." If the "guest" is a farmer, I consider him to be a parasite in the economic sense. La Fontaine explains this to me further on. What does man give to the cow, to the tree, to the steer, who give him milk, warmth, shelter, work, and food? What does he give? Death.

The system constructed here beginning with a production, temporarily placed in a black box, is parasitic in a cascade. But the cascade orders knowledge itself, of man and of life, making us change our terminology without changing the subject. It is an interesting circuit which we shall follow in order to understand one thing, various

---

*The word *imposteur* means both "tax-collector" and "impostor."—Trans.
†See *Le Festin et la Cène,* forthcoming.

landscapes, several epistemologies. Maybe polyphony is in order. I call
the language of many portals "philosophical."

But that's not all. You need the peasant's moral at the end of
the fable—the first member of the chain must be excluded. He will
never come back to the glorious sites of the feasts of the bourgeois and
rich farmer, this spot of terror and irreversible exploitation. He will not
or he cannot, it all depends. He does not feel at ease when he is anxious.
He leaves to go back to the flat countryside, to the peace of the fields,
to meet Horace, who is waiting for him. But who expels him? Noise.
One parasite chases another out. One parasite (static), in the sense that
information theory uses the word, chases another, in the anthropological
sense. Communication theory is in charge of the system; it can break it
down or let it function, depending on the signal. A parasite, physical,
acoustic, informational, belonging to order and disorder, a new voice,
an important one, in the contrapuntal matrix.

Let us stop for a moment. I am using words in an unusual way.
For the science called parasitology, a rat, a carrion-eater like the hyena,
a man, be he peasant or high official, are not parasites at all. They are,
quite simply, predàtors. The relation with a host presupposes a perma-
nent or semipermanent contact with him; such is the case for the louse,
the tapeworm, the *pasturella pestis*. Not only living *on* but also living
in—by him, with him, and in him. And thus a parasite cannot be large.
Parasitism pertains only to invertebrates, coming to an end with
mollusks, insects, and arthropods. There are no parasitic mammals. Not
the rat, not the hyena, not even the administrator.

Here's the answer. The basic vocabulary of this science comes
from such ancient and common customs and habits that the earliest
monuments of our culture tell of them, and we still see them, at least in
part: hospitality, conviviality, table manners, hostelry, general relations
with strangers. Thus the vocabulary is imported to this pure science and
bears several traces of anthropomorphism. The animal-host offers a meal
from the larder or from his own flesh; as a hotel or a hostel, he provides
a place to sleep, quite graciously, of course.

These customs and manners can be the object of anthropological
study; they were once the pleasures of idle reading, when literature still
existed. Literature made clear, even for the blind, a kind of figural,
instructive anthropology that was both accessible and profound, but
without theory, without awkward weight, not boring but intelligent.
Why do we have to pay nowadays with lead for what we used to get
from a quill pen? This way of obtaining knowledge was an enchanting
one. May our own science get to that point beyond the death instinct.

Horace or La Fontaine thus have two rats as companions, not a louse and a tapeworm—no worms in intestines for them. The importation does not have the same goal but nevertheless has the same meaning: it goes from man to animal but does not touch the same little bugs. The fable's anthropomorphism is the same as that of science; just the phyla are different.

Two arrows leave a common origin and arrive at different points. I am simply closing the triangle.

To parasite means to eat next to. Let us begin with this literal meaning. The country rat is invited by his colleague from town, who offers him supper. One would think that what is essential is their relation of resemblance or difference. But that is not enough; it never was. The relation of the guest is no longer simple. Giving or receiving, on the rug or on the tablecloth, goes through a black box. I don't know what happens in there, but it functions like an automatic corrector. There is no exchange, nor will there be one. Abuse appears before use. Gifted in some fashion, the one eating next to, soon eating at the expense of, always eats the same thing, the host, and this eternal host gives over and over, constantly, till he breaks, even till death, drugged, enchanted, fascinated. The host is not a prey, for he offers and continues to give. Not a prey, but the host. The other one is not a predator but a parasite. Would you say that the mother's breast is the child's prey? It is more or less the child's home. But this relation is of the simplest sort; there is none simpler or easier: it always goes in the same direction. The same one is the host; the same one takes and eats; there is no change of direction. This is true of all beings. Of lice and men.

I'll close the triangle, agreeing with science rather than with the fable. The intuition of the parasitologist makes him import a common relation of social manners to the habits of little animals, a relation so clear and distinct that we recognize it as being the simplest. Let's retrace our steps for a moment, going from these habits back to those manners, reversing anthropomorphism. We have made the louse in our image; let us see ourselves in his.

The intuition of the poet of the fable of the rats, and that of the philosopher who wrote of the eagle and the lamb, makes them import a very common relation in the realm of mammals and of the vertebrates in general, the relation of the hunt and of predatory behavior to human habits and customs. Man is a wolf for men, an eagle for sheep, a rat for rats. In truth, a *rara avis*. I've seen few men with the bravery of the rat, the courage of the wolf, the nobility of the eagle. I speak in figures to those who speak in figures; we know not what we say. We are in a labyrinth of images; we'll never get rid of these illusions. Let us leave the theater of representations, which can only become serious in the tragic instance of the unspeakable horror of metamorphosis of becoming a rat. Let's return to our writers. Quite curiously, the manners of this wolf, fox, lion, monkey, cat, or rat are never, or seldom, those of predators; in these stories, they are almost always those of parasites. In the guise of an attack, a theft, a power-play, in the person of these animals, the simple relation of the abusive companion reappears. Beneath the apologist, the parasitologist. Quite simply, what is essential is neither the image nor the deep meaning, neither the representation nor its hall of mirrored reflections, but the system of relations. The relation is that of guest to host [*hôte à hôte*]. Copying the relation of man to man brings us back to parasitism. Thus the writer agrees with the scientist and agrees with the intuition that makes the book enchanting. Of course, we may speak of rats, snakes, or hares and none of them can be assimilated to the louse or the tapeworm, and yet, what is in question will be nothing but the *Parasitic*.

The triangle is closed. At each of its points, through story or science, social science or biological science, just one relation appears, the simple, irreversible arrow.

One could draw up a list of attacks on human narcissism. That the center of the world be removed from the earth to the sun is an objective attack. That the Copernican revolution be interiorized in the mind, the clear or not so clear soul, work and economy, is a triple subjective attack. Our main object is decentered; the subject is decentered in turn, three times. Philosophy is still caught in the relation between subject and object.

The parasitic relation is intersubjective. It is the atomic form of our relations. Let us try to face it head-on, like death, like the sun. We are all attacked, together.

What is this sudden dangerous noise at the door that prevents me from finishing and leads me to other actions?

I must put three things together: habits or customs, animals, noises. At first glance, they are unrelated. Yet I am not putting them together haphazardly. I am forced to do so by my tongue: Latin, Greek, Roman. In this somewhat fuzzy spot, a parasite is an abusive guest, an unavoidable animal, a break in a message. In English this constellation does not exist: a break in a message is called static, from a different semantic field. And there are of course some groups, now dominant, for whom table conversation is not at all a means of living, is not an art at all, and in fact for whom such an art has no reference at all.

My linguistic reason is not sufficient: a semantic field is not a concept but a fuzzy set, a playing field for what amounts to, sometimes, only a play on words. Meaning, inevitably; play, obviously. A stronger reason is the tradition it belongs to. How can it be that such a simple and common fable associates, for these rats, table manners, a figuration of animality (though a predatory one), and static? Parasitism is never mentioned, but it is really a question *only* of that. This constellation is a constant one. We shall see this everywhere, from fable to history, from comedy to philosophy, from the imaginary to the scientific. Wily Odysseus leaves the cave of Polyphemus by hanging onto the belly of the ram, like some inhabitant of its unshorn wool; he dines with Alcinous, paying for his meal with his edifying stories; he frees himself from the song of the Sirens; he eliminates from his house the "pretenders," who themselves act like parasites. One of our first texts could have for its title, since it already has as its subject, our title and subject. Maybe I will write an odyssey too. Moreover, how many others wrote one despite themselves, or even hoping to do so? We'll soon see the impressive list, an unfinished one to be sure. What started out looking like a play on words is now compact and coherent. Here is a colossal tributary of our own history; we will soon be astonished that it had not been recognized earlier.

The word and the history are only paper. But the experience, especially the experience of suffering. Open your eyes and ears, open your door, open the leaves of your table, open your heart, open your homes, your arms. Open what philosophers most often seek to close. Everything but the mouth. Give what they hold back. So? So: the noise for your ears, stereotyped behavior for your eyes, the crowd who eat the last scraps from your table. The noise of their chewing produces a a noise in the organized cloud of those whom I can only call parasites.

My friend, the parasitologist, at the door, insists again. We never live in the animals we eat, he says. Indeed.

His objection, it seems to me, is the following: every parasitic animal lives, eats, and multiplies within the body of its host. Men, whom I call parasites, are never, as far as we know, inside another animal. Except the great beast, the 666, the Leviathan. Back to beasts of prey, back to hunting, and so forth.

First of all, hunting is not an answer. I have never found a group of men who did not go through with their action to the bitter end. The depopulation of the prey is immediate, brutal, explosive. I am willing to admit that we began with hunting, but this first stage, like the first seconds of the universe, was so short, so limited, that it is not worth the trouble of talking about it. From the dawn of time, there are no more prey.

Our relation to animals is more interesting—I mean to the animals we eat. We adore eating veal, lamb, beef, antelope, pheasant, or grouse, but we don't throw away their "leftovers." We dress in leather and adorn ourselves with feathers. Like the Chinese, we devour duck without wasting a bit; we eat the whole pig, from head to tail; but we get under these animals' skins as well, in their plumage or in their hide. Men in clothing live within the animals they devoured. And the same thing for plants. We eat rice, wheat, apples, the divine eggplant, the tender dandelion; but we also weave silk, linen, cotton; we live within the flora as much as we live within the fauna. We are parasites; thus we clothe ourselves. Thus we live within tents of skins like the gods within their tabernacles. Look at him well-dressed and adorned, magnificent; he shows—he showed—the clean carcass of his host. Of the soft parasite you can see only the clean-shaven face and the hands, sometimes without their kid gloves.

We parasite each other and live amidst parasites. Which is more or less a way of saying that they constitute our environment. We live in that black box called the collective; we live by it, on it, and in it. It so happens that this collective was given the form of an animal: Leviathan. We are certainly within something bestial; in more distinguished terms, we are speaking of an organic model for the members of a society. Our host? I don't know. But I do know that we are within. And that it is dark in there.

Hosts and parasites. We live, in the city or in the country, in the space of the two rats. Their fabulous feast is this book. A book that is oral and aural, about famine and murders, about knowledge and bondage. Both in the fable and in this book, it is a question of physics, of certain exact sciences, of certain techniques of telecommunications, a question of biophysics and of certain life sciences, of parasitology, a question of culture and of anthropology, of religions and literatures, a question of politics, of economics. I am not sure of the order in which these distinctions appear. But La Fontaine must have made them, just like Aesop, Horace, and Boursault. In another language, but what does it matter?

Stations and paths together form a system. Points and lines, beings and relations. What is interesting might be the construction of the system, the number and disposition of stations and paths. Or it might be the flow of messages passing through the lines. In other words, a complex system can be formally described (that of Leibniz, for example) and then a system in general. Or, one might have understood what is carried within the system, naming the carrier Hermes. One might have sought the formation and distribution of the lines, paths, and stations, their borders, edges, and forms. But one must write as well of the interceptions, of the accidents in the flow along the way between stations—of changes and metamorphoses. What passes might be a message but parasites (static) prevent it from being heard, and sometimes, from being sent. Like a hole in a canal that makes the water spill into the surrounding area. There are escapes and losses, obstacles and opacities. Doors and windows close; Hermes might faint or die among us. An angel passes.* Who stole the relation? Maybe someone, somewhere in the middle, made a detour. Does a third man exist? It is not only a question of the logicial. What travels along the path might be money, gold, or commodities, or even food—in short, material goods. You don't need much experience to know that goods do not always arrive so easily at their destination. There are always intercepters who work very hard to divert what is carried along these paths. Parasitism is the name most often given to these numerous and diverse activities, and I fear that they are the most common thing in the world.

One has to speak of Prometheus from the bird's-eye view—that of the eagle. Prometheus is one and the same as this greedy creature who finally, at the end of an evolutionary process, made its nest within the thoracic cavity of the producer in chains, now devoured.

Saying that this system includes the telephone, the telegraph, television, the highway system, maritime pathways and shipping lanes, the orbits of satellites, the circulation of messages and of raw materials, of language and foodstuffs, money and philosophical theory, is a way of speaking clearly and calmly. And looking to see who or what intercepts these different flows is also a way of speaking clearly and calmly. It is a complicated way of speaking, but it is really an easy way. I shall answer the question, for it can be answered.

And if the system in question were the collective as such? What relations do we really have with each other? How do we live together? What really is this system which collapses at the slightest noise? Who or what makes this noise? Who or what prevents me from hearing whom, from eating with whom, from sleeping with whom? How can I love,

*"Un ange passe" is said of a sudden silence during a conversation. —Trans.

whom should I love? Whom could I love and who will love me? Who forbids love?

Is this noise both the collective and the sound coming from the black box?

Look again at the diagram based on the story of the rats, paying attention to the succession of parasites in stepladder formation, and ask yourself if it is something added to a system, like a cancer of interceptions, flights, losses, holes, trapdoors—if it is a pathological growth in some spot or if it is quite simply the system itself. The rats climb onto the rug when the guests are not looking, when the lights are out, when the party's over. It's nighttime, black. What happens would be the obscure opposite of conscious and clear organization, happening behind everyone's back, the dark side of the system. But what do we call these nocturnal processes? Are they destructive or constructive? What happens at night on the rug covered with crumbs? Is it a still active trace of (an) origin? Or is it only a remainder of failed suppressions? We can, undoubtedly, decide the matter: the battle against rats is already lost; there is no house, ship, or palace that does not have its share. There is no system without parasites. This constant is a law. But how so?

Someone once compared the undertaking of Descartes to the action of a man who sets his house on fire in order to hear the noise the rats make in the attic at night. These noises of running, scurrying, chewing, and gnawing that interrupt his sleep. I want to sleep peacefully. Good-bye then. To hell with the building that the rats come to ruin. I want to think without an error, communicate without a parasite. So I set the house on fire, the house of my ancestors. Done correctly, I rebuild it without a rat. But in order to do that, as a mason I must work without sleeping, without turning my back, without leaving for a moment, without eating. But at night, the rats return to the foundation. I was thinking yesterday, What did you do in the meantime? You slept, if you please, you ate, dreamt, made love, and so forth. Well, the rats came back. They are, as the saying goes, always already there. Part of the building. Mistakes, wavy lines, confusion, obscurity are part of knowledge; noise is part of communication, part of the house. But is it the house itself?

A system is often described as a harmony. Maybe it's the same word, the same thing. In fact, what use is it to discuss matters, what use is it to be concerned with a system in disequilibrium, a system that does not function right? Yet we know of no system that functions perfectly, that is to say, without losses, flights, wear and tear, errors, accidents, opacity—a system whose return is one for one, where the yield is maximal, and so forth. Even the world itself does not work quite perfectly. The distance from equality, from perfect agreement, is history. Everything happens as if the following proposition were true: it works because it does not work. That must shock the old-school rationalism, but the rationalists of the generation before my own had the same relation to the rational [*la raison*] as old bigots have to virtue. It was more morality than research, more a social strategy than an intellectual one. I think it was a certain relation with cleanliness; but where do we put the dirt? Fluctuation, disorder, opacity, and noise are not and are no longer affronts to the rational; we no longer speak of this rational, we no longer divvy things up in isms, simple and stiff puzzles, strategic plans for the final conflict. Thus a system has interesting relations according to what is deemed to be its faults or depreciations. What then about its noises and parasites. Can we rewrite a system, in the way Leibniz understood the term, not in the key of preestablished harmony but in what he called seventh chords? Not with the equilibrium he loved to mention in mind but with the waves and shocks on the line in mind? Not with the taste of the exact pleasures of sapidity, that is to say, wisdom [*sapience*], but etched in acid, with a bitter, astringent taste? On the other side of the *Theodicy* where it was a question of the rare harmony. The classical system immediately fills these differences and distances, believed to make the enchantment of the perfect chords of their differential grow. Thus the rational resembles the system of numbers. Yet the irrational infinitely keeps its differences and distances without ever ceasing to be mathematic. Okay. The book of differences, noise, and disorder would only be the book of evil for someone who would prohibit the Author of the universe, through calculation, from a world that is uncorruptibly dependable. This, however, is not the case. The difference is part of the thing itself, and perhaps it even produces the thing. Maybe the radical origin of things is really that difference, even though classical rationalism damned it to hell. In the beginning was the noise.

Maybe we should construct the fable of the rats in reverse. At the door of the room, they heard a noise. . . .

Yet noise has a subject, the one who makes the noise, in the fable. No doubt it is the farmer, the parasited one. One of the first in the chain, he was thus cheated on behind his back. Awakened by the noise of the rats, cutting and nibbling, he suddenly opens the door. He jumps behind those who were eating behind his back and chases them. The parasited one parasites the parasites. One of the first, he jumps to the last position. But the one in the last position wins this game.

He has discovered the position of the philosopher.

Who is the host? The first rat for the second, the sleeper for the rats who eat his food, the taxed for the tax collecter (the tax farmer), and so forth along the chain. The host is in the row in front, the parasite behind him, a bit in his shadow or in his black ignorance. The host comes before and the parasite follows. Such is the case for every system where we eat at the expense of another, where we speak of him.

Who is the parasite here, who is the interrupter? Is it the noise, the creaking of the floorboards or of the door? Of course. It upsets the game, and the system collapses. If it stops, everything comes back, is re-formed and the meal continued. Think of another noise: the chain is broken again and everything vanishes in the bewildered flight. The noise temporarily stops the system, makes it oscillate indefinitely. To eliminate the noise, a nonstop signal would be necessary; then the signal would no longer be a signal and everything would start again, more briskly than usual. Theorem: noise gives rise to a new system, an order that is more complex than the simple chain. This parasite interrupts at first glance, consolidates when you look again. The city rat gets used to it, is vaccinated, becomes immune. The town makes noise, but the noise makes the town.

Who then is the real interrupter? It is the country rat. Broken himself by the interruptions, these uneasy feelings, the disruptions of his relaxing meal, it is he who definitively breaks the system. He could live on simple and easy chains, but he is horrified by the complex. He does not understand that chance, risk, anxiety, and even disorder can consolidate a system. He trusts only simple, rough, causal relations; he believes that disorder always destroys order. He is a rationalist, the kind we just spoke of. How many of these rough political rats are there around us? How many of them break things they don't understand? How many of these rats simplify? How many of them have built such homogeneous, cruel systems upon the horror of disorder and noise?

Soon the question becomes more general: such a parasite is responsible for the growth of the system's complexity, such a parasite stops it. The other question is still there: are we in the pathology of systems or in their emergence and evolution?

One of the rats goes to the fields. And so shall we.

Satyrs' Meals ──────────────

────────────────── *Host/Guest*

Everyone knows that satyrs have the tail and two legs of a goat. And being a goat, even half a goat, even the rear end, is really something. These dangerous beings live in forests, where they accompany Pan, the son of Hermes, the god of panic, the mother of all, the prince of fear and of wholes. Wild, they live in their lairs.

Having followed the procession of Dionysos or having been on the lookout for nymphs, they go home, ragged, to eat a good dinner with their wives and children on the mossy rocks. They're seldom seen like that, solid citizens, the way La Fontaine shows them, a family picture, all around the dinner table. Satyrs too wind up thinking about eating. No rugs, no shelter, no Persian carpet—here we are back in the fields. Can fear come to corrupt a wild den?

It is raining; a passer-by comes in. Here is the interrupted meal once more. Stopped for only a moment, since the traveller is asked to join the diners. His host does not have to ask him twice. He accepts the invitation and sits down in front of his bowl. The host is the satyr, dining at home; he is the donor. He calls to the passer-by, saying to him, be our guest. The guest is the stranger, the interrupter, the one who receives the soup, agrees to the meal. The host, the guest: the same word; he gives and receives, offers and accepts, invites and is invited, master and passer-by. The traveller, the homebody, the fixed and the moveable, client and hostler, here and there—city and country, for example. He is the object as well, for in the exchange of the word we cannot see where the exchange of the thing is. An invariable term through the transfer of the gift. It might be dangerous not to decide who is the host and who is the guest, who gives and who receives, who is the parasite and who is the *table d'hôte*, who has the gift and who has the loss, and where hostility begins within hospitality. Who hasn't trembled with fear in a shady hotel? Shady, obscure, badly lit. We like to know where we step. Again the same word, host and guest, active and passive, full of outrage and of generosity, of hatred and good-will. A word which hints at the inviter and the invited, the person warming himself by the fire and the one frozen from the cold rain, heat and cold.

The guest cools the soup and warms his hands; the host invites the traveller and sends him on his way, asks him in, asks him to sit down and eat and then asks him to leave, sends him away: don't sleep here, he says. The host, the guest, breathes twice, speaks twice, speaks with forked tongue, as it were. I don't know who the passer-by is or who the satyr is. Both are the host, the guest. And from one mouth they breathe and say yes and no. The traveller, moreover, interrupts the meal of his host; the satyr, moreover, interrupts the meal of his guest. Who cooled the soup, who spoke, but who didn't eat. The two rats here look alike. I would not be at all surprised if the passer-by's overcoat hid his tail and his goat's legs. Excluded even before he parasited the satyr.

But the excluded one, just a while ago, was making his way through the countryside; the passer-by goes out again in the rain that, as far as we know, never stops, beating incessantly on the roof of the host and guest. That noise too interrupted a process: a trip. And from this noise comes the story. Hosts and parasites are always in the process of passing by, being sent away, touring around, walking alone. They exchange places in a space soon to be defined.

There are some black spots in language. The field of the host is one such dark puddle. In the logic of exchange, or really instead of it, it manages to hide who the receiver is and who the sender is, which one wants war and which one wants peace and offers asylum. In the satyr's den, the host interrupts the guest and vice versa, and this is another black theorem. Or the non-zero sum of two things with opposite signs but the same value. We saw this shadow a short while back: we don't know what belongs to the system, what makes it up, and what is against the system, interrupting and endangering it. Whether the diagram of the rats is generative or corrupting.

Diminishing Returns ——————
—————— The Obscure and the Confused

Given a black thing, an obscure process, or a confused cloud of signals—what we shall soon call a problem. We intervene to illuminate it, define it, reduce it to something simple. Someone comes alone in these parts, no gloves, no hat. He opens the black box, Pandora's box with all its gifts. Attracted by such a source,* some others join the first, organize the work site, bringing light, equipment, documentation, increasing sophistication of means and the ever more complex organization of their group. Two things.

In the beginning, the investment is minimal and what one pulls out of the box is marvelous. The greatest results for the smallest outlay. The intoxicating ecstasy of the inventor, scorned and laughed at. History then assumes its rights, rights which are always the same everywhere. The load increases and the fruits decrease. Legions of researchers infinitely better equipped no longer find anything but bits and pieces. The first shepherd lays his hands on the treasure of the scrolls found in the cave; there are a hundred thousand. Now, with electronics and international relations, you glean rare, scattered, barely noticeable atoms of letters. Newton under the apple tree, all alone, gives the law of the world, leaving only a few marginal scraps for his innumerable offspring. Theorem: the history of science obeys the law of diminishing returns. The first attack on the narcissism of science. This law was not visible as long as we claimed to work on hypercomplex sets: the word, the organization of the biosphere, and so forth, whose information always exceeded the means of knowledge. But the narrow division into fields of

Source means "light," "river," "source." —Trans.

specialization reverses the situation, and the rule appears; it is simple and unparadoxical. Yet it still benefits a considerable group of people making their livelihood from it, a group that sometimes is going to drown the principal question with the din it makes. The direct relation to the object and the problem slowly is erased in favor of the internal relations of the group. Collective idealism marks the very end of diminution. Elsewhere, once more, another without a hat . . . The transformation of things and the world is in turn the object of science.

Secondly: if we examine the set made of the problem and of the actions that transform it, there is no doubt that it is, at the beginning, more complex than the thing itself or the process. Clearer perhaps, yet more complicated. The question can then be reexamined in order to try to illuminate this new complexity and, maybe, to transform it. Thus we form a set: the chain seems unending. The strategies of intervention, the interruption of the process or of the thing, observation that seeks to clarify, photon bombardment, the inseparable association of the knowers and the known—all make complexity increase, the price of which increases astronomically. A new obscurity accumulates in unexpected locations, spots that had tended toward clarity; we want to dislodge it but can only do so at ever-increasing prices and at the price of a new obscurity, blacker yet, with a deeper, darker shadow. Chase the parasite—he comes galloping back, accompanied, just like the demons of an exorcism, with a thousand like him, but more ferocious, hungrier, all bellowing, roaring, clamoring. Have I described the elementary link of a system of knowledge or its pathology? I do not know. Anyway, it makes work, gives sustenance. One parasite drives out another. The second attack on the narcissism of scientists. The shadow brought by knowledge increases by one order of magnitude at every reflection. Can we henceforth do without an epistemology of the parasite?

Let us return to exchange and to its equilibrium. I guess that in the neighborhood of the field occupied by the host and his guest we are rather near equilibrium: a little to the left or right, a little above or below. A simple fluctuation, a chance event, a circumstance, a noise, rain, creaking floorboards, and the like reverse the system head-to-tail, and the host changes function. The noise, chance, rain, a circumstance, produced a new system that in this case is inverted or contradictory, but that in general could be entirely different from the one that was interrupted. This is a new kind of logic and a strong one. We are rid of excess whose only use was relative to negative entropy, and we are finally free of the overly simple chains of contradictions whose use was rarely apparent. This new kind of logic opens up spaces of transformation in which the loci of metamorphic systems are separated by bits of noise. Islands randomly separated by bits.

Given the following diagram:

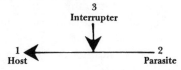

which is the elementary link of the parasitic chain.

During the night of the rats and the ortolans, we could not distinguish too clearly which one was the parasite—the rat or the noise— which one was in position 2 and which in position 3. In fact, they were both the parasite.

Here the rain, in position 3, disappears somewhat from the scene. Positions 1 and 2 apparently change: the host/guest prevents the guest/ host from eating. Satyr and passer-by parasite each other in passing, at will, in position 3 of the interrupter. The three positions are interchangeable; we would be better off with a new diagram in the form of a bifurcation:

The three positions are equivalent. Each is in a line with the others, and each can play the third.

Leibniz had already intuited that. In his *Theodicy,* all of a sudden he tells a few chance stories, of which he says there are an infinite number. Such and such a circumstance, unforeseen and slight, converts or perverts. Small circumstances, randomly distributed, are to the chain of things what little perceptions are to feeling. Unfortunately, it is a question of bifurcations. *Quod vitae sectabor iter:* will Hercules pick the path of virtue or that of vice? In the beginning, it does not matter much, but during the labors, it could matter quite a lot. Rewrite the twelve labors having supposed that the hero chose the path of vice. Often a little flick is sufficient for a decision to be made. Heads or tails, a book opened at random. Look at the story of the two Polish twins, two children: one was seized by Tartars, sold to the Turks, driven to apostasy (I like the word *apostasy,* which, once rid of its ecclesiastical relations, really means "away from equilibrium"), dwelling in impiety, dying in total despair; the other twin is somehow saved, having fallen into good hands, taught correctly, filled with the most solid truths of religion, dying with all the feelings of a good Christian. One feels sorry for the first, whom a small circumstance, perhaps, had prevented from being saved like his brother; it is astonishing that this small occurrence could have decided his lot for all eternity.

It is less a theological scandal than a logical scandal. The cause is minimal but the effect immense; the former is infinitesimal and the latter infinite; the first is chance and the second necessity. And yet, things are like that. These inclinations cannot be avoided, inclinations upon which the Epicureans built their world. The Classical era finds them again, but it is only now that we begin to understand their function. Now we know that order sometimes comes only from an explosion of noise. And that reason errs and cheats us when it looks for full causes and entire reasons.

The scandal is less theological than historical. History is the locus of full causes without effects, immense effects with futile reasons, strong consequences from insignificant causes, rigorous effects from chance occurrences. Now we know that this logic is at work in the physical world and the living one too; we have to know that it is at work in history. History is the river of circumstances and no longer the old orbit of the mechanists, bearing its conflicts and its relations of forces. Here we find the history of Poland. Of twin Poland, divided, in equilibrium between East and West, North and South, torn between the powers that condemn it while claiming to be working for its election to paradise. What makes the dualism and the bifurcation of the Polish twins is not Poland but the rivalry of powers and the war of ideas. Salvation and hell, good and evil, truth and error, the French and the Turks, the West and the Tartars. The balance perpetuates the battle lines. At this point, the theory of transformations is reduced to the poor choice of black and white, hot and cold, God and the Devil, true and false. Whence the twins and the random circumstance that inclines more to salvation than to damnation. Twinning resides both in the object and the subject. The twins are not only the Polish children but also the Turks and the good Christians. A Tartar pirate or an English corsair: were I being taken, I would not see much of a difference. Anyway, the story says that both children die very quickly. War, plunder, death—where is the conversion, where is the perversion? Hell is the separation of paradise and Hell, the Devil is the bifurcation between God and the Devil, evil is the crossroads of good and evil, and error is the dualism that only opposes twins.

Leibniz is surrounded by it: in fact, it is not necessary to have a large inclination to go from one twin to the other or from good to evil or from the Turks to the good Christians. They are more alike than different, almost re-plies, re-torts. Saved from dual violence, from heat and cold, satyr and passer-by, wild twins, the plurality of systems remains, where the logic of inclinations or of circumstances is fruitful. The bit of noise, the small random element, transforms one system or one order into another. To reduce this otherness to contradiction is to reduce everything to violence and war. It is not because we are a murderous species that everything bends to our law. The other is sometimes completely other. A statue of a god, then a table, then a washbasin. The affair told by the philosopher is less about theology, logic, or history than about theory—war theory. If I had to tell it again, the doubles and oppositions would disappear in favor of the plural and transformations; the Tartars and Turks would be replaced by an olive branch.

Though we have understood the dual logic of exchanges and exclusions, symmetries and equivalences, doubles, violence, goats' legs, hosts and guests, interrupted meals, noisy rain beating down, though we have understood everything that happens in the wild, quite different from what the country rat tells us, more often a case of war than of peace, though we have understood the birth of satire at the dinner table of interrupted revelries, the figure of hot and cold still remains, difficult to resolve. Let us look at it again.

Decisions, Incisions ───────────────
─────────── *The Excluded Third, Included*

A while back, a passer-by came in, frozen stiff. Chilled, iced, stiff, immobile, exhausted—it is the snake stretched out on the snow one winter's day. It asked for nothing; it was hibernating perhaps. A villager walking by, on his own land (note this well), gathers up the snake, brings it inside, stretches it out by the fire, where it immediately begins to awaken. From the outside to the inside, from numbness to life, from sleep to anger, from indifference to hatred: from cold to hot.

The passer-by asked for a haven, a bed and some food, soup, victuals—to sleep under the same roof. Asked for but did not negotiate; it is not a question of price: the satyr's hospitality is free. Thenceforth the risk is there, quite literally; one is at the other's mercy. On the contrary, in the villager's house, another country rat. As his action is meritorious—charity, my good sir—it is a question of rent. Rent, that is to say, a price for a space, a payment for territory. The one who is at home is my lessee: this double locative is a veritable hornet's nest where regulated hospitality passes many a time to hostility. Having come back from the cold into the warmth, the insect attacks: ingrate, says the villager, such is my pay!

But he figures wrong. The serpent is not a lessee; he was not looking for a haven; he was answered without having called. He was given an uncalled-for opinion. Someone made himself the serpent's benefactor, savior, and father. You are sleeping quite peacefully, and when you wake you find yourself in debt. You live with no other need, and suddenly, someone claims to have saved your country, protected your class, your interests, your family, and your table. And you have to pay him for that, vote for him, and other such grimaces. Thus the

22

serpent awakens obliged to another. Something to get angry about. But, moreover, the villager was taking a walk at home, then goes into his house, still at home. As far as he is concerned, he never changed territories, never crossed a border. For himself, he is at home. On the contrary, the serpent does change. It was undoubtedly in its nest and finds itself in a foreign land. More than having been given a spot, his own has been taken away. Another debt. Thus when the balance sheet is drawn up, the demanded payment is turned around. And the host is less a host than he thought. Less hospitable than he thought. Undoubtedly hostile, that's the thorny part, the hot spot. Who has to pay?

The litigation is serious. Who is the host and who is the guest? Where is the gift and where is the debt? Who is hospitable, who is hostile, again the same word, the same thing.* No third to judge in this case. It is true that elsewhere the third opens the oyster and eats it, devours the weasel and the rabbit, which surely means that he judges, that is to say, he decides, that is to say, he slices [tranche]. Like the esquire trenchant. We are drowning in words and in language. Host is subject, object, friend and enemy. Decide then. Yes, immediately. To decide is to cut. The villager thus takes up his hatchet. Notice: he does not judge, does not decide; he slices in three [tranche]. Trancher, a medieval word, from trinicare, from the Vulgar Latin for "to cut in three." Thus: he takes his hatchet, slices the animal in three, making three serpents from two blows, a trunk, a tail, and a head. Perrin Dandin slices the pilgrims' oyster correctly: crunches it and gives a shell to each. The arithmetic works out right: he takes the booty and sends the other two on their way, each with a worthless shell. Can this calculation be generalized? Which is the third part? Or who or what is the third, in this logic of the trenchant decision? Is the third excluded or not? Here we have a trivalent logic where we expected only a bivalent one.† The same at the head, the other at the tail, or being at the head and nonbeing at the tail, and this middle trunk that is both same and other, being and nonbeing, and so forth.

I think, however, that it can be decided. Here, La Fontaine, following Phaedrus or Aesop, writes from the peasant's point of view. Death to ingrates. At least we understand here that gratitude, in the hard logic of exchange, bears the risk of life or death. I have just written

*You can understand why the great hunter, face to face with the Eternal One, Saint Julian, becomes the Hospitaller. I shall speak of these curious hunts.

†"All of you who say that hot and cold or any two such principles are All, what is it that you attribute to both of them when you say that both and each are? What are we to understand by this 'are'? Is this a third principle besides those two others, and shall we suppose that the All is three, and not two any longer?" (Plato, The Sophist, 243D-E).

from the other point of view, that of the serpent. Which of the two is the ingrate, I ask you? Who among you allows himself to be displaced, carried from his home territory, permits himself to be the passive object of another's whim, that of the first passer-by? Who would thank, moreover, the one who decides for you? That would be the same as giving recognition to professional politicians. To those who see and consider others as if they were rocks, cold stones. To those who force others to be only objects, which can then be carried. To those who are astonished when the passive object suddenly wakes up and lashes out in anger. The one who did not lash out against his benefactors, saviors, and fathers would be forgetting all his duties, as would he who did not pass from cold passivity to the heat of battle. Ready to die. Sliced in three.

I was saying that it could be decided. Look for a third before reaching for the hatchet. Strike but listen first. Let's try the ingrates, says the snake in the bag. My life is in your hands, the snake says to the man; cut me up but be aware that *you* are the ingrate. We'll go to the cow; let her be the judge. She says: I give my milk and my children to man and he has never given me anything but death. The steer, a new third party who will judge, says that he works and is beaten in return and that his life is ended with a sacrifice on the altar of the gods. All of them give to man, then, who never gives anything in return. But let us descend to the level of the tree. It gives shelter, decoration, flowers, fruits, and shade. And in return for its wages or more accurately for its rent—for it shelters and produces a territory—it is felled. The tree judges man to be an ingrate. Man milks the cow, makes the steer work, makes a roof from the tree; they have all decided who the parasite is. It is man. Everything is born for him, animals and beings. In the moral, La Fontaine is euhermerist, sociologist, or politician enough to please his reader. The great and powerful, he says, act this way. Yes, of course, but the others? The farmer of the cow, the carpenter of the roof, and the priest who kills the steer are not great people. History says so without symbols, without translations or displacements. But history hides the fact that man is the universal parasite, that everything and everyone around him is a hospitable space. Plants and animals are always his hosts; man is always necessarily their guest. Always taking, never giving. He bends the logic of exchange and of giving in his favor when he is dealing with nature as a whole. When he is dealing with his kind, he continues to do so; he wants to be the parasite of man as well. And his kind want to be so too. Hence rivalry. Hence the sudden, explosive perception of animal humanity, hence the world of animals of the fables. If my kind were cattle, calves, pigs, and poultry, I could quietly maintain with them the same relations I have with nature. Such is the peaceful dream of my contemporaries, descendants, and ancestors. Always talking, never giving, staying in a good position in irreversible logic. The louse is a man for the wolf. Metaphors move around, metamorphose.

The Lion's Share —————————————
————————————————————— The Simple Arrow

You remember the relation of order and of him who plays to the hilt in the position of the king.* The one who occupies this site receives everything and gives nothing in exchange. This defines a space where a wild den is at the extreme limit. If I were a fox, I would tell you why: I would see how to get in but not how to get out. All flows are oriented to the aforementioned position, and none come from it. All the footprints point toward the lion's den, but none come away. A rigorous diagram of a space structured by the relation of order, bearing a maximized point. Oddly enough, here, it is the spot of power, of absolute power, that of the lion, the king's place. But it is also a trap, an open maw. He who is well-placed has the right to eat the others. It is always a question of a meal, of visitors, and of guests. What does the lion give in exchange for his good? Nothing? Not entirely. An edict, a document, a passport, words and writing. He pays for his meal in well-turned, well-written phrases. And thus he is in the position of a parasite, a universal parasite. One day we will have to understand why the strongest is the parasite— that is to say, the weakest—why the one whose only function is to eat is the one who commands. And speaks. We have just found the place of politics.

Why? Invert the described space and you will see the king grown old. He does not receive visits and game but is kicked, bitten, butted. He is excluded and sacrificed. He dies twice from the donkey's kick. The maximized point suddenly is minimized. The host/guest is universal, eater of all and eaten by all.

*"Le Jeu du loup," in *Hermes IV. La distribution*, pp. 89–104.

26

The rats, the country- and the city-dweller, have shown us that the system of parasites in stepladder formation is not very different from an ordinary system. Who will ever know if parasitism is an obstacle to its proper functioning or if it is its very dynamics? Daily, general patterns of behavior depend on the answer to this question. If we eliminate these tie-ups, would a system still remain? Is the system a set of constraints on our attempts at optimization, or do these latter, quite simply, produce the system itself? The question is asked globally here.

In the case of the lion, it is asked locally. The space is full of relations of order. All lines go in one direction, none in the other. They literally go to one opening: the gaping maw of the universal parasite. Or to a common misery: the broken back of the universal victim. Questions: is the king victim or parasite, is the parasite king or victim? It is the same question, not asked of the whole network, but at a local division, a single point of the system, undoubtedly at its *extremum*. It is the same question as that of the host/guest. But here we already have an idea (a rare one) of what might be a point of decision: the den where the game is eaten ravenously and where, one day, someone else risks being cut up.

The space is strewn with simple arrows, pointing in only one direction.

Athlete's Meals
Difference and the Construction of the Real

Rarely is an object of praise in and of itself worth the trouble—with the exception, of course, of the gods and a tender mistress. La Fontaine adds the king, for alimentary reasons. And thus for him, the fable is over before it starts; he has paid the king with this word and he eats. How do you praise a champion? He is only what he is, once you have said that he won the race. You can speak of him only by evoking the gods, giants, heroes of the games. This is what Simonides the Elder does, just like some newspaper reporter. He spoke of Castor and Pollux; it was no hyperbole, that is to say, no exaggeration, but a parable.* He throws himself aside, the fabulist says. He makes a distance, a difference [écart]. We are indefinitely on the side, the proof of which is the fact that the word *parole* (speech, word) derives, I don't know how, from this parable, parabola. Between the word and the thing a parasite makes one move aside. The parable was the divine word; Castor and Pollux always return. No, I cannot speak without a god or a mistress, who are always present in the distances of my words. No one ever totally speaks of the thing; it is written in serious books—a Philadelphia lawyer [*Gascon*]† knows that and a Greek, even more so. Why are we always on the side? Let's see. I have never really understood all the fine points of the morality of lying nor what is currently being said about the referent. You would have to speak only—and always—of algebra. Simonides spoke, parabolically, of twins. The Dioscuri. The praise was,

*_Parabole_, in the French, means both "parable" and "parabola." —Trans.
†The French has *Gascon*, that is to say, a native of Gascony; proverbially, Gascons are wanglers, sly and slightly unscrupulous. —Trans.

28

as was necessary, outside the discourse. Professors also judge things to
be outside the subject, a proof that they know better than I do where
the line is drawn. Scissors and knives. Simonides thought that an example was necessary. You will more easily understand it if you know
that his athlete was a wrestler and that the gods of the fable were twins.
Wrestlers are well aware of twin forces: my hand, your hand, your arm,
my arm, our equilibrium. One of them will win if he throws himself to
one side of this equilibrium. Then the other one is pinned. Wrestling:
twins who have braced themselves, then a distance at the end between
the winner and the loser beneath him. A distance which in the end could
be considered a parabola. Consequently, the wrestling match: the parable of the twins. And inevitably, Castor and Pollux enter the picture.
This is the example, the poet says. And well he does. Again a double
and a twin, bearing a difference. There is even one known language in
which *champion* and *example* are the same word. Better yet, *example* is
a word whose prefix says "difference" and whose root says "buying"
and "selling." As if it were a way of getting out of exchange, something
taken away, something removed from the purchase. Like a distance
from the equilibrium of the payment, like a parable of twins. The example elevates combats; La Fontaine says that Simonides said so. This
elevation says the same thing again.* We will never be able to finish
measuring on the same scale all the words used in this calculation of
glory. I am measuring the "too much" [*trop*] of the beginning of the
fable.

Simonides, however, sliced the thing up by speaking of the
champion in one third of the text and of the Twins in the other parts.
A trunk, a tail, and a head. A text in three parts is well-balanced, they
say. In the poem at least, the athlete's adversary was missing, while each
of the brothers had his own. The figures are exact: the double is split
without deciding exactly. A text in three parts—a dialectic—has a
forked tongue and the head of a viper. The twin thesis and antithesis
divinely produce the athletic synthesis: the synthesis waits for its adversary or its double in the wrestling match. A good show, in truth,
where mythology gives birth to dialectic.

Simonides sells this triangle to the athlete who recognizes only
one of its sides. The estimate and the contract promised a talent, but
the champion takes care of only one-third of it; the gods, he says, have

*I like the example here, so close to praise [*éloge*]. I ask you, says Socrates
to the Sophist, for some definitions; you give me praise and examples. Later on,
Socrates says that he too sells them.

to pay for their publicity. The moral of this story is an exact reckoning and quite clear. Here there is a difference relative to the estimate, relative to the balance sheet, relative to the balance of equilibrium; the series of differences begins again, from *parole*-parable-parabola to example, to wrestling. The debit balance takes these depreciations into account. I am still measuring the "too much," the athlete calculates it, and the fable writes it down.

But the story is not over even if the moral has already been told. We know that after business is over there is a feast, like a supplement to the palavering about the combats and to the signatures on the treaties. It is the meal that is cut short, the interrupted banquet, that of the Stone Guest. Come dine with me, says the Hercules of the fairgrounds. It is not the thought that he owed something to Simonides, for the accounts have already been adjusted; but you have to say "thank you," *merci, gracias,* and the like. "Thank you" is said when everything else is said, when there is nothing left to say about the treaties and the contracts. "Thank you" is also said when everything is written. Such speaking and giving outside writing. The thank-you of gratitude and the free giving [*gré*]—Simonides does not want to lose that in addition to what he owed and lost. For there is what is owed and what is freely given. They have two different kinds of logic and two different economies, and perhaps two ways of living as well. In the logic and economy of the law and of possession, exchange reigns, weighing and measuring, figuring out the balance; in the logic and economy of the freely given, exchange is not there. In one group, owing dominates; in another, the freely given. Two incomparable societies. In the second, there are lots of communal meals, lots of invitations to feasts, repasts, banquets.

I am thinking of a story barely indicated by the fable. Among modern men, here and now, be they poets or fighters, known or unknown, the freely given occurs only after the owing, the feast after the payment; maybe they fear losing, besides what is owed them, the thanks of praise, freely given. Exchange first; the celebrations, if possible, later. Business before pleasure. For the gods, the situation is the inverse; the given comes before the owed: the Twins appear, thanking the poet first and then, in payment for his verse, warn him of an imminent danger. Exchange word for word, praise for warning. Thank you; we'll talk later of payment: this is certainly the world upsidedown. The world turns in one direction; history has its economy where exchange is fundamental: it is called the meaning of history. It stops a moment, turns in the other direction, and in this new (hi)story, exchange appears after everything was freely given. It is not a new story; on the contrary, it is an ancient one, lost in the dark recesses of memory; it is the story of the gods. Now I understand why the gods were always eating and drinking. Now I understand why the meal was interrupted—by the see-saw of history. By a catastrophe that I still do not really understand. The societies of giving have disappeared; even in antiquity they were thought to be divine. They have left a place for the collectives of giving and having. There are only barely perceptible traces of the history of giving in texts and on monuments. Since then, we have been caught up in economic history, a time of calculation of exchanges and of making up for losses. Does this history have an outside? That is precisely the subject of this book. I have not finished yet. When history and time are measured by the calculation of exchanges and brought back to this cal-culation, I fear that here and there there will be some insolvents. People who can give nothing but their children, their muscles, their bodies, a pound of flesh. It is a time of death and a history of death. People who can give only their life and their bodies, bit by bit. How many times have men sent up a cauldron filled with scattered limbs to the table of the gods? I can only give my approach to death; I can only pay with my courage in the face of this shadow; I can only write of its immediacy. This time and history are invaginated around nothingness. They need a zero to be calculated; there has to be a nothingness for their meta-physics. Now I understand why the gods seemed immortal to men; at least I think I know what ambrosia did not contain.

Let's return to the banquet of men, always interrupted. So who are the gods? The ones whose meals are never interrupted. The immortal is the eternal reveller. Look at Simonides at the banquet: he eats and drinks as he pleases, quite in the position of a parasite. He stuffs himself and gets drunk for his freely given verse; he pays his select table com-panions and their good food in word. But someone disturbed the dinner. At the door of the room, they heard a noise. Simonides runs off, but no one else follows him. No one of the cohort misses a bite. But the cohort is wrong, for its members are about to die.

For the first time we know who knocks at the door, who makes a noise behind the door-frame. The gods. Who warn us to move, for the sky is about to fall. The Twins run off; Simonides follows them. They move to one side, parabolically.

The word is made flesh. The difference becomes static. A pillar is missing, and it is cast aside. Everything is soon cast aside: the *parole*-parabola-parable, the example, the elogy, the owed and the freely given, the poet and the gods, the column and the coping. We always calculate the too much. The too much and the *para*. Parabola, parable, parasite. The parasite pays in parables. Here, the list of differences, their order, title, or collection.

A pillar missing, and we pass from the logicial to the material, from the word to the flesh, to stone, from the word to its referent. Who is avenged? The divine being, the poet, or the thing itself? You don't live in language and words for very long before the object comes back once, before a foot is suddenly missing. Before the real falls down on your head. I am thinking of a triangular room, with a ceiling with three architraves, ogees, bays—that is all predicted by the calculation of the static, by the word, the logicial. Had the triclinium been square, a missing column would not necessarily have been an irreparable tragedy, for the cantilever could have resisted. But a column is missing, and the ceiling finds nothing to lean on. It had three beams, like the elogy, three feet, three supports, three theses, like the discourse. Two for the twin gods, one for you, mortal, who one day, one night, one evening, will be missing. Two stable columns, one unstable one. Triangle: the elementary link of static equilibrium, of the distribution of space, of the arrangement of positions, of topology, of measure, of the immobile arrangement of forces, of the syllogism, of reason. Material, logicial. Do away with one of the feet of the tripod, everything collapses; cross out a thesis, a term, everything vanishes. Everything falls on the athlete's feet; the guests are crippled. A miracle is sought, and the miracle is just that the same distance is kept between small energies and large and that the real world is thus comprehensible. That the parable of the parasite and the paralysis of the guest are quite precisely parallel. The next day, the athlete as well as the guests are cast aside, lame. They are missing a pillar; they need walking sticks. Like the old man in the riddle of the Sphinx. Like Hephaistos. Those who limp are the discoverers; inclination is the beginning of the world.

One can never praise enough; here is the list of excess, fault, difference. It appears in the logic of reasoning, in calculation, in accounting; it appears in language, in words and in poems, in parables and paraphrase; it appears in order, plans, space; it appears in exchange and in money, in what is owed and what is freely given, pay doubled once more, that of the poet and that of the gods, the cursed part; it appears at the edge of the beam, at the top of the threatening pillar, in the cantilever and the coping; it appears now in physical systems, in the difficult equilibrium between stone and marble; it appears in living systems, walking, running like the crippled, fighting twins until one of the pillars of the struggle gives way and makes a winner a loser, paralytic in his body and the elementary paradigm of the social group in combat.

I count this impressive advance as a knowledgeable construction of the real, just like those the classical age often made.

The prefix *para* is counted, calculated, weighed in its difference from equilibrium. But it is also placed and situated. When the column holds the beam up, one line goes to the end of the second; here, the vertical joins the edge of the horizontal. That makes a right angle at the top. In any case, it makes an angle and a top. Move the pillar, mark a cantilever—a loss or difference, *para.* In the diagram, the line no longer goes to the end of the second line, but to another spot along the way. The parasite has a relation with the relation and not with the station. And it puts the relation in the form of a cantilever. The simplest diagram appears. *Static,* in English: parasite.

In one word and not only in one prefix, the whole text and the whole story. Then and then only can it be understood that it is an origin for the art of memory. The discourse, the course taken [*parcours*], is of canonical simplicity: it is deductive, it constructs reality, it constructs the real by starting with the difference. In a variety bestrewn with simple arrows, the difference is in the place of the inclination.

Picaresques and Cybernetics ———————
——————————— The New Balance

The parasite is invited to the *table d'hôte;* in return, he must regale the other diners with his stories and his mirth. To be exact, he exchanges good talk for good food; he buys his dinner, paying for it in words. It is the oldest profession in the world. Traces of it are found in the oldest documents. There are a thousand known variations on this law of justice—rarely simple and often complicated—practiced in social, friendly, tribal, and familial everyday life, just like in the oldest comedy or the most recondite story. For example, the sponger pays in morals and the host gives, filled with guilt by this great yet imaginary duty. The moral is one discourse among many, some sort of specie that is legal tender. Each society allows a linguistic specie that can be exchanged advantageously for food. Influential and powerful groups are able to diffuse a forced lexicon in that way. Today it is economic, just as it was humanist not long ago, Voltairean before that, and religious a long time ago.

A vagrant, dying of hunger, found himself one evening at the kitchen window of a well-known restaurant. The aromas were delicious. He filled himself on them and that calmed his hunger pangs a bit. One of the scullions discovered the trick and, quickly coming outside, demanded money for what could be called the service rendered. The passer-by and the scullion were about to fight over their disagreement when a third person came by who offered to settle the matter. Give me a coin, he said. The wretch did so, frowning. He put the coin down on the sidewalk and with the heel of his shoe made it ring a bit. This noise, he said, giving his decision, is pay enough for the aroma of the tasty

34

dishes. The roast is the thing eaten, and an aroma comes from it. The coin is the thing exchanged, and a sound comes from it. If the coin is worth the roast, then the sound of the coin is worth the aroma of the food. And he returned the coin to the passer-by. Justice is done.

An old tale that demonstrates a wise bit of knowledge. We are hollow and empty; we cannot fill ourselves with air and with sound. We need something substantial to mend us. Two positions and two orders: substances and solids here, and there air and sound. According to this bit of wisdom, if there is to be an exchange, it must be of the same order. That is philosophy, the justice of the stomach. Solid for solid, substance for substance, and meal for coin of the realm; elsewhere, air for sound and vice versa. There are infrastructures—a serious matter—and there are superstructures where hot air is sold. The consistent and the diffuse. Every author and every language notes this division in its own way. And the heavy philosophers consecrate it.

The parasite invents something new. Since he does not eat like everyone else, he builds a new logic. He crosses the exchange, makes it into a diagonal. He does not barter; he exchanges money. He wants to give his voice for matter, (hot) air for solid, superstructure for infrastructure. People laugh, the parasite is expelled, he is made fun of, he is beaten, he cheats us; but he invents anew. This novelty must be analyzed. This sound, this aroma, passing for money or roast.

A paralytic was crawling about on hands and knees. Was it our athlete, wounded? A few steps away from a sumptuous repast, Tantalus, you can die of hunger if you are unable to move. He was collapsing in misery, rotting away in a black corner. One fine day, he saw a blind man who was bumping into a thousand obstacles and who thereby almost broke his neck. He could die by falling into a well if its lip were low and seemed to be a step and if his outstretched arms only touched the air. The paralytic calls him and offers to strike a bargain. The blind man will carry him and the cripple will be the guide. The two of them form one normal person.

An old tale that pushes the wise bit of knowledge out. You laughed at the parasite, but you do not laugh at the exchange of legs for eyes. Nevertheless: The blind man gives solidity, force, transportation, power that can be calculated in calories produced by such and such a food from a meal. In other words, energy on the normal scale. What does the cripple give in exchange in this new picture? He speaks, and that is that. He announces obstacles, he watches, he proposes a direction. Perched on the shoulders of a black force, he clarifies it and illuminates it. Soon we will have to say that he directs it, that he gives the force orders. After all, the contract he proposed to the blind man was a parasitic pact. For he pays in information, in energy on the microscopic level. He offers words for the force—yes, his voice, air, for a solid substance. Worse yet, he takes control and governs.

The parasite invents something new. He obtains energy and pays for it in information. He obtains the roast and pays for it with stories. Two ways of writing the new contract. He establishes an unjust pact; relative to the old type of balance, he builds a new one. He speaks in a logic considered irrational up to now, a new epistemology and a new theory of equilibrium. He makes the order of things as well as the states of things—solid and gas—into diagonals. He evaluates information. Even better: he discovers information in his voice and good words; he discovers the Spirit in the wind and the breath of air. He invents cybernetics. The blind man and the cripple are a crossed association of the material and the logicial, an exchange of the solid for a voice—that is the oldest story of the rudder [*gouvernail*]. And if the bolt of lightning governs the universe, here it is the look and the invitation to create a slant. The person who limps is the inclination. He is the difference, and he says so.

There are several fine balances in this. First of all, not all voices bear information; not all winds bear tidings. Not all smooth talkers are invited to dine: good *raconteurs* are distinguished from tiresome braggarts and from stubborn cavillers. The king of Prussia could choose; he preferred Voltaire, and the tsarina, Diderot. They would not have invited the ridiculous Jean-François Rameau. There is a market for good words, sometimes at a fixed price. Bad money often chases out the good. But this balance is evolved, sophisticated; it is useless at first.

Let us return to the paralytic, that is to say, to the governor. The one with energy, the producer of movement, can sometimes distinguish the useful message in the voices of the wind. Yet his blindness forbids him from ever regulating the message's usefulness. The cripple, perched atop his blind stare, could make him fall into a ditch. The blind man must trust the cripple. And the latter could be anyone. For the blind man cannot choose his mahout. Of course, he can distinguish messages from noise, but his lack of control allows him to be lied to. I shall warn you about all obstacles, and I shall lead you where you want to go. And so he goes quite like a sheep.

From that point on, anyone who wants to sit on the shoulders of an athlete does not want him to see well. He who likes to command can do so, but on one condition: the eyes of the producers, of the energetic and the strong, have to be poked out. Those who have energy necessarily cannot have information; thus, those with information can do without energy. Information is as precious as it is rare. Thus this rarity has to be provoked. The blind man and the paralytic already established these theorems and the new balance as well. They began with symbiosis, but that did not last very long. The parasite came back.

The balance of rarity functions perfectly in a space or an environment without information. Here the first signal that appears is worth all the money in the world, is worth life itself. The first bolt of lightning that inclines in chaos. The first olive branch in the beak of the dove on the flooded plains. Afterwards follows all the meaning. And history itself is derived from this spark. Begin with the black box, night, blindness.

Thus you have to begin by removing all sources of information for the workers and producers. Horses are trained by putting blinders on them. Calves and chickens are placed in the dark, in school, as if they were simple, small men. You have to begin by dividing the work. The manual laborer has to be blind in relation to the paralyzed intellectual. The helmsman has no porthole; he hears his master's voice, he listens, he repeats, and he obeys. Just like the blind man a while back, who followed a voice. One furnishes energy; the other, information. One gives the force to work; the other, the directions. Matter and voice. Again this is an iniquitous exchange, but it works in history and not only in comedy. They must have found the parasitic diagonal very serious. They must have found the new balance intelligent. For the division surges up and makes a system very quickly: the intellectual producer is blind relative to the administrative paralytic and blinded by him, and so forth. This cybernetics gets more and more complicated, makes a chain, then a network. Yet it is founded on the theft of information, quite a simple thing. It is merely necessary to edit the laws and to withdraw knowledge from the greatest number. In the end, power is nothing else. It is measured on this balance. It is the relation and literally the balance beam between the loci in which information is stocked and those from which it is withdrawn. Who put out whose eyes? Where is knowledge located, and from what space is it absent? It is true enough that the division of manual and intellectual functions more or less matches the old relation of city and country, for example; this is what the rats show us.

This power, which could be called bureaucratic, seems to me to be stronger and stabler than that of force, which is never strong enough, or that of law, which is never just enough. It is based on knowledge, and worse yet, on information, on the signal, almost at the level of a reflex. Yet its genesis is paradoxical. That of strong powers is simple: it is a question of violence and death, warfare, muscles, and strategy. That of just powers is simple as well: it is a question of faith and of sacrifices, of martyrs and fanatics. Nothing out of the ordinary, nothing rare, nothing rare, nothing ridiculous. Here, the ancestor is a parasite. He is ridiculous, a joke. He claims to exchange his daring words for good food. But he is the only one we hear at the table. He is the only one we see on stage in Plautus. Him and his loud voice. Everyone laughs. By what miracle does everyone suddenly cry then? In the meanwhile, the master has lost the power to exclude him. He is there, well entrenched. Ruins the father, screws the mother, leads the children, runs the household. We can no longer do without him; he is our system itself: he commands, he has the power, his voice has become that of the master, he speaks so he is heard everywhere, no one else can talk. From the *table d'hôte* to the table of Orion—now he is on the shoulders, the master, Zeus-like. How could this have happened? How could the producers have suddenly been blinded? What hit them?

The producer plays the contents, the parasite, the position. The one who plays the position will always beat the one who plays the contents. The latter is simple and naive; the former is complex and mediatized. The parasite always beats the producer. The producer, always attentive to the game of the things themselves, supposes that the other does not cheat, since the things themselves are fine but loyal, as physicists say.

The one who plays the contents plays the object. He is an artisan; he is a scientist as well, but it is only the mastery of the world, subtle, wily, but not cheating. The one who plays the position plays the relations between subjects; thus, he masters men. And the master of men is the master of the masters of the world.

Some are of fire and some of location. Some whose word is of fire and some whose word is location. Those of location without fire are the masters—the cold ones. Those of fire without location burn madly, so strongly that around them, objects change as if in a furnace or near a forge. Flame of fire in the wind; the wind comes from where it will, blows where it will to stir up the fire. They are not the masters; they can be the slaves, but they are the beginnings. They are the noise of the world, the sounds of birth and of transformations.

To play the position or to play the location is to dominate the relation. It is to have a relation only with the relation itself. Never with the stations from which it comes, to which it goes, and by which it passes. Never to the things as such and, undoubtedly, never to subjects as such. Or rather, to those points as operators, as sources of relations. And that is the meaning of the prefix *para-* in the word *parasite:* it is on the side, next to, shifted; it is not on the thing, but on its relation. It has relations, as they say, and makes a system of them. It is always mediate and never immediate. It has a relation to the relation, a tie to the tie; it branches onto the canal.

There are those of sources and those of canals.

The whole question of the system now is to analyze what a point, a being, and a station are. They are crossed by a network of relations; they are crossroads, interchanges, sorters. But is that not analysis itself: saying that this thing is at the intersection of several series. From then on, the thing is nothing else but a center of relations, crossroads or passages. It is nothing but a position or situation. And the parasite has won.

Pentecost

Et factus est repente de caelo, and suddenly a sound came from heaven, sonus, tamquam advenientis spiritus vehementis, like the rush of a mighty wind, ἦχος ὥσπερ φερομένης πνοῆς βιαίας, un bruit comme celui d'un vent impétueux, et replevit totam domum ubi erant sedentes, and it filled all the house where they were sitting. Et apparuerunt illis dispertitae linguae tamquam ignis, and there appeared to them tongues as of fire, διαμεριζόμεναι γλῶσσαι ὡσεὶ πυρός, des langues séparées les unes des autres que étaient comme de feu, a distribution of tongues as of fire, cloven tongues, divided, split like flames, seditque supra singulos eorum, distributed and resting on each one of them; et repleti sunt omnes Spiritu Sancto, καὶ ἐπλήσθησαν πάντες πνεύματος ἁγίου, and they were all filled with the Holy Spirit, and began to speak in other tongues, et coeperunt loqui variis linguis, λαλεῖν ἑτέραις γλώσσαις, à parler diverses langues, as the Spirit gave them utterance, dabat, καθὼς τὸ πνεῦμα ἐδίδου, selon que l'Esprit-Saint leur donnait de s'exprimer, gave them, dabat, ἐδίδου, gave them.

Tongues that came from wind and noise. To speak in tongues after the fire, after the noise. At the door of the room, they heard a great wind.

Now there were dwelling in Jerusalem Jews, devout men from every nation under heaven. Facta autem hac voce, convenit multitudo, and at this sound the multitude came together, γενομένης δὲ τῆς φωνῆς ταύτης συνῆλθεν τὸ πλῆθος, après que ce bruit se fut fait entendre, ils accoururent en foule, hac voce, φωνῆς, this sound, ce bruit, voice or noise, the agreement is suddenly broken, as are the rhythm and the meaning, but the two are mixed and it is both voice and noise, message and

40

parasite, and each one heard them speaking in his own language, audiebat unusquisque lingua sua illos loquentes, et chacun les entendait parler dans sa propre langue, ἤκουον ἒις ἕκαστος τῇ ἰδίᾳ διαλέκτῳ λαλούντων αὐτῶν. Parthians and Medes and Elamites and residents of Mesopotamia, Judea and Cappadocia, Pontus and Asia, Phrygia and Pamphylia, Egypt and the parts of Libya belonging to Cyrene, and visitors from Rome, both Jews and proselytes, Cretans and Arabians, we hear them telling in our own tongues the mighty works of God, mirabilia, merveilles, μεγαλεῖα, mighty works.

The new meaning spread everywhere starting from wind and noise. Not a single language translated in several languages, but several spoken and several heard at the same time.

The course of events is exact seen from our rational points of view. All of a sudden, without warning, the noise, a noise coming from the sky, a sound like that of the wind when it blows hard. It is produced locally, in a single direction and soon it fills the space, the whole space. In an unforeseeable fashion, it passes from the local to the global. It was a noise, a sound. It was an event in a corner of the system; it penetrates, invades, and occupies the whole house. It was heard; it is seen. They saw it appear. The noise is a chance occurrence, a disorder, and the wind is a flow. What they saw was first a distribution, a dispersion, but a division as well. What they saw is also what is generally heard, like noise. Tongues. Divided tongues, or distributed. But tongues of fire. It is the fire that pushes the winds, the heat that produces the gusts of air, the fire that crackles, that produces the chance occurrence, sputtering and crackling; it is the fire of force and of clarity of energy, light, power, and information. The noise is made message before the word is made flesh. It is a noise, a sound, the tongue of fire, and the meaning of the tongue of fire. The meaning that is cloven, inclined, divided like a bolt of lightning, the illuminated meaning. Toward declination and by the flame that announces itself to the eyes and ears. It is the beginning and the transformation; and it is in such a way that systems change order so easily. A fluctuation, a noise, a spark of chance: the state of things changes states according to this correct sequence. I have changed voices, and my tongue is split; I am speaking in rational language.

What change? Let us imagine a crowd, here, brought together, attracted by the noises and the voices. It has no unity: Come from Pamphylia, Phrygia, Judea, Asia, and Cappadocia: they are there, Mediterraneans and Persians. The noise, wind, sound, voices, are received.

But the tongues? In other words, the local event invading the spot momentarily provokes the crowd. A system is formed, but only for the bits, points, units, and elements. It is not yet a system. How can these monads communicate, Medes and Parthians, Elamites and Romans? Someone gets up and speaks. He speaks Aramaic, Greek, or Latin. What did he say? The translator comes forward. First the Persian translator, then the Assyrian interpreter, and so forth. Everything is in place.

Look at the caduceus of Hermes. Two snakes cross repetitively on it. The elementary chain of the picture looks like an hourglass. An hourglass relates two sets or two crowds through the intermediary of a very fine neck. So thin that one grain could take its place. That is the place of the speaker. He speaks alone. He speaks alone to several, who in turn speak to others, and so forth. The hierarchy is in place. The first to speak—or the strongest, etc.—imposes his own tongue at the neck. That is the description of Hermes as well as that of any shop-keeper. He produces, alone, a relation among an incongruous mixture of subjects and practices and an incongruous set of objects and merchan-dise. He sets the price or discusses it. The essential is that he has the isolated spot—unique, at the intersection, the knot, the neck, of the two parts of the hourglass. The one who holds this position produces, with himself as origin, divisions and dichotomies. Those of translation, for example: the Latin he speaks is translated into Greek, the Greek into Aramaic, the Latin, again, into Persian, and so forth. This is the naive description of "forked tongues," divided, cloven, translated tongues that come to rest on each and every one of us. This is the usual organi-gram of all beginnings. A net of divisions that go back to a common point. The noise, the wind of the Paraclete, overturn and transform this system, replacing it with another, a new one. Improbable and miraculous.

The hourglass, the elementary link of the caduceus of Hermes, describes relations of the sort many-one-many. Many tongues, one speaker, a crowd of tongues; a set of objects, a shopkeeper, a group of clients, etc. Let us now imagine that any speaker speaks in his own language and that every hearer understands in his own, whatever the language and whatever the location. In that case, the relations can be considered to be many-many and the network that describes them is decentered. With neither exchange nor crossroads. Such a graph has never been seen. Hermes agonizes along his way—the exchanger has un-tied his knots.

The translator places himself in the center or at the heart of the hourglass, or of any sub-hourglass. As does the shopkeeper, as does Max-well's demon. They transform the flows that pass through the exchanger. They ease passage, control it, and relate to the one-to-one. One language for this hearer, one molecule recognized as being slower, one item for such a client. Everything travels through the hands of Hermes. He is well-placed; hence, there are good places. Everything passes through his hands, because, more or less, everything is transformed in his hands. The exchanger is also a transformer. At least by the change of directions, at least by the division of flows, by bifurcation, at least by semiconduction, one-way streets and no entries, at least by orientation. Hermes is the god of the crossroads and is the god of whom Maxwell made a demon. Thus the message, passing through his hands in the location of the exchanger, is changer. It arrives neither pure nor unvarying nor stable. I am willing to have it improve, but that is a judgement. And if it were to worsen? I don't know and won't decide. What is true is that the message is burdened and arrives thus burdened. To speak correctly, it is parasited. The parasite has placed itself in the most profitable positions, at the intersection of relations. The elementary link of his individual activity was to relate to a relation; its performances are far better in spots where several relations cross or meet. It is at the knots of regulation, and suddenly, it relates to the collective. The one who succeeds in the relation of many-one, forms it and makes it work, is the politician and has found power. As is often said, he has the power of decision: of course, since he is at the crossings, the intercuttings: here, the intersections.

If the orator is heard as is, the network is decentered, even locally: there is no longer an intercepter, no longer a crossroads or intermediate; there is no longer a town; Hermes, the father of Pan, died on the Pentecost. A miracle, they say; such things don't happen. I can speak and hear from West to East; the walls come tumbling down from gusts of wind, from blares of music. I can have a relation directly to some object without an intercepter coming in between either to intercede or to forbid [*interdire*]. Is the absence of a parasite so rare? Is immediacy so miraculous? Must the word [*parole*] always be a parable, that is to say, always aside, *para-*? No. If it is not a miracle, can we build it?

I'll begin again. The first known system of communication is that of Leibniz. It is both radical and simple. No one relates to anyone or anything; doors and windows are not only closed but absent; everything and everyone relates to everything else by the intermediate of God. As the unique mediator, he is all-knowing and all-powerful. What the messages are that are exchanged by God among the monads is another question. This system is perfect, can be mathematically determined in its parts, *de jure* and *de facto*. Inversely, this mathematics is optimal communication. Every parasite is reduced to almost nothing in it, a grain of sand or of salt, a seventh. The problem of evil is brought back to harmony by the calculation of the optimum.

The second system is that of Hermes. He is a polytheist, is multi-centered, a chain of hourglasses, a network of such chains. The angels that pass, be they gods or demons, occupy the crossroads: knots of exchange, changes, cuts, bifurcations of decision, spindles, bundles, where the many come in one single hand. The beginnings of politics. The messages and flows move according to their energy and according to interceptions. What is received is what is sent, plus or minus the parasites. Sometimes the difference is considerable: what arrives, sometimes, is almost nothing. Distances destroy the hungry. The system of Leibniz is a limit of this system.

This network may remain at equilibrium for a while, but it can also come apart under the influence of great heat. Fire brings back disorder. The only thing heard is noise. That of the wind. And in this new beginning is distribution.

The third system connects many to many without an intermediate. It is the invention of the Paraclete, on the Pentecost. The many regulate themselves. This is something quite new, so new that it is believed to be the result of a miracle. In the second network, the demons and gods are many and well-known: local kinglets and chieftains, little leaders and procurers—of money or ideology, blackmail or information, single despots of regional rackets. In the first, everything reaches its limit; the local moves toward the global and the plural to the singular. In the center, the King is seated, that is to say, the Sun King, the Sun. God is the name Leibniz gives him. He is the universal in communication, the common language, Esperanto, Volapük, music, algebra, the universal characteric, or the *calculus ratiocinator*. It is the calculation that, as it is produced, produces the world. To communicate here is to calculate, that it to say, to encode. This universal can also be called money, another code, another general equivalent. For each denomination there is an exchanger, a unique change for the set of the network. If you speak theology, you will call it God; if you speak like an economist, you will call it money; if you adopt the language of philosophy, you will translate it or rather explain it by using terms like *code, general equivalent;* and so forth. And these translations leave everything unchanged, even—and especially—when they say: Reason. We live in a universe of rationalities. Those who change language fight amongst themselves as much as they affirm the same thing.

It is a question of knowing whether a network without constraints of crossroads, interchanges, intersections with parasites can be constructed. Where a given element can have a relation to another element without the constraints of mediation. This is the model of

Pentecost. We have to write a philosophy without any interchanges. I have just begun.

The ancient, venerable theology of the Paraclete matches in part the anthropology of exchange. When the Holy Ghost comes, so do gifts. He is the gift-giver, *munerum dator,* and his gifts are seven in number, *septiformis munere, sacrum septenarium.* The paths of the wind are not reversible; its origin is at only one point of the compass, and the flow never goes back to that point. The gift has a source but is not a point of reception. There is no exchange. What come from it are Wisdom, Knowledge, Intelligence, Advice, Force, Piety, the Fear of God. Eliminating from the list what is properly considered to be divine, what remains is what has the characteristics of what we call information.

Fire, from which wind comes, which comes from noise, from which gifts come, is paradoxical. It heats: *fove quid est frigidum, ignem accende;* it burns; but it cools. *Dulce refrigerium, in aeste temperies.* From this source, from this mouth, both hot and cold blow.

The most overused words in the world sometimes have unheard-of pomp. No exchange could take place, no gift could be given in any of the languages I have heard spoken, if the final receiver did not say "thank you" at the end of the line. The terminal offers thanks. The phrase is only a gust of wind; it is indispensible nonetheless. It throws this thank-you on the scale of the freely given. Without it, there have been wars: the ingrates against the magnificent, the parasites against the euergetes. What purpose would giving serve, I ask you, if this minimal recognition did not recognize the superb and the generous? Moreover, the thanker moves away from the last position, one, by the way, that is rather difficult to maintain. To have the last word is to leave the last position to the other and to jump to the penultimate. Thus the host or the gift-giver quickly answers: "Don't mention it; you're welcome; at your service," and thereby brings back the receiver to his place.

I never understood this supplementary response before having had the chance to use it in Greek. In other languages, its mechanical use had left it in the dark.

In saying "thank you," the Hellene says *eucharist.* "Good graces." Everything is clear now. This word for this thing and this is my body. I do not know if this form of polite answer in an exchange explains the aforementioned transsubstantiation, or if the mystery illuminates the everyday, but I am sure that, since the clear laughter of the Cretan peasant, it is a question of the same act and the same operation. Eucharist: the word is worth the thing; the logicial enters the secrets of the material. Eucharist: God is in our relation; our relation is

God himself, incarnate. Eucharist: the exchange ends in a prayer, and when we pray together, Christ is there as the third among us. Eucharist: the word is made flesh and the bread is made word. Εὐχαριστῶ πολὶ.

Παρακαλῶ is, as we know, the closing response. Don't mention it and, yes, you're welcome. I call you, I call, I beg you. Who is invited, the one prayed to, the one called to? Say his name, say your name, say a name. Παράκλητος, the Paraclete, the common name of the Holy Ghost, the third person. He intervenes, interrupts, comes in through the walls, during meals or meetings; he intercedes and proceeds both from the Father and the Son. He is the wind, the being of the wind, the gust, the one the Jews called *Ruach*. He is the gift, the being of the gift, the universal donor. You say you're welcome because he has received, because it is he who gives. Fire flies above exchange and above the group, jumps from last place to first, closes the irreversible chain and constitutes the community. The parasite Paraclete becomes the host. At the door of the room, they heard a noise that day. Divided in tongues of fire on their heads, the third—included—is henceforth at every position. It is possible for this fire to bring some light into the black box that we are. Hermes died one day of interference.

Eucharist and Paraclete, the second and third persons together, in common words of everyday usage: the preceding description was of a trinity, without our knowing so. And the gods are here.

We undoubtedly know and maybe one day we will fully understand the things of the world. We will never know if they are created nor who might have created them. This mystery is entirely out of our grasp. It is not at all sure that religious matters have anything at all to do with the world—that is to say, with physics. Behind the thickness of things, the one called God is almost infinitely hidden. Our classics hid Him under the conditions of the infinity of exact thought. This distance is as long in the clear subject as in the shaded object.

But I want to say that there is something divine in this word, divine things. What I am saying is really beside the real, direct question: *God* is a noun, a name; *divine* is an adjective, thrown to the side. The world is divine and is full of divine things. This sea, this plain, this river, the ice floe, the tree, light and life. I know it, I see it, I feel it, I am illuminated by it, burning. The wine-dark sea and divine life. The adjective, placed to one side, at a distance from the names and notions of philosophy is enough for me as a parable. Yes, the divine is there; I touch it; these things are improbable miracles; I never stopped loving the world and seeing that it is beautiful. Yes, my philosophy is adjectival; it is awe-struck. The real is not rational; it is improbable and miraculous.

We will perhaps never know what passes and what happens in

our collective. What passes is the object or the word that is exchanged. What happens after giving? The gods come down slowly into this black box, the adjective Paraclete, the gift-giving guest, lit by a flame. It is not at all certain that religious matters do not have everything to do with intersubjective relations. God is lost behind physics. God is lost behind objects. God is lost behind the subject, be he intelligent or pathetic, of knowledge or of feeling. The one my forefathers called the Father, infinitely hidden, remains absent. The canonical proofs, along the paths of the world or the function of rigor, are out of bounds. When philosophy is neither in the object nor in the subject nor in their obsolete relation, the religious is not thinkable. I have lost forever the power and the glory, total knowledge and the abundance of the Creation.

I live among things—divine things—and I am plunged in the obscure group. They are easier to understand than it is—not more simple, for they are exquisitely complex. I find happiness in the divinity of things themselves; they push me toward pantheism; I suffer quite often in the group and in the dark, in my intelligence and in my life. Soon, in order to make the collective clearer, I shall use the notion of quasi-object. It circulates, it passes among us. I give it; I receive it. Thank you; you're welcome. Eucharist and Paraclete. We are the second and third persons, submerged in the incarnation and in the wind of the Pentecost, leaving the Father to infinity for all eternity. Grace passes in the fuzzy area between words and things, between the canals where substantial foods and sonorous voices flow, between the exchanges of energy and information, an intermediate space, a space of equivalence where language is born, where fire is born, where it makes the things of which it speaks appear, an unstable distance of ecstasy and existence, of incarnation and ascension, of bread and birds. I move forward a bit in the black box. I hear the invitation to live together in the space in which the material and the logical are exchanged. The third appears; the third is included. Maybe he is each and every one of us.

Part Two

More Interrupted Meals

Technique, Work

Rats' Dinner ———————————
——————————— *Diode, Triode*

The city rat feasts with the country rat; the story, however, is not just about two rats. Someone troubles the feast, interrupts the meal, intervenes. Who is this third person? He makes noise; he is, most assuredly, a prosopopoeia of noise. Noise is a person—that is the lesson of Pentecost: it is the third person.

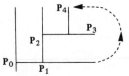

The banquet is a relation of the two rats, a relation presented almost theatrically, on the carpet with the door in the back making a hole in the scenery, but it is a real relation where they eat ortolan and enjoy themselves—a relation, believe me, among the best. And the third person intercepts it, parasites it by means of a parasitic noise. He makes it stop.

But everything has not yet been said with these first figures. The third, probably, was the parasited one. The master of the household, awakened from his sleep by the sounds of the rodents and the noise of their teeth on the birds' carcasses, comes back to where the feast had been and where the dirty dishes and leftovers are still spread about. Suddenly, the system we had sketched closes. In the nesting series of vampires, the first, as if by luck, jumps to the last position and, in one fell swoop, eliminates the intermediates, who leave in a hurry. A good bit of feedback, like a slap on the cheek to get rid of a mosquito: destructions and flattenings of the system. It was nothing or almost nothing. The host counter-parasites his guests, not by taking away his food from them (first meaning) but by making noise (second meaning). Theorem: if the first becomes the last, the intermediates are cancelled.

Question: how does the noise scare the robbers? And how is it that worms and rats work in secret, silently, at night? How is it that this is not said? An obscure relation between the thing to be taken, and the substance, and the winds and voices. Black horror, anguish, the only thing that made Rousseau drop his pen, the only thing that interrupted his confession. The parasite is afraid, and the host knows this. Thus, he uses an alarm, securing his doors with warning signals. He never stops giving the signal. Thus, the nightingale sings and the dog barks to define their nests and their property. The signal and the thing are not as cut off from one another as they say. The *Cratylus* plays on the flight of the rats at the first sound from the building. If the door creaks a bit, I drop the booty. No one would enter a deafening area, even if it were filled to the brim with precious stones. The more valuable the things in the vault, the louder the alarm. The voices of the gods, on the mountain-tops, in lightning and thunder. The most nominalist of my contemporaries could not refuse to repel the cuckoos from the birds' nest, and he would yell were the nest robbed. A relation of alarm between the thing and the sign.

The system is cancelled when the parasited one makes noise in feedback. But this signal does not last. You cannot spend your whole life singing, nor can you continually protect your possessions, for you have to acquire, repair, work: without that the winter winds come, and one begs for food in vain. Noise stops for a moment—it is a function of time; even the grasshopper stops. A signal that did not stop would thereby stop being a signal. And thus the third man withdraws. The system immediately is put back in order. Rats in the country. At the first noise, the system is cancelled: if the noise stops, everything comes back to where it was. That shows at least that the parasites are always there, even in the absence of a signal. Only the noticeable signal cancels them. They are inevitable, like white noise. White noise [*bruit de fond*] is the heart [*fond*] of being; parasitism is the heart of relation. White noise is the base—"white space," as it were; the parasite is the base of the canal traced on this space. Parasitism is only a linear noise. The system is oscillating, and it can be easily constructed. It exists as a whole; it returns to nothingness according to the noise, its duration, and its time. The noise, through its presence and absence, the intermittence of the signal, produces the new system, that is to say, oscillation. It oscillates twice in Aesop's text but La Fontaine, as far as I can tell, was not looking for that.

There is, however, a condition for this variable stability, for this invariance by instabilities. The city rat reinvites the country cousin. If the latter accepts, the system is reinstalled, as I've noted, until the next noise. This, however, is not the case. The country rat leaves; enough of that signal for him. And he goes off to the country, where the city rat does not follow. Thus, now it is the country rat who interrupts the meal. It is no longer the noise, since it has already stopped. The guest thus becomes the interrupter. The parasite in the first sense of the word becomes the parasite in the second sense, for he cuts the relation; he does not want to hear the message of the invitation. The setup of the system is somewhat more complex than we had thought.

For it to remain as simple as the aforementioned oscillation, the country rat has to resemble the city rat; he has to learn which noises are which; he has to become domesticated. All the oscillation provoked by the noise depends on the equality of the rats, maybe on their being twins. They resemble each other—they are rats; they are not twins—they are not equals. Put that into an equation—nothing is easier—and the system can be constructed. As they are unequal, another system is added to the first. The country rat becomes the interrupter, like the noise. The broken relation is that of the city rat and the guest, that of the city rat and the noise. For the city dweller, immunized to aggressions of this caliber, moves away a bit and then returns to the meal. He would not eat without being thus inured. Thus he has a constant relation with the interruptions; they are familiar to him; he knows how to tame them; he is acclimated to them. He is vaccinated by the parasites. His guest suddenly breaks these habits. From that point on, the parasite changes his place. Who is, as I was saying, the third? Noise. Of course, and moreover, it was the host, the master of the household. Now it is the guest. The third is the second, the second becomes the third. The system oscillated; now its very mechanics change.

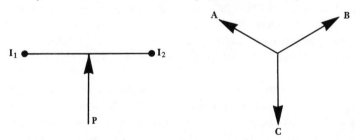

Given, two interlocutors and the channel that attaches them to one another. The parasite, nesting on the flow of the relation, is in third position. Up to now, this model was adequate; it was the elementary link of the system. But now, the positions change. The guest becomes the interrupter; the noise becomes interlocutor; part of the channel becomes obstacle, and vice versa. Questions: who and where is the third man? These questions have fluctuating answers, functions of noise, time, and of the new relations of equality or similarity between the terms. The same and the other change places with the third. A clear-cut logic, at least since the Plato of the *Sophist* and "The Villager and the Snake." A diagram is needed where the branches are not determined and where the cuts are not specified.

Another example. The rats resembled each other a bit, being of the same species if not of the same locality; the third interrupts the feast. This young man, Socrates, is snub-nosed, like you, with prominent eyes, like you; he looks like you, both his face and his body; as for the latter, he is your homonym. The one to whom I am introducing you is a stranger. From Elea, from Mantinea, besides not of the same deme as our ancestors were. The analogs and the host, those here and those there, those of the *Symposium,* those who interrupt the feast and those who make it work, homologous with the newly arrived stranger. Now conversations without parasite. Xenophon's is too affected. He is affected; he is a mime.

Simonides, however, is at the banquet and is interrupted like the rats. He runs to the door, and no one follows him. Here he is, an epiphany, in the presence of the divine twins. Castor and Pollux resemble each other to the point of being easily confused with one another. And the situation, which was fluctuating in the room with the Persian rug, is completely reversed. Two rats dine, the third is at the door and makes noise; a poet dines, two men at the door make noise; the rats flee, Simonides runs, the animals are analogs and the gods, twins. The diagrams are asymmetrical. The city rat made a mistake: the first creak can precede the catastrophe.

To avoid the catastrophe, the country rat turns the whole thing around himself, and the guest becomes the interrupter. By the grace of the gods, the same model is completely turned around: the interrupters are two in number and similar, like interlocutors. If positions, roles, and controls change, it is better to have a diagram with indeterminate divisions.

Once again, who is Simonides? A guest among other guests. He participates in a festive communication at the feast. But as a poet of odes of triumph, he has paid for his place at the table with words, be they freely given or owed, and he is thus a parasite. Is he part of the channel or part of the obstacle? That is not something to be decided but to be cut in three. And each branch can have all the values. To put it another way: Alcibiades interrupts the banquet, makes a lot of noise at the door of the court; in a besotted voice he yells at the top of his lungs, and is accompanied by a flute player whose voice we hear as well;

gilded youth, parasitic as much as you wish—economically, politically, festively—and here, as well, on the operations of communication. These disorganized noises will introduce disorganization into the system and then, a new order. But the guests at this symposium are paying for their participation in the feast with discourses—voices and winds. They are parasites, like Simonides. I no longer really know how to say it: the parasite parasites the parasites. In other words, any given position in the ternary model is, *ad libitum,* parasitic. Who is the third? Someone, anyone. The noise stops; someone leaves. Someone, anyone: both formal and random.

Logic of the Fuzzy*

Who, then, is making such a racket at the door? The gods, come here to save from a possible danger the one who deals with the divine through style. The benefactors, the benevolent, the messengers, the angels. Who is making this noise, this wind, these voices, these tongues? The Holy Ghost, the Paraclete, the gift-giver. The interrupter is an intercessor and a favorable one.

No. Say no to the powers of noise to be able to hear oneself, listen to oneself, understand oneself. Get thee behind me, Satan. Eliminate the parasites from the channel so the message can go through as best it can. The imperative of purge. Thus exclude the third, the Demon, prosopopoeia of noise. If we want peace, if we want an agreement between object and subject, the object appearing at the moment of the agreement, at the Last Supper as well as in the laboratory, in the dialogue as on the blackboard, we have to get together, assembling, resembling, against whoever troubles our relations, the water of our channel. He is on the other bank [*rive*], the rival is. He is our common enemy. Our collective is the expulsion of the stranger, of the enemy, of the parasite. The laws of hospitality become laws of hostility. Whatever the size of the group, from two on up to all human kind, the transcendental condition of its constitution is the existence of the Demon.

The Devil or the Good Lord? Exclusion, inclusion? I don't know. But in any case I know these archaic questions. Struggles between

---

Flou means "nebulous," "blurry," "fuzzy," "cloudy," and so forth. I have chosen *fuzzy* as a translation because of the use of the word in mathematics in the term "fuzzy set." The reader should bear in mind, however, the other meanings of the word *flou*. —Trans.

two men are never anything but theater: appearance, representation (show), scenery, moral, amusements. As soon as we are two, we are already three or four. We learned that a long time ago. In order to succeed, the dialogue needs an excluded third; our logic requires the same thing. Maybe they also require an included fourth. The very lesson is written all around. Saint George face to face with the dragon plays the strongman facing his equal; both are associated, in fact, to cut up into pieces the bodies that crumble under the stable arch of their bridge. These bivalent logics and dialectics are useful only as advertisements, promos, commercials, for those involved. The wolf and the lamb, alone, each on a bank of the river, populate their space with dogs, shepherds, families, kings.

The Devil or the Good Lord? Exclusion, inclusion? Thesis or antithesis? The answer is a spectrum, a band, a continuum. We will no longer answer with a simple yes or no to such questions of sides. Inside or outside? Between yes and no, between zero and one, an infinite number of values appear, and thus an infinite number of anwers. Mathematicians call this new rigor "fuzzy": fuzzy subsets, fuzzy topology. They should be thanked: we have needed this fuzziness for centuries. While waiting for it, we seemed to be playing the piano with boxing gloves on, in our world of stiff logic with our broad concepts. Our methods can now be fine-tuned and in the process, increased in number. Henceforth, my book is rigorously fuzzy. Geometry has made its peace with finesse.

——— *The Master and the Counter-Master**

The master and the slave are never face to face. The master is wily enough to avoid such a confrontation, which would endanger his mastery and possession. This ruse is mastery itself and the way of keeping it. The master leaves the battleground as soon as the battle is won. The master is not there. The slave constantly looks for him everywhere but does not find him. No one has ever killed an absent adversary. The master is lost as soon as he is found. Struggle is rare, an exceptional case, in which the master has allowed himself to be found; it is the most optimistic figure in history. In fact, the master is afraid; he lives as if he is hunted; he lies down and hides. He sends out emissaries, sends lieutenants to fight in his place. If the one-instead [*tenant-lieu*] wins, the master wins; if he loses, it is not the master who has lost. As soon as the master is master, he fears death and lives with death, the reality of his power.

He is right to fear death, for he is more or less alone among a rare population of masters. The slave is a crowd; he is in the greater number. How a very few people manage to enslave the greatest number— more or less all of humanity—that is the miracle and is the exception to every law. Thus it is a mistake to posit the relation between the master and the slave as a one-to-one relation, two single heroes fighting on the lists, the object at stake; their relation is at least that of one-to-many, if not that of one to the quasi-totality. By having conceived this relation as one of individuals or of singularities, whatever the symbol, the inventor of this struggle sketched out a maximally optimistic figure of history. If there were always a one-to-one relation, there would be two

---

Contre-maître more properly means "foreman." I have chosen the more awkward "counter-master" in order to maintain the implied opposition. —Trans.

equally strong subsets, that of mastery and that of slavery, which would constantly be changing places; there would be neither miracle nor exception. There would never be slavery but rather the image of a title at stake every fall and awarded every spring, the illusion of sportive glory, with the titleholder changing. It is thus that, for the past two centuries, philosophy has offered the spectacle of a medieval tournament or of Olympic games, opium.

But this is never the case. The oppressor is rare; the slave is ordinary—in droves. The relation between a master and his slaves is always a relation between one and many. The classes are never equally strong, and it is almost never a division of classes: more often, number and rarity. The master exploits the positive strength of life, the energy and the time, the production of forces, the work, and so forth, of this immense number. The crowd produces; the small number decides and channels movement. To exploit means to prepare the space, decide, channel, etc., to specify the strategies. Long columns of ants move at fixed times along the streets and roads and place themselves at their intended posts. The master is always a geometer, a topologist, and someone who knows space first of all; the empire is large in the first place. The master always knows where the slave goes and will go; he has marked the entrances and exits and has stamped the passports. Sometimes, among the innumerable ants, the noise of revolt rears it head and other energies appear, different from those that accept channeling toward their work. Then the slaves begin to struggle with the master. And sometimes, they force him to appear.

Sometimes the crowd lashes out and pillages everything in its path. That, however, is rare. It seems that that is feared. Why, I don't know, but I do know that it is feared. And that many things are built up to avoid what is called an unleashing. In general, and in reality, the large number *delegates*. Among the slaves, at the same time the noise appears among the slaves, one or several individual heroes appear who represent, as they say, the angry crowd or the struggling class. They are directly produced by the energies that could be called the negative energies of the mass, not those of work, but those of rebellion. The master parasites some of them, and these heroes are produced by others.

Thus, with their own class, the heroes have relations of one-to-many, the same relations—formally at first and then very quickly made concrete—that the masters had with the slaves. This slave becomes a master, that is certainly true, but far from becoming a master of the master, he becomes another master of the slaves. As such, as the representative of the slaves, he struggles with the master. And the latter recognizes this. He allows himself to be found. Then there are no longer relations of one-to-many, but that of one-to-one, the relation of individual combat, of tournaments, of the lists. The master and slave face each other; they have equal chances of winning, or at least, the outcome is in doubt. The Horatii and the Curiatii, under the clamoring militants, enlisted men. Then the slave can become the master of the master, and so forth. He is, precisely, a counter-master. Another master against the master. Opposed to him and right next to him. In his fuzzy environment.

And it is thus that the master once began his career.

More Rats' Meals ———————————
————————————— *Machines and Engines*

With a few pieces of wood and some rushes or strands of hemp, small, simple machines can be constructed that have an exquisite relation to the business at hand. A tortoise, awkward and slow like any tortoise of its size and carrying his house around on his back, tires of travelling back roads and wants to see the country. Two ducks like the project and create a flying machine to carry the pilgrim. They put a piece of wood sideways in his mouth, and each grabs one end of the stick. Hold tight, they say: take-off. The formal plan, seen from here, is described at three thousand feet: the twin birds and the parasite, whose teeth are hooked onto the middle of the stick. A miracle! cry the gawkers; philosophy, relations and diagrams, flies way above our heads. Above your heads, you fools, answers the passenger, who, letting go of the stick to chatter, falls and dies at the feet of the passers-by. The parasite must keep quiet, even if the noise of the crowd accords him highest honors. Profit from ducks, pigeons, and fools, but never say a single word about it, for the penalty for that is falling down from the heavens into the disordered noise of the disseminated crowd. The talking-machine is mortal. And the unwise or stupidly talkative third is excluded from it. And put to death all the more cruelly, the greater his difference from his interlocutors, who resemble each other. Airborne species or earth-bound reptile, travellers in the air or in the water and a homebody with a moveable house, a global view, a bird's-eye view, and myopia. What is this third getting into?

It is of no small interest to notice here that the well-run machine does not copy the bodies of animals and their organic system, but rather our relations among ourselves. Can we conceive of an intersubjective origin for simple machines? For the lever? For the scale? For technology in general? The answer to this question is affirmative. And it is still affirmative for machines that are not so simple.

The ducks—as we expected—build a machine with acoustic parasites. By varying the logicial, the material is changed. By speaking, the tortoise interrupts the channel, that is to say, the trip. The machine works if the third says nothing. As for the birds, they can squawk and chatter to their hearts' delight. But the hawk, the bird of prey, discovers a machine with ordinary parasites, those looking to eat well. Thus a frog wanted to eat a rat; for that to happen, these stories must be fables. Given a big fat rat, obese, never fasting, a parasite who succeeds without interruption. The frog invites the rat to dinner, and the story begins to be interesting: eating goes on everywhere in the story and all the time: the rat eats without a pause, the frog eats the rat, and the hawk, even before the frog eats the rat, eats the both of them. Come to my house, the frog says. But we'll have to swim in the swamp. Hence the machine, the new engine, the link. A supple relation, not stiff like a stick, but a rush does the trick. The frog and the rat are tied together at the feet; the first pulls the second out into the reeds. And already,the frog is ready to devour the rat. To do so, noise first, brekekekex. The feast changes hosts, and the guest changes roles; from the subject of the banquet, the rat becomes the object: once a parasite, now the main course. My body is only this. Is it really rare that the guest is eaten? The fear and anxiety of the passer-by in the den of the satyr: were these really the memories of ancient anthropophagy? Do all these stories hide some forgotten cannibalism? And have these interrupted banquets only interrupted the chewing of like by like? A while back, the ducks, analogues, let a talkative tortoise fall; and now we have two tied together who are very different in nature, so different that, tied at the feet, they come to blows [en venir aux mains], and see the third swoop down on them. Instead of being excluded, he arrives. Instead of dying, he kills them. And the diagram is symmetrical. Who is hostile, who is hospitable? Everyone. From the point of view of the third, the thing is always double, everyone is both fish and fowl, host and guest, and enemy to boot. The channel is bad; the third is the master. But we already know how a subject can become an object. But if that happens for one, it happens immediately for the other. And for the relation as well. This is my body; this is my blood.

And suddenly, I no longer know if we have built a model, if from wood or rushes we have been able to produce a model of relations, or if, in this practice, we have discovered the origins of technology, of tools, of means. This roundabout means. These media always between us.

For once—a rare occurrence—Aesop is above La Fontaine. His naive moral brings a goddess with her justice and her scales, and the beam of the scales is a yoke, the equilibrium of a yoke. But I have already seen this setup: the hawk holds the middle of the beam securely and the frog and the rat are tied together by this yoke. It is the same thing with the tortoise and the two ducks. Let us put scales and justice —the usual moral of the story—aside for a moment and return to the action. Or, more exactly, let us return to all the actions told here, a thousand of which have been told since the world became the world, that is to say, since the beginning of history. The relation here is never simple, a canal or a road, a stick or channel between two ducks or anyone else. The parasite always plugs into the system; the parasite is always there; it is inevitable. The parasite is the third in a trivial model, the three-branched star. Here now is the relation that cannot be analyzed; that is to say, there is none simpler. Here then is the beginning of intersubjectivity. The third is always there, god or demon, reason or noise.

A third exists before the second. A third exists before the other. As Zeno the Elder would say, I have to go through the middle before reaching the end. There is always a mediate, a middle, an intermediary. And in this three-handed game, the middle term can be any one of the three, depending. If it is a man, he is a slave, servant, or butler: or king, or prey, or sacrificed, or eaten, or excluded, or triumphant conqueror. Loved, hated: deified, chased into the underworld; obstacle or aide: things don't necessarily go two by two. He is the being of the relation, coming from it as it comes from him. His roles or incarnations are a function of the relation, the relation is a function of the parasite, in a circular causality, in feedback loops.

If the parasite is a man, he is all that, tortoise or hawk, lion without rivals or grown old; if he is a man, he is the whole animal kingdom, through his fabulous metamorphoses. If you do not recognize the parasite, it is precisely because he goes through the whole fable and the whole system and that he is transformed as if by magic. Thus the Holy Ghost speaks every tongue, and everyone hears him in his own; this is the absolute metamorphosis of the essence of the relation. He is sometimes a horde of rats making noise in the attic, sometimes the king's court, and the king in the palaces where people bow to him. Pumpkin and carriage, char-girl and princess. Only a fable says that. Only the fable and its metempsychosis allow me to see the same third man in the nest, in the cave, at my table, and on the throne. If he is a man, he is nothing; like a neutral element, a joker, he is nothing but grimace and greasepaint. This morning, he defends the humble, justice; at noon, he is only one who can be heard; this evening, he takes all the spots;

tomorrow, he is king. Or it can occur differently. And this power comes simply from the fact that he is the relation and not fixed in the essence, that he is not fixed in a station but is in the functioning of the relations in his being part of the warp and woof, that he is relational and thus that he is multiple and collective. As he is, without knowing exactly what he is, in the black box of the socius, he is seen in various guises. He is a Sophist and a politician. It is in his interest for everyone to be fixed in place and fixed in essence. The mobile relation wants to prolong the permanence of Being. If he is a man, he is an actor. He goes on stage, sets up the scenery, invents theater, and imposes theater. He is all the faces on the screen. If he is a man, he is at the origin of comedy, tragedy, the circus and the farce, and of public meetings, where he gathers the noises of legitimacy. If he is a man, he is the joker in the free systems of collectivities. He is social technique and knows how to play at the mastery of men and at their domestication.

If he is an animal, he is a servant. Once upon a time, says the fable, a time that wasn't fabulous, where there weren't as many banquets or weddings. You didn't eat so often nor so well nor together before the miraculous Neolithic Age, when agriculture and animal husbandry were invented. No banquets, no mounts for horses, no feasts, no beasts of burden. La Fontaine says these things in parallel, a parallel which instructs us today.* The wedding is a result of domestication and of the farmyard; without that, where would the sheep, calves, chickens and broods, all be? No feast without a parasite, as I was saying. That is understood twice, and the second time we hear that animal husbandry is in fact parasitic. The scrounger is not only the one we think. It is the guest, the host, the farmer. All our results together again. A horse hated a deer and ran after him, the reverse of the story of the frog who, through his desire, attracted the rat. The horse didn't catch the deer; what deer do, they do quickly. The horse calls man, who saddles the horse, who invents, shall we say, hunting, and who doesn't let the stallion go free after the kill. The same diagram is as effective as ever. The man in third position masters the link between the horse and the deer. We notice too that hunting is not primitive; we thought as much. Before hunting, hunting dogs have to be raised. Horses and dogs—read Xenophon about the latter. And parasitism is fundamental, first to acquire these indispensable foods of history. The horse dies in the stables where he drags his link, his reins changed from hatred to servitude, reoriented from the second, the deer, to the third, the man: the man who always thinks of playing the third position in order to become master. Now he can have a relation to the deer; he can speak of hunting and

*La Fontaine, "Le Cheval s'étant voulu se venger du cerf."—Trans.

game and then say of the horse that it is in the third position. If he is an animal, he is domesticated. He is in the stables, in the farmyard, in the pig sty—in short, in school.

And if the third is an object, it is a technical object. For the past few minutes I have only been speaking about technique and technology: social, biological, that is to say, used in or on complex systems where blind practice seems to precede any theory at a great distance. But this distinction or this precession might mean nothing at all. It is undoubtedly relative and undoubtedly dominated by narrow cultural categories. In short, it is exactly the same thing as the discovery of the origin and function of slavery or domestication or husbandry or tools or engines. It is the growing objectification of our intersubjective relations.

In this field of research, the theory of knowledge, the history of praxes, the only thing ever considered is the set of relations of the subject, be it personal or collective, with the object, be it local or global. On these relations, be they direct or reversed, only schools and sects, laden with signs and names, swords and guns, have been built; only contradictions and impossibilities, harmony, miracles or illusions have been found. Or vulgar banalities, like the extension of organs in a hammer, in a telescope, or in tongs. Vaguely obscene. And naive: how does this philosophy of the hoe account for—I am not yet saying a computer— but simply, a simple machine?

Here then, we have discovered how. By that I mean the intermediary, the milieu. A trunk, the tail, and the head: the trunk of the relation between head and tail. The milieu, the mediate. What is between, what exists between. The middle term. The means and the means to an end. The means and the tool; the tool and its use; the means and the use.

The Means, the Milieu

At the door of the room, they heard a noise. What happened? The master is there; he disrupts the rats' feast. Why? He was sleeping soundly, after a good meal of ortolans, a heavy dish. Suddenly he awakens. He has heard a noise. Uneasy and anxious, he gets up and bit by bit opens the door. No one. The rats have left. A dream; he goes back to bed. Who, then, made the noise? The rats, of course. A feast makes noise. Here are the guests, with their little paws; it seems like thunder above the ceiling. Here are the gnashing of their teeth and the scratching of the rodents. All that wakes him up. The noise, then, was called for by noise. At the door of the room, he heard a noise. He gets up, the rats flee . . . A change of position for the observer.

At the feast everyone is talking. At the door of the room there is a ringing noise, the telephone. Communication cuts conversation, the noise interrupting the messages. As soon as I start to talk with this new interlocutor, the sounds of the banquet become noise for the new "us." The system has shifted. If I approach the table, the noise slowly becomes conversation. In the system, noise and message exchange roles according to the position of the observer and the action of the actor, but they are transformed into one another as well as a function of time and of the system. They make order or disorder.

This case, like that of the rats is more interesting than it appears. In the room, there are two systems, the feast and the telephone. A given noise, the sound of the conversation in the room, is a noise for the conversation I am having with my interlocutor on the phone, but it is a message for my guests. And for them, my conversation is a noise for their own. It all depends on the position of the observer. The result is well-known. But the sound of the phone interrupted the conversation of the table: this system of messages collapsed into noise. It announces the exchange of messages on the telephone; the sound opens up a new system. It depends no longer on the observer but only on time. The noise is the end of a system and the formation of a new one. That is exactly the *apologia* of the rats. The feast is interrupted by the host, and when it starts again, the conditions are transformed for the ordinary meal in town and the banquet going on in the countryside. The noise separates them and forms a complex system with two different feasts. Noise is a sign of the increase in complexity. It would seem that the separation of city and country was a decisive one in history: there were simple rats and complex rats afterwards.

The noise is a joker. It has at least two values, like the third man: a value of destruction and a value of construction. It must be included and excluded. This is both the story of the rats and that of a complex system. Computer science and anthropology are joined together. Does that amount to saying that the former, through its technical intervention, will have as great an impact as the other through its analyses? Or does that mean that science is making objective what old wives' tales have said all along? In this new type of rationalism, that takes into account both the exact and the human, everything can be said.

Where am I now? Somewhere between the feast and the telephone. I have found a spot where, give or take one vibration, moving a hair's breadth in either direction causes the noises to become messages and the messages, noises. Of course this crest is jagged, random, stochastic. Whoever watched me in my comings and goings would think that he was watching a fly. I guide myself by sound. I am on the saw's teeth of the mountain, at the edges of noise. Not an echo, not at the center of everything like a sonorous echo, but on the edges of messages, at the birth of noises. This erratic path follows the paths of invention exactly. These are also edges common to the exact and human sciences. Diode, triode, method.*

Bivalent systems get lost around here. The value of belonging passes through space, through the spectrum that separates or unites the two old values. The mathematics of the "fuzzy" explores this milieu, this means, this medium.

A given system is in place. The rats' feast or our own or any other organization. It works and makes noise. It gets used up; it ages; it heads toward noise. But the usual function is a set of messages. Look

*See "Randonnée," in *Hermès V. Le passage du Nord-Ouest*, pp. 11-24, 93-113.

at the conversation of the banquet, look at a classical machine, look at a communication circuit, look at a living organism. The couple noise-message is part of the system, and its relation is a good index of the operation and the age of the system.

This couple and their relation are set apart by an observer seated within the system. In a way he overvalues the message and undervalues the noise if he belongs to the functioning of the system. He represses the parasites in order to send or receive communications better and to make them circulate in a distinct and workable fashion. This repression is also religious excommunication, political imprisonment, the isolation of the sick, garbage collection, public health, the pasteurization of milk, and so forth, as much as it is repression in the psychoanalytical sense. But it also has to do with a history, the history of science in particular: whoever belongs to the system perceives noises less and represses them more, the more he is a functioning part of the system. He never stops being in the good, the just, the true, the natural, the normal. All dogmatism lives on this division, be it blind or decided.

For this couple to appear and for the message to be brutally undervalued, all that is necessary is to leave the system. One can leave the system in several ways: by one's own difference or by the gesture of exclusion that I have just called repression. It is not so simple. If systems were univocal or if they had one norm, this description would be enough. But systems function with several norms at a time, the proof of which is that one often arrives at the center by playing the periphery. In other words, the game of exclusion can be played without ever leaving the system, and, on the contrary, getting more and more into the system. The best way to succeed in it is to misconstrue it. The counter-norm is never a noise of the norm but the same norm reversed, that is to say, its twin. If you make a motor turn in reverse, you do not break it: you build a refrigerator. Since Bergson, who invented this whole business about opened and closed, interior and exterior, systems have been immunized by becoming more complex. They became stronger by becoming more tolerant. They were acclimated to the revolutionary, the madman, the deviant, the dissident: an organism lives very well with its microbes; it lives better and is hardened by them. The implacable power of systems with several norms and several variables grouping each time a norm and a counternorm and the function of inclusion of these systems have to be added to the cruelty of systems with one norm and a gesture of exclusion. On one side you kill; on the other, you castrate. On one side you put away; on the other, you festoon. Tolerance is part of the panoply of intolerance. Thus, the genius never undoes the system; he generalizes it, introducing into it a supplementary variable with its countervariable. He never questions the validity of science, but one of its paradigms or incarnations, and that is what science is, they say—the broken series of these incarnations. He never questions reason or history, but one of its moments or states or specific cases, for that is what history or reason is, they say—the discontinuous series of moments. The recovery of the simple through the complex. But it is not because it is more complex that it is not the same thing.

These descriptions or phenomenologies, sometimes in logic, sometimes in topology,* repeated for almost a century in a variety of guises, express the system. They are the voices of the system. They show how to transform it in order to reinforce it. How to use exclusion or a counternorm to enrich complexity. Let us suppose a moving observer. First of all he perceives the set of working messages—the conversation of the banquet. He nears the border. More and more, he has the voice of the repressed. The border he crosses is not linear. Outside, he hears only noise, the to-do made by the guests, the gnashing of the rodents' teeth. The border is wide; it is the crown or torus of reversal. The border goes from the message with repressed noise to noise with repressed message. The couple fluctuates in the torus. The torus is the space of transformation of noise into message, and vice versa, for the observer.

It is the same for every banquet and every system. I have moved away from the table (of the gods); I listen to my new interlocutor on the phone. Near the phone, in such and such a condition, our message represses and expulses the sounds of the meal. If I move away, the sounds become conversation again, and the new interlocutor becomes inaudible. A new crown around the system, a new torus, a new bottle, a new space of transformation. The rats' feast makes noise for the host; the host makes noise for the rats. The noises of the former awaken the third from a deep sleep, and his awakening puts an end to the rats' gettogethers. That is to say, the systems interfere with one another.

The philosophies about which I have just spoken come into play in this imaginary world where there is only one system and where this one system is constructed on only one norm or one principle. In fact, all systems are very complex; in fact, there are several of them. They come into play in an ideal world of light and dark where there is only one exterior and one interior, only one shadow and one light. This imaginary world is on the moon. Without any atmosphere, where a screen separates space into black and white, furnace and glacier, blinding light and opaque night. In both cases, no one can see a thing. But the atmosphere,

*These notions of open and closed, of closure and enclosure, that have served, at least since Bergson's time, as operators for the rhetoric of history, are often only representations in space, projections in a topology like that of Jordan, of Hegelian dialectics. Instead of speaking logically a space is described. But nothing is changed by transposition.

the air, the milieu (the medium), make light diffuse; it outlines obstacles, lights the other side of walls, single-point light sources producing scallops and patterns. In order to have only light, one would have to live at the single-point light source, or the medium would have to be removed, creating a vacuum. As soon as the medium intervenes, the ray of light wanders about the world. We see only because we see badly. It works only because it works badly. Every system is a set of messages; in order to hear the message alone, one would have to be identical to the sender. As soon as love flees, the noise comes back in. As soon as the discussion of love lessens, Alcibiades is at the door, yelling at the top of his lungs, accompanied by his flute-player. As soon as we are two, there is a medium between us, the light ray is lost in the air, the message is lost in the interceptions, there is only a space of transformation. The torus and the crown devour the system. There is no need to move away from the system for the fluctuating couple of message and noise to appear. Maybe I understand the message only because of the noise.

A while back I thought that fundamental transformations were at work between systems, in their intersections or interferences, in a conditional space in which they were all immersed. I thought that my method was a trip through the transcendental space of this immersion. I thought that it followed the stochastic crests and the jagged edges of its sierras: the capricious ups and downs of the divisions between message and noise. To one side or the other I hear a noise or the beginnings of a message; thus the crest is rather sharp, and in order to stay atop it, one must move around a great deal in the crown or the torus or in the intersection of these volumes.

My method was certainly a capricious trip in the space prejudged as transcendental in which the systems are immersed.

But the systems are not that different from this milieu itself. The milieu is only the extension of one particular system. The transcendental is only the extension in the conditional of a system of singular events. An analysis of the space of immersion can be applied to the transcendental. The conditional space is not that different from systematic space. And it is equally as relative.

Spaces of Transformation

Individual spots, categories or phenomena, praxes or wrought objects, placed together under the name of Hermes—these were the spaces of transformation encountered at first.

Interference is an aural and visual phenomenon, a phenomenon of physics; it is a metaphor and an art of invention. The exchanger is a builder where the moving parts are sorted as to meaning and move along according to that sorting, a sort of winnowing machine with several hoppers where the transformation is only cinematic. At the crossroads, the morals turn around the decision, sometimes murders are committed; bifurcation, that of space and of logic, suddenly rises to a fantastic level and takes charge of old tales where language is as close as possible to its birthplace; one's reason for living—one's reason, quite simply—is changed. The discourse speaks of the path taken and follows its meanderings. The well, the bridge, the labyrinth: these are vignettes or figurings, games, strategies, chances or random occurrences, circumstances, built or constructed monuments, phenomena as well since death soon comes around, but still fantasies and still exact theorems for changes of phase. A rich series of varied spaces, separated, for multiple transformations, maybe the richest or the most baroque. On the contrary, the open, chaotic space of the Norman heaths, at Lessay, loses a bit, loses a lot of its features, too well defined by a god who is too determined, though mobile, to become simple, both formally and concretely. How can we cross the heath? How can we cross the sea? What does it mean to cross the sea? Images. The space of transformation as such emerges from this hodge-podge of abundance whose merit lies in having taken diagonally, askew, crosswise, many of the usual and stupid distinctions of philosophy. Translation is both a praxis and a theory; turbulence is a stable and unstable phenomenon where liquid moves and stays in a randomly fixed

71

form; the organism—my body—is now an exchanger of time. At this point in time, several chronies intertwine. Perhaps I have encountered only spaces of transformation, singular spots or slack varieties. The simplest of these, absolutely, is the void, the void in which the atoms fall, in which, suddenly, bursts the clinamen: be it an order brought to its elementary state, elements of distribution for an element of order, a void purged of all determination; be it a transformer brought to its elementary state; be it a minimal operator, a difference of angle, the smallest change of direction. Then a second order appears, a volume in the fall brought about by a small volute attached to the bursting spark of chance. The space of transformation here is brought back to the first and simplest states, almost to the zero state, both in the theoretical and in the concrete. From that, however, a global system is formed, a world in the universe of worlds. The distance of performance is as large as the origin is near nothing and the final phase is near totality. Given, the following sequence: a distribution, a signal, a system. The hum of the universe—chaos, the blink of an eye, the world. Thus the space of transformation came back to physics and to phenomena typical of sight and hearing.

States change phase, and systems change state, by transitions of phases or of states. But the system itself is never stable. Its equilibrium is ideal, abstract, and never reached. The state, in the first meaning of the word, is outside time. The state is the contrary of history, for history tries to block and to fix the state. The state is the mortal enemy of history. And it can kill history. We are not far from this now. It moves ahead like the beam on the unstable wall when the winds blow and the earth shakes. It falls, it does not fall; it rights itself, it falls. It wears away; it is abraded; it is split by the flow. An aggregation, it loses parts like a vase covered with cracks. A miracle reunites its fragments and makes its synthesis blaze; time slowly disaggregates it. That is what existence is: facing death, being in perpetual difference from equilibrium. These flows never stop running over lacunar lands. To devour them, parasite them, nourish them, and make them live. The fall kills us and creates us. We move unfailingly toward noise, but we come from noise. Oxygen feeds the heat of our lives, but aging is an oxidation. It works because it doesn't work. The system is very badly named. Maybe there is not or never was a system. As soon as the world came into being, its transformation began. The system in itself is a space of transformation. There are only *metabolas*. What we take as an equilibrium is only a slowing down of metabolic processes. My body is an exchanger of time. It is filled with signals, noises, messages, and parasites. And it is not at all exceptional in this vast world. It is true of animals and plants, of air crystals, of cells and atoms, of groups and constructed objects. Transformation, deformation of information.

I thought that the exchangers were intermediaries, that interference was on the fringe, that the translator was between instances, that the bridge connected two banks, that the path went from the origin to the goal. But there are no instances. Or more correctly, instances, systems, banks, and so forth are analyzable in turn as exchangers, paths, translations, and so forth. The only instances or systems are black boxes. When we do not understand, when we defer our knowledge to a later date, when the thing is too complex for the means at hand, when we put everything in a temporary black box, we prejudge the existence of a system. When we can finally open the box, we see that it works like a space of transformation. The only systems, instances, and substances come from our lack of knowledge. The system is nonknowledge. The other side of nonknowledge. One side of nonknowledge is chaos; the other, system. Knowledge forms a bridge between the two banks. Knowledge as such is a space of transformation.

This whole question is fractal.

Leibniz described fractal reality, formed of pools and fish, filled in turn, with fish and pools, *ad infinitum*. Mandelbrot repeats this of the world, inventing the world, and undoubtedly, the thing. I am saying the same thing of the process of knowledge.

Lunar Meals

Of the fox and the wolf, which one is better, the stronger or the smarter? I think, by playing this game of competition, playing this game of slyer, stronger, crueler, these species have disappeared, leaving man alone to play this game of destruction. But before there were no more foxes or wolves, a question about intelligence could be asked. In fact, it was this question that killed the foxes and the wolves. Aesop chose the fox and La Fontaine, the wolf; teachers like to classify things. I think that they are equivalent, and I think that it all depends. Sometimes it's Achilles, sometimes Ulysses; sometimes the pendulum swings one way, sometimes the other. This game is a machine that comes and goes like the balance beam of an assay scale. Our justice or our scourge?

We all know that the naked truth is found at the bottom of a well. They say that you have to go look for it there. Or at least, that was the advice of Renard, after Thales or the astronomer. Leaning over the edge, he saw the full moon, pale in the water, and he took it for a wheel of cheese. Starving, he jumps in the bucket which tumbles down in the noise of clashing chains and which erases the cheese, now a network of waves. His hunger increases from this stupid illusion. How truth does flee from the place we thought it hidden! So Renard the fox, because of his short-sightedness, dies of hunger. One fine evening, looking up, he sees Master Wolf leaning over the same water. Look at the beautiful cheese, he says. I have eaten a part of it; I invite you to eat the other part. On the aquatic rug the table is set. Get into the second bucket to make the trip. The wolf gets into the machine and goes down as the fox goes up. Who was the stupider? Look at them: the fox a while back, the wolf today. Stupid? Not at all. Who thought that the pure

74

unvarnished truth was found where he was taught it would be found? It fluctuates, oscillates.

I don't want to play any more. Neither at the game of who is smarter nor that of the truth. For you can die of hunger, of cold, of drowning, while playing. I want to eat some good cheese. Not the best, nor the true, seen in the mirrors as images. I want to be wise. And I want my little piece of the banquet, the object.

There are three of them. The sly fox and the stupid wolf. There are three of them, two idiots and the moon. Who is the stronger, who is the stupider? The answer to this question spins like a top. As the balance goes up and down, as the precision balance changes and varies, as the struggle with fifty-fifty chances continues, with its shared murders, with its reversible entrances and exits, the story moves toward its end, during the exchange of arms and ruses, of merit, money, blows, power, words, injuries, victories and losses, gifts, laurels, caresses, blood, attacks and assassinations, during the exchange that never ends, while the fox below brings the wolf down and the wolf, stupidly sitting in the bucket, raises up the fox, while these subjects see-saw, dying of hunger, buried alive, the object—cheese—slowly goes up to the heavens or down into the well and becomes an illusion, an image, an idea. You can't eat an image but you can fight to the death for an idea. The longer struggle is all the rage, and the longer it goes on, the more the objects disappear. In a world lambent with lights and shadows, the war goes on. History.

There are three of them. Two symmetrically arranged in a relation of forces, alternating, in phases, like the moon. The master and the quartermaster. Which of them thought that by turning the winch, sometimes this way, sometimes the other, they would end up drying out the well with the chains of truth? Or history, with their dialectical tourniquet? No, they're just baying at the moon.

Exchange without use and subjects without an object.

Abuse value.

The two subjects with the same desire are infinitely distant from the object. Or, the object disappears, it is seen to be illusory, by a changing of subjects or by their mutual homicide. Or again, it is a feast, an interrupted banquet. Or again, the relation between subjects can be infinite. But there has never been a winch whose chain was infinitely long. When the chain is unwound, it has to be rewound. It turns, eternally. Like the moon. Or, the more war there is, the more representation there is. Or inversely, the more representation there is, the more the struggle is all the rage. Or again, dialectic is the logic of phenomenology, that is to say, appearance. The moon and its image.

Or again, two parallel parasites have only illusions to eat. And finally: the hyper-Hell of the Danaides where the condemned sisters sit in the bucket.

Meals of the Lord in Paradise

For a moment, I'd like to talk about paradise. Given a plot of onions, sorrel, and eggplant. It seems to me that, like the inhabitants of the Persian paradise, the gourmet loves a garden; it is his dream. It is easy, if not vulgar, to like sweets and meat. Fruits and game. But beans, dandelions, and turnips! The gourmet likes vegetables. Everything else goes along as a side dish, accompanying the court of the queen of foods, the eggplant. Here is the garden and around it some flower beds, a space cultivated for flowers for Margot, to make a spray for her hair, to perfume the sheets. Onions and jasmine, the table and the bed, one celebration, maybe one garden.

Someone new has interrupted the feast at this interrupted meal. The hare eats the lettuce. I suspect that our good friend La Fontaine wanted to say that the rodent destroys the flower beds and the plots of vegetables—which is what he said—and wanted to say as well—what I say too—that at a meal, meat and even game disrupt the vegetable a bit. But it also disrupts love with Margot. The bother must be excluded. He is a parasite on the relation between the gardener and his garden, his vegetable, and his Margot. The parasite must be chased away. The preying hare, a parasite, like a man.

To chase: push out, drive out, uproot, dismiss, purge, repress. We repress what bothers us. What is repressed, but remains anyway, still parasites communication. The hare is in the third position, and thus, he must be excluded. He must be chased, hunted down.* I fear that this is the origin of hunting. The only things hunted are those that have to be chased away. In the end, there are two kinds of animals: those that are invited and those that are hunted. Guests and quarry. Tame and wild.

Chasser means both "to chase" and "to hunt." —Trans.

The wolf and the dog whose neck is irritated by the collar. It is said that
once hyenas and cranes were domesticated and then chased away. Why?
I don't know, but did the hyena learn to be a parasite and to eat carrion
at that time? There are animals whom we parasite and those who might
supplant us and whom we chase away, hunt, and eventually eliminate.

The repressed returns to parasite what I'm talking about. Such a
force is in the third position that I repress. It could be my father, my
mother, my child; we now know how to turn endlessly on this three-
branched star. It could be that this interrupts communication. It could be
a parasite in the biological sense, this child raised by the father, who eats
at the master's table, who coos graciously; whom the mother carried, who
sucked at her breast, whom theory causes to bear the weight of the sins
of the world. Whoever wants to kill his dog says that the dog has scabies.
Acarus or parasitic sarcoptid. Polymorphously perverse, kills his father
and rapes his mother: the massacre of the Innocents. Hide Abraham behind the Oedipus complex; hide the ram behind swollen feet. It could be
a parasite in the acoustic sense, the producer of slips of the tongue and
mispronunciations. Analytical theory, though obscurely, is also looking
for a way to make the three meanings of our concept coherent. Could
health be the silence of organs? And sickness makes noise. It is always
talking, always making noise at the door while we are doing something; it
never stops scratching in the attic during our sleep. We get up, look;
there is nothing there. We go back to bed and it starts again. The feast is
troubled, the meal interrupted. Let's go then to the country, where such
anxiety has not yet disturbed anything: a movement toward a spot
purged of parasites. But alas! the rats go to the country too, and everything starts again. The parasite is indeed this repressed one, the chased
entity that always returns: look at the rats or the hare. The other makes
light of the traps, rocks, and sticks. If you expel him, he inevitably returns. I have undoubtedly found a good definition of the parasitic function. It is ineluctable and almost a necessity. The force that excludes it is
immediately overturned to bring it back. What is repressed is always there.
You can chase it away only if there is another parasite. One parasite chases another and takes its place. The master parasites Miraut, who
chases the old hare. Look for the parasite who reestablishes a healthy
situation. Theory or praxis, a set of parasitic and parasitized discourses.

Weren't we happy, Margot, don't you remember, when our
problems, were, as they say, not yet resolved.

Rigorously speaking, there is never silence. The white noise is
always there. If health is defined by silence, health does not exist.

Health remains the couple message-noise. Systems work because they do not work. Nonfunctioning remains essential for functioning. And that can be formalized. Given, two stations and a channel. They exchange messages. If the relation succeeds, if it is perfect, optimum, and immediate; it disappears as a relation. If it is there, if it exists, that means that it failed. It is only mediation. Relation is nonrelation. And that is what the parasite is. The channel carries the flow, but it cannot disappear as a channel, and it brakes (breaks) the flow, more or less. But perfect, successful, optimum communication no longer includes any mediation. And the canal disappears into immediacy. There would be no spaces of transformation anywhere. There are channels, and thus there must be noise. No canal without noise. The real is not rational. The best relation would be no relation. By definition it does not exist; if it exists, it is not observable.

This is the paradox of the parasite. It is very simple but has great import. The parasite is the essence of relation. It is necessary for the relation and ineluctable by the overturning of the force that tries to exclude it. But this relation is nonrelation. The parasite is being and nonbeing at the same time. Not being and nonbeing that are the names (or the nonnames) of stations; but arrow and nonarrow, relation and nonrelation. Hence its metamorphoses and the difficulty we have in defining it. The ancient topic depended on an ontology, an ontology of the pure, simple, and unique relation. The *Sophist* and the *Statesman* are inside the functioning of the *Dialogues*. The same goes for the *Symposium*. Or rather, the sophist and the politician (the statesman) are interceptors of every relation in general; they are the relation itself and, as I have said, the collective. The parasite is being and nonbeing, relation and nonrelation. This is the case with the politician, for example. Nothing exists more than he does since he is always there in our relations and in the system in which we live, but nothing exists less than he does since a certain noise makes him immediately disappear. He is a noise of the system that can only be supplanted by noise. Thus noise—I am passing here from the human to the exact sciences; my discourse remains the same—thus noise is the fall into disorder and the beginning of an order.

We shall go back to the Persian paradise, the master's garden. The hare must be excluded; our first relatives, who ate the fruit of the tree of the master, must be chased away. An interrupted banquet, the very first feast. They are all there in a group at the dawn of history: the two that are part of the relation where the other is so much the same that he is drawn to the side of the same, and the third intervening. The parasitic guests are chased away. We must return to paradise lost, where the thirds were the Devil and the Good Lord. For all I know, the two of them stayed. I now know the path to take back to Eden; it is neither lost nor promised. This hare is a magician, says the inhabitant of the small town to his own master, the local king, half-bourgeois and half-squire, local king of the town, but more importantly, of hunting; he is a magician, I tell you; he plays on my strengths, laughing at my tricks. He is a magician. He is the Devil: we're now back in well-known surroundings. René Girard has shown us how the hunted becomes God and how he becomes the Devil as well. In equilibrium on the crest, not yet expelled, not yet victim, doing well, waiting for death, lynching in the crowd and the ruckus they raise, the beast is both God and Devil: magician, thaumaturge, sorcerer. The beast is in the third position, the middle term between the somewhat bourgeois gardener and his garden or his Margot; the beast has the means, the capability, and the power to confront the gardener's attacks. It has a thaumaturgic power that can be supplanted only by another thaumaturgic power.

Let's go back a bit, in feedback. Given two stations and a channel. They exchange messages. However, a third is necessary for the channel. The relation is there in third position, and it is there in first position. Exchanges are possible only if a relation is instituted. Thus the third man precedes the exchange. Anterior and conditional. The parasite precedes the exchanger, the broker, I don't know what to call him. The parasitic relation precedes exchange in general. There is always a hare in the garden. There always was a hare, even when the plot lay fallow, even when Margot was still a virgin and no one was there. For the simple reason that the one who gathers grass for rabbits is a rabbit as well and that the gardener, bourgeois and yokel at once, is also a hare after a fashion. One makes holes and the other furrows. That is why the relation of exchange is always dangerous, why the gift is always a forfeit, and why the relation can attain catastrophic levels. It always takes place on a mine field. The exchanged things travel in a channel that is already parasited. The balance of exchange is always weighed and measured, calculated, taking into account a relation without exchange, an abusive relation. The term *abusive* is a term of usage. Abuse doesn't prevent use. The *abuse value,* complete, irrevocable consummation, precedes use- and exchange-value. Quite simply, it is the arrow with only one direction.

Thus the Quirinus of the lettuce, parasited by the Jupiter of hares, the thaumaturge, immediately goes and fetches the Mars of the nearby castle, the sovereign of the garden. Hence we see the constitution of the theory of three functions in which each parasites the relation of the other two. It can be superimposed on our diagram with three parts. I am still not very sure, as I have not yet examined what a producer is exactly. Is a producer a reproducer? It would be nothing else but a parasite. There are still a lot of questions to be asked. Mars comes as soon as he is aked, the angel with the sword of fire; it is his job to chase and to hunt. Will he race after the hare, following swiftly in his tracks? Read the admirable Xenophon, and you will see to your surprise that the noble Greeks chased after the hare on foot. To run after such a swift racer—I'd like to see my contemporaries, suited up as if for Agincourt, and armed to the gills, to exterminate what is already dead, Tartarin plus the Would-be Gentleman plus Tarzan of the Jungle when it's a safari—I'd like to see them chase after the antelope, the gazelle, or the warthog. They would become chess players and would no longer pillage our world. I'm getting sidetracked, running after the parasite. No, the master doesn't move at all, just like the modern hunter. He sends Miraut after the hare. The hunter is a parasite, first and foremost. Not only the hunted, but also the hunter. He makes the dog, falcon, or sparrow hawk do what he cannot or does not know how to do. Hunting is above all a cynegetic art—an art of leading dogs. Dogs, a pack of dogs, horses, birds of prey. Dogs, horses, and grooms, all with hearty appetites. The master, the hunter, is a Mars for the sake of appearances, or rather, Mars is only war through interposed slaves. Just like the hunter has dogs, the warrior has men. They are only called men in this case. Tally-ho? Miraut. *Morituri te salutamus.*

The second feast. The first one, as I said, was composed of vegetables. It was the feast of Quirinus. But I fear that it was also that of Cain, tiller of the soil and the sacrificial giver of the first fruits. Vegetarian. The second feast is composed of meats, for Mars. Abel passed by, animal husbandry replaced agriculture, and the firstborn of the herd are offered in sacrifice. Quirinus is double, at least. Here, he is close to Mars, the bloodthirsty meat-eater. This meal will not be interrupted. For the moment, the master is the strongest parasite.

The master parasites Miraut to catch the hare, parasites the gardener to caress Margot, parasites production to eat as he likes. It's the same story as the parable of the horse who wanted to avenge himself on the deer. He gives orders in the host's home. There is always the same mystery of the guest of the master who becomes the master of the master.

Understand why the hunt needs music and why the horn sounds off. With a great deal of clamor, it announces to the frightened game that it is not man who is chasing and hunting, but the dogs, the horses, the falcons, better-trained animals. It announces his parasitic din from

far away. He pays in words, in sounds, in signals. He pays for his material benefit with the logicial. Like the fly, he makes noise. He moves
the dogs and horses with his voice, whistles for the falcon, and blows
trumpets and horns so that the rats flee.

We shall soon discuss what "own" means; we can talk about this
when we have some land, a garden, a nest. It will also be necessary to
discuss what open and closed have meant since Rousseau. The gardener
has a garden proper and the enclosed area next to it. But he was not the
first to enclose this space and say this is mine. This is mine because it's
closed. It is no longer mine, is less mine, if there is a hole in the hedge,
not a hole but a wound. This garden is somewhat my body, or the extension of my body proper. It is in order and will no longer be mine,
will be less mine in a miserable state.

The gardener makes his vegetables grow for his soup and makes
his flowers grow to adorn Margot. Later on I shall say whether the
animal farmer parasites the fauna or part of the fauna and whether the
vegetable gardener parasites, in turn, part of the flora. Or better, if he
parasites their reproduction. The production of living systems is their
reproduction. Animal-raising and vegetable farming are practices that
are parasitic on the reproduction of living things. The tree and the cow
told us that man never returned or recognized the gifts of flora and
fauna. He uses and abuses them but does not exchange with them. He
gives food to the animals, you say. Yessir, he gives flora to the fauna,
fauna to the fauna, gives inert material to the flora. What does he give
of himself? Does he give himself to be eaten? The one who does so will
utter a timeless word. One word, *host*. That of the Eucharist.

The gardener has only his body and the extensions of his body.
He gardens, raises pigs and poultry, keeps Margot by his side. I no
longer know whether Margot is his mistress or daughter. The garden of
Venus or the garden of my father. I am lost in this profusion of gardens.
He chases the hare just as he spades the plants or calls the rooster. With
his hand or with his mouth. With sticks and stones. He thrashes the
terrier, stones the on-coming fireball. This direct kind of chasing is in-
effective. He chases and hunt with traps. And what is trapped are feet.
Oedipus. I don't have the time now to talk of this. To be continued.
Why are these hunts not effective? Because the villager has neither
Miraut nor dogs nor horses nor squires like those of the Would-be
Gentleman. Does the lord of the manor hunt? I no longer am sure. I
don't know what hunting is. Who blows and makes noise in the loud
din of the hunt? The horns. Who gallops? The horse. Who traps and
bites? The pack of dogs. Who organizes the battue? The squires. The
hunter does everything while doing nothing. What does the hunter ex-

change with the horses, the dogs, the squires, the horn-players, the whippers-in, the trumpeters, the falconers? What is the master doing here? What the gardener was doing. Could Mars and Quirinus be twins?

The master and the gardener are not as different as we were led to believe in elementary school, the institution founded by the all-powerful bourgeoisie, who wanted us to believe that. The bourgeoisie pushes us to storm the Bastille, the castles, and the bishoprics so we never think of taking its absolute power and its safes. The villager who is half-rustic is also half-bourgeois. The master is of the town, half-bourgeois and half-noble. These halves fit together and can be added. When the bourgeois comes into being, he will shove the nobles (and the clergy) in front of the yokels as a lure. He will be in the third position in their useless struggle. He will parasite a pointless combat because it is accomplished and kept up by him placed by him in front of the scenery. Thus a dominating class can peacefully enjoy the class struggle. A three-player game where one makes the other two play.

Here the intersection master-gardener is not empty; both are bourgeois together. The gardener parasites the vegetables; the master refrains from doing that. The gardener parasites pigs and poultry, the master, the horses and dogs, all of them animals, edible or not. The difference is in the mediation and only in the mediation. Horses and dogs are mediate, mediators, as far as I know. The man of the gardens is of the immediate. The vegetables go into the soup and the fat pigs to the smokehouse. To cultivate vegetables and to raise animals, desire must be deferred. Eating must be deferred, so that the seed can be chosen, so that the races can be bred, so that the gardener can hoe, plant, feed, and cut. The gardener, like a parasite, is already the man of the mediate. But of the mediate that directly bears on table matters. Pork and cabbage a bit later but pork and cabbage just the same. The moral of the ant and not the grasshopper. The grasshopper has just failed; it couldn't pay for a fly or for a cabbage for the winter with its summer song. The danger of playing the mediate on the mediate. The grasshopper is expelled as a recognized parasite. But the master sings too: he sounds the trumpet and the horn, whistles for his dogs, excites his horses, an astonishing din. He is the master of mediations. And that is why at first he is not concerned with vegetables. What is there to do with flora except to go directly to the goal, without a hitch: eat them. The master defers eating at a higher level than the gardener. He defers deferring. The one who defers is always the master. Here now is the moment of the grasshoppers. Now the time has come that the grasshoppers win. Where a word, noise, voice, sound, win over things and substances. The master has time, he waits. He stocks neither pork nor sorrel, neither capons nor eggplants; he forms packs of dogs and brings life to the stable. The god goes where the master tells him to; the dog returns, carrying a partridge; the horse runs, jumps, gallops and trots; the master whistles, yells, sings, calls, names. Night and day, like the grasshopper, he sings. He experiments with the power of the logicial. He trains, tames, subdues. He trains the horses and the dogs, who listen attentively. He trains the squires and the men. With his voice. The gardener uses his hand; the master, his voice. What are dogs or horses relative to the animals in the farmyard? Relations. The stronger the voice the longer the relation. Horses and dogs sometimes multiply it to endless lengths: by that I mean the world. The gardener puts his hand on the immediate. The voice of the master is borne a distance by the mediate. The gardener closes in his land so that everything is at arm's reach. The master makes a hole in the hedge so that the dogs can pass through, so that relations can be established, so that he can leave the garden on horseback. Master of the closed, master of the open. Hence the first founder was the first who, having made a hole in a hedge that enclosed an area, said: this is my passage; he found gardeners weak enough to believe him, to allow him to do it, indeed, to call him. Opposition of the traveller and the homebody, the pastor and the peasant, the right of passage and the right of ownership.

But there are two kinds of farming. The second is that of flowers if the first is that of vegetables. Eating is again deferred, for another motive, a sweeter one. The bouquet of Margot, jasmine, is also a relation. Again, it is rather close; soon it is immediate, immediacy itself. There are two kinds of farming, but there is really only one, when all is said and done. Agriculture is culture. Bed and board.

But there are two kinds of animal husbandry: that of the farmyard and that of hunting. To eat, to run after what will be eaten. That of the farmyard and that of work. To eat, to prepare what will be eaten. There are also two kinds of parasitism. The first, more direct, though very wily and devious; the second, more mediate, thematizes the relation, complicates it, raises it to relations of relations. As if the paraparasite were being invented, as if the difference were differed, as if the distance were distanced. A first ruse, a ruse of the ruse, *ad infinitum*. Do, then have done. From the hand to the voice, from the blind man to the paralytic, the doubling passes to the logicial. Again, cybernetics. Suddenly I see that there was no work before there was an order. The gardener, without his master, enjoys: he enjoys his sorrel; he enjoys his Margot. The fruition of the fruit. Of course this use value is totally ideal; in fact, it belongs to paradise. For there to be world enough and time, the system must be absolutely closed. But it is open, since the hare came in. The fact that there is always a hare in the garden, an insect in the vineyard, or a serpent in Eden proves that they are open. All relations would have to be removed, a monad with neither hole nor door. And still it would not have use, for it would no longer have any relation to what it enjoys. All would come from inside. What we enjoy we have a relation with and thus we parasite. The revenue, the fruit of the gardener, never comes back to the one who offers it. Calling it revenue (returns) is a lie. It is an abuse of a word and of things as well. The original relation is that of abuse. It never stops. It is contemporaneous with the relation; it is the relation itself and the opening of the system. To go into the garden, the hare and the serpent used a door, but by what right? Through this hole has passed history. Through this hole, the horse and his master come out. Through this hole, this wound, our forefathers passed after the Fall. The system is open; it is the only real thing; there are always relations and parasites. The hole, mediation, to go far, with dogs, on horses.

I am here alone in my garden. My land is my blank space; my hoe is my pen; I make furrows for sowing. I am a farmer, like my father, in my closed field, harming no one. Wanting to do good is often so cruel. I admit that I have never worked; I have had the unbelievable, unheard-of, and miraculous opportunity not to know what work is. There, intuition and joy grow as they will. I never wanted anything more than some soup, a cobbler for the children, and some dessert on Sunday. My beautiful sweet garden of fervor, of constant prayer, my waiting for dawn, hoping for the light. Before daybreak, I am drawn toward white revelation. Time is dense and incandescent. Space is transparent. I see the immeasurable smile of the world. I am not working; I would like to be in paradise. But the hedge is crawling with wounds. I write. For example, I have to name the animals, just like Adam. And the din begins, messages and noises. The *tohu-bohu* (chaos) from which everything came has never stopped. It crosses both space and time. Disorder engenders order and moves through it. We don't move—Margot and I—and yet a thousand masters are there whom we never called but who offer to chase the hare from the disorder. At the door of my room, they make a never-ending noise. They cross this page on horseback, send their pack of dogs into my words, and their men, their grooms, their whippers-in, their trumpeters, into my sentences. Suddenly, I work. And I work myself to death so that amidst all this mess something transparent remains, so that a bit of light can be saved in this medley. I am expelled from paradise; I work; I shall die, drowned by disorder; I lie down among all this sadness and misery; I have lost my immortality.

Work

What is work? Undoubtedly, it is a struggle against noise. If we allowed things to happen without intervening, stables would fill up with manure, the fox would eat the chickens, and the phylloxera would cross the seas to dry out the vine leaves. The channel is filled with mud. At low tide, you see the port filled with sand. Soon, the ships will not be able to get through. Things mix; don't move, don't stir with the spoon; the sugar will sooner or later dissolve in the water. Sometimes there are convenient, useful mixtures, but most of them are obstructions or encumbrances. To work is to sort. Maxwell's demon is unavoidable, just like the parasite. Alas, they are twins perhaps. There is an objective base or work without which the temporal flow toward disorder or complexity would be quicker. Contrary to what is said in both classical and contemporary philosophy, men are not the only ones who work. We are never that exceptional. Animals work, as do living organisms. What I mean by that is that life itself works—that it is life through its struggle against the tendency to death, through sorting, through the activity of Maxwell's demon. The organism gets order and energy, chews them up, sorts them, classifies them, and re-forms its own order and its own energy, eliminating the losses. Does a miller do otherwise? Is the treatment of aggregates in a river another activity? What is production in a factory? People will say that I am projecting our own organization of work into a natural system. Maybe so. I tend to think that here we are not finding a cause and an effect, but two parallel effects or a circle of cause-effect. I no longer see the difference between the bee and the architect.

Work flows from me like honey, like the spider's web. I don't know with what external order I nourished this second order; my body is transformer of itself, but also a transformer for this linguistic wax, a long secretion come from my five fingers; I work hard, I don't work at all; it comes easily, just like what an animal does when it follows its own instinct in doing this or that. I am a bee or a spider, a tree. I no longer can tell the difference between work and secretion. But noise is also there, in the very acts in which an order is set up. The chaos of the zero state, before the first day, endures throughout the week and even enters paradise. The spider's web loses the angles of its spirals; the plots of sorrel and cabbages are trimmed by the hare; there is no honey without wax and no discourse without obscurity. But it is not a question of this second state. The very production of order, secretion, the organism itself undertaking production, are all struggling to exist, struggling against a never-ending noise, against being dragged down toward the mortal fate of mixtures. Thus they work madly to move the point of application of forces to a point upstream from this dragging down.

Living systems are at work, are work. The act of writing this book and the life of the one writing it are one and the same action. This writing and this body. Carry the hawser about the upstream bit relative to the flowing river. Mechanical work: moving the point of application of forces; thermodynamic: fighting entropy; information: to be able to distinguish two points. Life and the organic system are this very page; life is this cabbage patch, these beehives and these webs, fragile orders, frail, ready to exfoliate, refusing to be cast away. Death is always accepting death. Death is the end of work. Life is work, simply, and work is life itself.

Certain pale, cadaverous shades move about, wandering in a world like some netherworld, almost dead already, and even greedier, thirstier, for fresh blood, the blood of those who work. Innumerable vampires and bloodsuckers attached in packets to the rather rare bodies of the workers. To every major work is attached a descent into the underworld as an index that there really is a work. As soon as a Homer, a Vergil, a Plato, appears, their bodies cross the pale fields where souls drink blood. All of them are hosts. They eat and drink from their own writing, as do their contemporaries and their successors. Life needs work so much that, to survive, one must work oneself or look elsewhere. One can accept being derivative. It is thus that the parasite condemns himself to death or at least to disappear if Ulysses does not come by. He who works has a relation to life, walks between the earth and the sky, comes out of the infernal abyss when he decides to, knows the path that leads out of the underworld, the path of work. Large, pale bodies without work, riveted to death, wait for the living to pass within their reach. They organize a world that is completely policed, in which they condemn whole populations to live without work, condemning them thus to death, condemning the living, tied to their work, condemning

them to give their flesh and their blood. They have accepted death—
their own and that of others. You can always accept the fact that veins
fill with mud, like ports and canals, that communication dries up. As
soon as Prometheus puts down the fire, an eagle starts to tear out his
liver. Death is always a suicide. Maxwell's demons stop working.

Life works; life is work, energy, power, information. It is impossible to translate this description into an ethical discourse. It is thus,
must be thus; I really don't know. The work of life is labor and order
but does not occur without borrowing from elsewhere. It makes order
here but undoes order there. And it reinforces disorder and noise. There
is a lot of work involved in chasing the hare from one's garden so that
the lettuce can grow in a more orderly fashion, but the master makes a
mess, which means that he installs himself in a dwelling to court Margot,
to eat the hams, to replace the lover of the garden. He installs himself
like a hare, like a carnivorous hare. One parasite chases out the other, as
one disorder chases out the other. The master will plunder, not the sorrel, but the courtyard and the farmyard. The replacement parasite
changes the key, changes order, adds a mediation. He eats the poultry
that peck at the grain. He devours the fauna that devour the flora. It is
not that he changes positions in the garden itself, but rather that he
adds one loop to the parasitic system. He increases its complexity. La
Fontaine numerically evaluates this mutation. One hour of the second
is worth a century of the whole species. As if an individual were a
species, as if the unity of his time were equal to history: a century, an
era, a historical epoch of the species to which he is compared. The order
—as in order of magnitude—is changed. The human parasite is of another
order relative to that of the animal parasite: the latter is one, the former,
a set; the latter is time, the former, history; the latter is a garden, the
former, a province. To destroy a garden or to destroy a world.

Things are not yet moral, but they are becoming serious. Cultivate your garden, but first of all do not destroy the garden, do not let it
be destroyed. The Greek word for "chaff" or "weed" is zizania—that is
to say, "discord." The introduction of zizania; weeds, discord, the hare.
This book, as you have seen, is the book of evil, the book of the problem
of evil. Don't chase the hare out; you would need the entire armed
forces to do so. Don't chase the hare out; you'll wind up like St. Julian,
who was a hunter and then a hospitaller, who having chased out all the
animals, began to invite men, who having excluded, began to include.
Good morning, hare; stay if you like. As long as you have one hare in
the garden, only one hare, it's better to make your peace with it. Bacteria cannot be exterminated, but they can be used for cheese: milk can
be fertilized with this pestilence to create the gods' ambrosia. The hare
is a magician, a devil—a good devil. The others, I think, are all worse.

Tolerance begins here, and maybe morality as well. Jupiter, Mars, and Quirinus were interchangeable. They only knew how to chase out the parasites.

I want to know who destroys the garden. There have to be two kinds of work. And the moralizers of the work society are becoming dangerous today.

Weren't we happy, Margot, don't you remember, when our problems, were, as they say, not yet resolved . . .

Our forefathers were excluded from paradise. I left too; we were all chased out. The more we chase, the more we are chased. The more we exclude, the more we are excluded. But we spend our whole life excluding.

Our forefathers were excluded from paradise. You will work; you will bear children in pain; you will die. Repetitions or redundancies.

The newborn is chased out by its mother. Birth is an exclusion; childbirth, a dismissal—a discharge. Ostracism, quarantine, banishment. Would that the gods could make all exile a birth, all dismissal childbirth. The little protean parasite is eliminated by its good hostess, chased out of paradise.

The old, the dying, the hurt, leave the feast of life. They pay back the nitrogen cycle and the environment with the four basic atoms that they had borrowed plus a few rare earth metals that made them hard. Return to the world and one payment. Return to dust, suddenly ceasing to parasite the vital banquet. The dying are excluded from the host-world, chased from paradise.

Between these two discharges, between these two meals, we never stop working: excluding mildew to drink the fruit of the vine, excluding the hare to eat the sorrel, removing disorder and the noise of the world to impose our own order. Never ceasing to chase beings from their paradise and always chased by others from our own.

Repetitions and redundancies. There was only one curse; it begins again, never stopping.

Chased from the tree of knowledge, excluded from knowledge. Prohibitions always come between—in the channel—between the being and the act of knowledge. The serpent, unrolling, rolling up, between the world and ourselves.

I shall leave life just as I've left the table thousands of times. I'll have heard a noise at the door that interrupts the feast; I'll recognize it. I don't know if it will be a bell, or a voice, or a gust of wind. But I know that I'll understand it.

For a moment I'll have to look back. Before following the burst of sound, I'll have to look for my host, smile at him, be courteous, not leaving before I've thanked him.

In turn, have I been a good guest? Did I pay for having been here, both night and day, with some swift words, some happy notes, some conversation? Did I keep up my end of the conversation? Maybe now I can pay for it all in one fell swoop. Quickly passing, there is a moment in which voice is worth a whole life.

Thank whom though? Where is my host? Who invited me here? I see only strangers, like myself, around the table, only diners who will return home this evening. The master's place is empty. Whom then shall I give this moment of dense equivalence to?

The last look is over. Nevermore will I be able to say "thank you." Thank you for this or that, for this miracle, for the turbulent sea and the fuzzy horizon, for the clouds, the river and fire, thanks for heat, fire, and flames, thanks for winds and sounds, for the pen and the violin, thanks for the enormous meal of language, thanks for love and suffering, for sadness and for femininity . . . no I'm not done yet; I'm just beginning to remember who must be thanked; I've barely begun my hymn of thanks and my turn is over.

I am the lightning bolt, the wind, the noise. Blinded, blown away, deafened. I've barely begun, tearfully, to say "thank you," the equivalent of grace.

"You're welcome," says the noise or the wind or the sound from behind the door. You're welcome and be my guest, you're welcome.

Insects' Meals

The adventures of the grasshopper at the closed door of the ant. These adventures are archaic in comparison to those of the hare and those of the rats, and maybe to all the others, perhaps even prehistoric. The exchange of singing and food is evoked but remains impossible. We are still at the level of distinguishing the proper substances to feed us when we are empty from winds and voices. Instead of singing, collect worms. The ant does not have as its dinner guest a flute-player or a folk-singer, whose voices constantly fill space. Thus, the ant excludes the parasite. This history is strictly classical. The dismissal of the parasite does not cost a thing. Chasing out the hare, on the contrary, costs the master, that is to say, results in servitude; it is dearly bought. Chasing the grasshopper costs only a word; it is almost free. Be on your way, the savage says. A gesture. The passer-by doesn't stay, nor does the grasshopper. It is not yet a question of the return of the repressed. The house-cleaning is still rather naive. No one comes to replace or to supplant the grasshopper sent off to dance. In other words, the ant hill is a system proper. What is real for the ant is rational and can be rational through and through. The work costs nothing. The work is solely and wholly good and gives rise to a moral. The ant, of course, is one of Maxwell's demons, who excludes grasshoppers and includes worms. You could call it Maxwell's ethics. The moral is free and in fact is a moral because it is free.

The ant is at home, is rational and works. It works by chasing out disorder. It constituted order, classifying its seeds, flies, worms; chasing away the singers and dancers; building the collective city through its collections: well-run large cities, perfectly controlled. What is also noticeable is the equivalence of work to the police. Maxwell's demon checks the permits, acting as a customs officer. The elimination of noise

91

is the aim of both these activities. Every society founded on work and
economics is a police state: we have known this since Aesop; man has
known it since the story of the ant; humanity has known it since the
élan vital of certain collective animals ceded its place to the mechanical
instinct of social life. Workers and soldiers. The ant who talks to the
grasshopper is a soldier, furthering the moral of work, stocking up, and
order. To watch over a stock is to work to create order and to exclude.
It is also to go back from winter to summer.

Animal cities no longer have anything but consumers, soldiers,
and workers. It is a rational society through and through. Was Aesop
aware that he was representing the exact gesture of the worker and the
bestial nature of economics? Working is always chasing the grasshopper
or the drone, gathering, stocking, direction, organizing flows—in the
end it comes down to eliminating grasshoppers. We can guess our horizon, the point of entry into the shadows of the perfect anthill, crumbl-
ing into animal rationalism. A return to the fabulous good old days, to
rigorous prehistory. Economists, policeman, and workers are all defined
at once as street-sweepers.

The ant works and is at home in pure reason. The ant forms a
system or a city by making order. There is no end to it; disorder has to
be eliminated and to do so, there must be work. No, the fable is not
naive: it's a snapshot of the ant at a given moment during its movements. Work never stops: armies of soldiers are needed to eliminate the
grasshoppers, armies of street-sweepers to remove the trash. That is to
say, workers and economists to make the best use of the movements. It
is hoped that, through the work of the street-sweepers, the system will
be clean. A clean garden and the adjoining plot of land. We will finally
be at home when everything is clean. This is all foreseen by the stercoral
theory of the origin of property rights. Collective property must be
clean as a whistle. You work yourself to death so you can finally be at
home. The work is inhabitable when it is clean, appropriate to our own
uses. The aim of philosophy is to make the world inhabitable. Thus it
only speaks of order and disorder, of work, of economy. How much
energy do these myrmecoid demons need to eliminate all the singers
and dancers? How much do these soldiers in black chitin have to eat to
exclude the refuse? So much that they make a lot of noise and thus, a
lot of disorder to eliminate. The ant who eats and does not speak, speaks
nevertheless to chase out the grasshopper. The ant produces parasites
in eliminating others. There is perpetual movement in working and in
appropriating the world and that is why, in traditional philosophy, it
seemed to be the motor of the world. Tomorrow—Sunday—you will be
at home in the promised land abounding in milk and honey. At home—
that is to say, in the land of your forefathers. Why, then, this long

detour, since our ancestors were there? I already told you: they were chased out, undoubtedly by some street-sweeper. Suddenly, work is no longer free; it has a price—of energy, power, time. And of loss as well. The cost of work: you have to work to be able to work. The moral changes positions, as do all the questions.

The ant works so as to be at home, for the ant is rational. But I would like to know what reason is in this case. Pure reason is inflation. Inaccessible purity raises its prices.

Energy, Information

If all the merit, honor, and glory are usually given to the populace of the anthill, sometimes they are given to the grasshoppers. All that is necessary is to have enough of them in the system for us to be happy. As usual, good and evil are divided, and the corresponding marker is sometimes given to the worker, sometimes to the singer. By making the system more flexible, it is made more complex, more dynamic; it is saved, given life, multiplied; now it is as large as a set of anthills. Things are further along; knowledge is greater too. But the constraints, even in their flexibility, are even more ferocious.

Music has been a fundamental part of my life. I could not conceive of life without music. But now, I've begun to hate it. It is everywhere nowadays, trapping me everywhere. I knew that we had entered the motor age when the noise coming from motors filled space everywhere. There was no space without a motor. Even in the most rural country spots, the chain saw, acute like a dentist's drill, replaced the grasshoppers. What I mean is that the ant had understood, that the ant had understood all the fables. The ant had understood that the producer can seize power only if he takes the place of the parasite as well. Thus the motor, an expansive phenomenon, filled space and was the founding fact of property. Noise is stercoral: it makes the occupation of an expanse intolerable and thus gets it for itself. The grasshopper counterattacks. At a distance from the anthill, it sings, filling space. The ant cannot get rid of this cry: here is a parasite that it cannot eliminate. The parasite has to find a phenomenon against which the producer can do nothing. A noise is not chased out but covered. From this point on, the ant makes motors that backfire in the streets. The grasshopper counterattacks with loudspeakers. Hi-fi, full strength, earphones: the motor is

beaten. Music culture—that is to say, the culture of communication—
has just wiped out the industrial revolution, the revolution of productions. Little packets of energy chase out bigger ones. One parasite chases
out another. One power chases out another. One owner chases out
another. An expansion chases out the preceding one. What counts is
changing environments, having the means to change environments. Alas,
I do hate music.

The parasite gets power less because he occupies the center than
because he fills the environment. The grasshopper occupies space, the
media, the environment, the milieu—his property because it is the owner
who emits an extensive phenomenon in this place.

Power, a while back, occupied the center. For it to come from
this center, for it to be effective to its edges, for it to be carried to the
periphery, a necessary condition is that there be no obstacle and that
the space be homogeneous around its action. In short, the space must
be deparasited. In order to be obeyed, for example, one must be heard,
listened to: the message of order must pass through silence. There must
be silence. The parasites must be chased. The ant puts itself to it, sending away the grasshoppers to die of hunger. I return to the three functions, in which I no longer see distinctions but only analogies. The
holder of the juridical and sacred function purifies the space, eliminates
the garbage in the temple of Vesta, cuts up temples, glazing them with
blood or water all over. The profane is outside, where evil abounds; the
holy is inside, at the center in the inner sanctum. The space inside
is rather homogeneous, isotropic, and deparasited. The head of martial
functions guards the edges, protects the doors and borders with his
sword of fire, strewing death throughout the garden. In both cases,
violence for the sake of peace. But the active participants in the function
of production organize work and economics in the same way, creating
order and exluding disorder, in a gesture that is not different from those
of the two co-gods. All three are Mars for their violence, Jupiter for
exclusion, Quirinus. They form clean spaces, and the closer you go to
the center, the cleaner they are: center, closed spaces, surrounded by an
unknown barbaric desert where evil abounds and where the grasshoppers
can always sing and dance. Three gods, religion, three concepts, meta-
physics, or three functions, history, in any case three powers, one
power and the same model where the same activity is organized. The
same anthill. The activity that the three works have in common is the
deparasiting of a finite location. This is the oldest trick in the book, the
most common in history, the most reproduced in our institutions, cultures, and sciences. Cut, center, purify. You will find it in everything

from agriculture to systems analysis. Maybe it is the fundamental model or structure of producers' cultures. How can we advance from the center? Leave the border constant for a while and then move it forward. Power at the center organizes, from the center on out, a closed space that expands, an order that advances, a world in expansion. Production or moving forward. We are all Indo-Europeans. For that, in fact, is what production is: this growth—the advance of closure in a Rousseauesque garden, the progressive conquest of space, the absorption of the desert, bit by bit. Informing the desert, changing disorder into information, transforming the face of the globe. That is what production is for Indo-Europeans. The three functions must be there, or one god in three incarnations, one god in three persons. And that is exactly what our history is. The Roman (or Persian or Greek or British) Empire and dialectics: thesis—the garden subset; antithesis—the complement; synthesis —the garden and the adjacent land.

Have we left this anchoring and this progression all of a sudden [*d'un coup*]? The worker ants slowly drag their booty through closed space. The grasshopper sings, passes through space. The ant works in time, crossing in caravans loaded with cloths, perfumes, and china; the deserts surrounding the space are closed off with temporary walls. The ant moves through space and decelerates time: *festina lente*. All of a sudden, the grasshopper fills the surrounding area. The grasshopper doesn't need time to fill a space. No, the grasshopper is not a producer, it has a very different power. Neither Jupiter, nor Mars, nor Quirinus. Something else. Where are you? I don't know. Where are you going? It doesn't matter. The grasshopper wanders every which way. In other words, the emitters can be randomly distributed. The center loses its place, its function, and its importance. Where are you going? Everywhere. All spaces bathe in its power. The parasite is everywhere. Its voice expands, filling the space, wherever he is and wherever he goes. Voice, wind, sound and noise. Now is the reign of the Paraclete. The reign of the spirit, Hegel finally actualized. The reign of the Beatles, that is to say, of the shit-eaters. Those who eat the garbage disposed of by the ants.

Grasshopper and ant, the closed-off garden of the workers about to embark on imperialism, and suddenly, the space is occupied by the explosion of voices, the blare of horns. Grasshopper and ant; the Sun King, I think. The center here and the expansive shining that fills the world from the dawn. We have changed all that. Henceforth, expansion is enough. You can do without the center. Circumstantial emitters are enough. The world empire of IBM, tomorrow, the absolute empire of relation. The end of substance.

Substantialism was and is the refusal of voices and wind. From now on, only relations, only waves.

Thus, we must look for what is expanding. Noises, odors, and waves. And maybe Reason as well. Reason, *ratio,* the Hellenic logos, the voice once more. Reason is spread by the voice. By calculation and measurement that presuppose long chains of reasons. The old Cartesian chains were slow and hyperbolically deparasited. Today the chains move at the speed of light and the parasites have them in their grasp.

Once again, look at the fable of the ant and the grasshopper. Singing is not exchangeable; singing is not coin of the realm; singing is self-condemnation to dying of hunger. Plato excludes the poets from the city by virtue of strict justice. Speaking is not eating. Solid and wind. The parasite is chased out and the teller of the tale is invited to dance in front of the table.

Everything else will be the revenge of the grasshoppers. Those who come to look for hospitality—don't reject them, for they are gods. You will be metamorphosed. The grasshopper is avenged. Metamorphosed into a fox, it changes the crow into the phoenix of the hosts. The grasshopper did not caress the ant, did not tell the ant that it was superb, did not scrounge, and has not yet made it sing. You were singing? No, says the grasshopper, returning, you, sing! And the croaking bird drops the cheese. They do not lend? Then they'll have to give. The return of the grasshoppers will never stop, the return of the excluded, the return of the repressed, of the poets of the tale-tellers, of the parasites at the dinner table of the Chateau de Vaux.

The first fable is archaic, but is an exception. The rest of the fables announce our world.

—— *The Gods, the Perpetual Host* ——

With precision and certainty our master chooses the tale of the hospitables from the *Metamorphoses*. Philemon and Baucis, just like Saint Julian, will become immortal but not without having been the occasion or cause of a flood of violence: the whole town disappears with its animals and denizens; they have no choice; they are dragged by the rise, the reappearance, the crisis of violence, just like the hunted animals are massacred down in the valley. Maybe this is the way the plague is seen through the eyes of an ass.

The two old, poor people are the only ones who open their door to Hermes, preceding Zeus himself. Disguised as pilgrims, the gods had found no room at the inn. No one around them would shelter them. No room at the inn: is a god about to be born, a host such that no hotel would have him?

Philemon and Baucis prepare the feast for their guest.

Milk and fruit, poor, sober gifts. The travellers are thirsty, and the hosts pour spring water mixed with wine from the vase. An interrupted meal, interrupted by a miracle. The more poured from the vase, the less it became empty. Two miracles.

La Fontaine.* An outpouring, an overflow, never running dry. Divine fables: the more the author writes, the more he has left to write. The production could not dry up. It is not a miracle but it is true, perhaps the only true perpetual motion. The more one writes, the more one writes. Always thirsty and always giving drink. The

*Serres is playing on the name La Fontaine, which also means "the fountain." —Trans.

98

immortality of the work, the feast of immortality. Finally, an uninterrupted meal.

A parasitic meal. The more you give me to eat or drink—I, a god —the more you will get from these fables, for which I never lack. Paying for wine with words and for food with information is so cheap, so free, that I shall never lack for money. Consequently, the motion is perpetual. That is the miracle, but it is also every miracle. No sooner said than done. It only costs a few words to acquire something. At that price, nothing stops, nothing runs dry. If information were equal to energy, we would be gods. A miracle as in power, a miracle as in physics. But this impossible gesture is accomplished by the guest. It is the daily miracle of the parasite. It is always the *table d'hôte* and the phoenix of the hosts. Parasitism doesn't stop. The host repeatedly is reborn from his ashes, from the ashes expelled through the stercoral door. Sit down at the *table d'hôte;* the host always makes the meal. He is there for that. The host is reborn from his consumption, from his consumption by fire, and the wine springs again from his destruction. That goes on and on. There is never any equilibrium: the table is wobbly, it is missing a support, it leans to one side; it is righted by a potsherd. And the table still abounds; the vase pours, the table pours, an abundant pitcher of verse [*verseau des vers*].

The host's pouring is infinite. His debt is never-ending.

If he is inhospitable, he is condemned to death, and his corpse is washed away by the flood. If he is hospitable, he pays forever. He pours, continuously.

There is as much wine to be poured as there are men to be killed down in the valley, in the town, beneath the waters. To put it another way: there is as much water poured from the vase as there is in the downpour of the flood.

The guest—the stranger—comes to the table; he does not parasite an individual, but the reproduction of individuals. Not their production, which is exceptional and rare, but their reproduction, which is rather common. That, in fact, never stops. One parasites the life of another: sometimes his ontogenous life and always his phylogenous life. The thing that is always pouring is phylogeny. They reproduce for that: they can be the substrate for ammunition, murder, work, eating, instruction, ordering, giving birth. Yes, life is inextinguishable. And the gods are thirsty.

What would fable be without metamorphoses? Men must be changed into animals with a wave of the magic wand. And how can that be? The secret of the fable is metamorphosis in the fable. It has to do with a miracle of hospitality—or with an infinite number of parasitic relations.

Interlude

Full-Length Portrait of the Parasite

Confessed Meals

The pen is falling from my hands ... It doesn't fall out of Rousseau's hands for just any reason. He admits being wrong, on other occasions, for having taken it up sometimes without need. A reason for taking it up, a reason for losing it. He never loses it when he admits his morose sexuality, nor when he tells of being found out flashing a girl by the well. There he holds it tight for the enchantment of the commentators who are thrilled to take the place of the girls. Courage now! ... The pen is falling from my hands.

He has just been caught stealing apples. Not by having opened the door of the pantry where they were stored, looting the treasure quite boldly, but by trying to get them through a little hole, through a jalousie. He needs tools for such an undertaking: a skewer, a slat of wood, a knife. Look at the master's hunt now, the hunt of game, what Rousseau calls the hunt of the apples, distorting the meaning of the world. It is true that this reserve, the storeroom of the master, holds the products of the master's hunt as well as his arms and tools. Thus the apprentice seeks to use both the game—or the harvest—and the skewer for his own profit. The master is a predator—which remains to be seen— and the worker is a parasite. It is never a question of conquering the garden of Hesperides nor of slaying a dragon but rather of eating at his expense, furtively.

Too short a skewer, now a bit longer, a recalcitrant apple, too narrow an opening, a knife that cuts, and a dragon that sleeps with one eye open, the anguish of being caught red-handed: all this regales the psychoanalyst, and even more so because the pen is falling from my hands. And even more so because it has to do with a garden, in fact, the garden that, in the *Ninth Promenade,* the little Savoyard woman carries in front of her in her basket for the great desire of the Savoyard men.

103

Translating here would be tantamount to trivializing the matter. And thus, directly, it has to do with apples, fruit that we eat, fruit that we eat when we are hungry, and when the boss has sent you away from the table, at the best part of the meal. It makes you roguish and avid.

I like to eat, he says, without being greedy: I'm sensual and not piggish. Too many other tastes pulled me away from that one. I never took care of my mouth except when my heart was unoccupied; and that happened so infrequently in my life that I hardly ever had the time to think about the choice dishes.

Indeed. We must always believe what he says and never what he says he says. For on almost every page, the aforementioned choice dishes appear. The question then is knowing where they go. But for now, the apples remain where they are.

But the asparagus. As far as I know, an asparagus is not the same thing as an apple. But here the theft remains unpunished. Every morning I went to pick the most beautiful asparagus. The interest here, as I've just said, is in knowing where they go. Rousseau doesn't eat them but gives them to another, for his profit—to the son of the owner (again, the garden, the mother's garden, the feast continues, and a garden of asparagus, and did you know that the man's name was Verrat ["Worm-rat"] ?), the son who himself splits the profit from the sale with another friend. The young apprentice is no longer a parasite but is parasited. The model of the apples is reversed. A while back, the master—the host, just like the mother is the hostess here of her own son—accumulated wealth through a means of production, hunting or harvesting. And the apprentice used the products for his own benefit. It is this detour of the products that is described with a wealth of details and circumstances, large and small skewer, the slat of wood and the knife, the whole and its parts, the hole in the jalousie: this is the parasitic circle, with its wily detours, always complex, duplicated, always with eccentric orbits and epicycles. A producer, a predator, is always a simple person. But if you meet a complicated man, ask yourself at whose table he eats. Or read scientific treatises: you will admire the sumptuous detours and the baroque ruses of parasites, to the point of believing that these animals are intelligent and to the point of believing that one day, it was these animals that invented intelligence. *Parasitus sapiens.* In the matter of the asparagus, Rousseau is in a symmetric position: he doesn't eat what he gathers but is just someone else's pawn. Someone else behind him, who directs him and uses the harvest and the hunt for himself. (That is to say, the botanical hunt, *à la* Rousseau; apple or asparagus—what else does the narrator do but botanize?) Two paired stories—really only one. In the complete model, the surprised thief and the thief thieved from occupy two interesting positions, opposite or symmetric, relative to the one who thieves or surprises. There is always a third—look at *La Nouvelle Héloïse*—just as in science, where the third is excluded. But we are not yet at this level. Here, quite simply, it is a question of eating, perhaps of surviving. Here I am, and here is the apple. And here is the third in position. He is, over there, the source of the apples, and here, at the opening of the asparagus. I am the opening of the apples and the source of the asparagus. Immediately, the good position appears, discovered by comparing the two stories: you have to hold fast and never give way. Hence, the trial-and-error method. First, the thief thieved from, then the thief surprised—we're making progress. The good position has been recovered, and the apprentice, for his trial efforts, remains an apprentice. At first he is satisfied with bits and pieces, gets no wine, and then, gets nothing, not even a piece of an apple. He will never forget this lesson. It is so important that it is the only time in the *Confessions* that the pen falls from his hand, like the little skewer. It is a lesson worth all the cheese in the world. (In the *Emile*, commenting on this verse of La Fontaine, Rousseau notes: the thought is a good one.)*

Cheese. Departure for Turin. I imagined rustic feasts, delicious fruit on the trees, and vats of milk and cream on the hills. Even in Turin, the reflex is rather a conditioned one: at the time that the bell of the last rites scared me, the bell for mass or vespers brought to mind a lunch, a dinner, fresh butter, fruit, dairy products. The viaticum of last rites is food for a trip, for a special trip, taken alone, that of our death. The last trip—the last *Promenade*—unfinished. A few steps from the Contrà Nova, not far from the table and the breast of Mme Basile: with dairy products, some greens, cheese (I'm no longer too happy with this; this gastronomy of the milky, the creamy, the mammary, is decidedly not very evolved, undoubtedly infantile, Protestant perhaps, and Anglo-Saxon thereafter; but for the honor of French literature, Rousseau does not detest good wine), cheese, I was saying, some brown bread and some drinkable wine—with all that you can always be sure of regaling me. The regal is not autonomous though; it [*régaler*] is not a reflexive verb. Yes, the position is well held. One is sure. Who is sure? The one who regales me. The one who invites me to his table. The one who nourishes me. My host. Here, for your benefit is my menu, for you who read me, for you who might have me at your table some night. Cover it, then, with cream. And to drink this wine, why shouldn't I think of the celebrated cup that served as a mold for the most beautiful breast in the world? Is the best parasite the one who is the least weaned? Of course, it is a question of Jean-Jacques, of Maman and the governess, of the milky and the

*Jean-Jacques Rousseau, *Emile*, in *Oeuvres complètes* (Paris: Gallimard, 1969), 4:355; La Fontaine, "Le Corbeau et le renard." —Trans.

infantile, of the motherless orphan and of the expert who recommended that mothers nurse their children. Of course, it is a question of the person who lacks for his mother's breast and looked for it and who loses his children in order to have no one to nourish, that is to say, in order to keep what I have called the good position. But this person, so he tells us, shows himself in his true nature. I am not making any hypothesis on as controversial affair as human nature. But I don't think I have ever met a completely weaned person. They all seem to bear either a pump or a sucker, whether visible or invisible. Parasites and poorly weaned individuals: I don't know which of the two is the cause of the other, but I suspect that each is cause and effect. Certainly badly weaned: Rousseau is called the Little One next to his Maman.*

The customs of sumptuous tables have not changed the simplicity of my tastes at all. Some milk. But no maitre d', no servants, no lackeys. Everyone sees the good republican, poet, and peasant in this. No. He who was a servant knows the position perfectly. It is the good position. Rousseau's real rival is in a position to replace him here. For example: the lackey named Dupont, who wrote very well and to whom I paid ten *écus* from my own pocket and who never paid me back. Dupont—a copyist or a writer?—both times the double of the model. Further on, confessions: the reason my tastes stay simple is that any unequal association is disadvantageous to the weaker party. So be it, and long live equality; we will make or have made the Revolution for that. Let's examine this a bit in detail. Living not far from opulence, I see myself forced to copy the habits of the rich. They have their servants; I have no valet. But the hospitality of the master makes me another master for the same servants. If someone knows all too well that I am not a master, it is the servant. He laughs at me behind my back: rogue, rascal, lookout, the knave. This arrogance must be paid for. Whence the innumerable gifts, inside and outside the house, to the lackeys, the porters, the coachmen; it never ends. Without considering the laundry or the barber. Say, twenty-five *écus* to sleep only four times at Mme d'Houdetot's house; it's ridiculous. (Mme d'Houdetot is the great love of his life.) In fact, the disadvantage of an unequal association does not come directly from the great, the rich, or from princes, but from the small, the people on the bottom. Such skinflints. It's unbearable. I did lots of little favors for the servants, and I never received any from them except for money. Whereas the great were always at my service for having understood my

*My little household, my little chatter, my little business. The France of the "little" goes back to Rousseau, that of the "little meal," the "little beach," and the "little, local wine." Before Rousseau, France was the land of the great and of grandeur.

little chatter. The great are despicable because of the small; the rich, because of the poor around them. Good-bye, Revolution. In short, the parasite has but one enemy: the one who can replace him in his position of parasite. Give me food, and let there be no additional expense required.*

Let's return to the departure for Turin; I was going to find feasts (again), friends ready to serve me, mistresses hurrying to please me. Here is what is enough for me: my ambition was limited to one chateau. I was the favorite of the master and of his wife, the lover of their daughter, the friend of her brother, and the protector of the neighbors; I was happy, needing nothing else. Irony, of course, colors the picture but does not adulterate it at all. The confession remains the same. And it is so true that life itself, like the novel, will try to attain this state. In the meantime, peasants I knew welcomed me, housed me, nourished me; look at the letter to Julie where Saint-Preux tells of the peasant of the Valais and the peasant women with big breasts, who all gave quite freely of their hospitality to the traveler-philosopher, to the wanderer in love. And with no surcharge [service compris]—the service is assured by the aforementioned women.

The model is slowly constructed. The first first-rate host, M. de Pontverre, a descendant of the gentlemen of the Spoon. This famous name, he says, struck me. I too am enchanted by his glass [verre] and spoon. He gives me dinner—it is inevitable. Henceforth, things are serious; it is the war of religions, priests against ministers. Jean-Jacques finishes his lesson with the minister and dines with the priest. Theology is discussed. I found, he says, little to respond to arguments that ended this way (read: at the table), and I decided that the priests at whose houses one ate so well were at least worth our ministers. I was too good a dinner companion to be a good theologian: my superiority (at the theoretical level) was not worth the price of his wine of Frangy. A dinner is certainly worth a mass. And even more so, since a mass, after all, is another feast, communion. Abjuration will soon follow: it is negotiated at the table d'hôte. He changed religions, says Emile, to have bread. The voice of one's conscience cannot be heard by someone whose stomach is rumbling. Go back to the same letter to Julie where Saint-Preux tells how to get drunk free among the vintners of the Valais. The wine there is violent and good, and hospitality requires you not to refuse it. Hence, not being able to pay with money, I paid with my reason.

*Rousseau's hatred of servants and lackeys is implacable. To see the infamy of paternalism, one must read about how they are treated in La Nouvelle Héloïse. We know that the French Revolution cut off their heads: they were the social group that suffered the most from the guillotine.

Reason for wine, religion for bread: the exchange remains Eucharistic. Here then is a first profession of faith, in the *Confessions,* in Savoy: I wasn't thinking about changing religions; I allowed it to be imposed on me; I played the role of a coquette, just like upright women (the word is not wrong here: a chaste coquette offers but does not give, and gets without paying), for hunger was nipping at my heels. One must live. Good-bye, minister, I'm a priest. Excuse me, vicar. The word *vicar* is rather interesting, as is the role indicated by the word. Vicarious, supplementary, substitute; situated beneath the priest, at the lowest level. There is no one beneath the vicar, yet he can replace the priest. *Vicar* is a word of exchange, like *vice versa.* And it is a word of paths and passage—of promenades. The good priest of Pontverre has a vicar, a replacement: Mme de Warens. She too sold her faith for the King of Sardinia and several hundred pounds of income and it is in her house that the rabble will sell its religion.

The parasite detours for his own benefit. For example: this good young man, now a roomer (?) at the Savoyard vicar's house, sees the money for charity pass through the hands of the priest, money that goes from the giver to the needy. The parasite seeks to branch onto the channel. He asks for a part of this money, for, he tells us, he has this despicable side to his character. It is true that it is easier, although finer: he is not a poor person asking for alms and to whom they are given; he detours a flow for his own benefit, according to the usual rules of behavior. The vicar immediately refuses and gives him his own money, of which he doesn't have enough. The gift is thus direct, without detours, vicariousness, or replacements. No one is replaced. It appears that this lesson was not lost on him. Again.

The parasite makes a detour. I still don't know why. Toward Annecy. The trip takes one day; it took me three. I wandered left and right, from chateau to chateau, singing under the windows. Suddenly this becomes very serious. A trip, yes; a promenade, already; the beginning of an outing. Whose rules are those of irregularity: never take the shortest path, move to the left or the right, be carried away, singing, if you please. It is a path but not *the* path. Why should the good, true path be overemphasized as the best one: the simplest, the easiest, and the straightest? Question: it is agreed that the method is the path; how then can one discourse on the method, if one has left *the* path? The answer is interesting.*

Sudden arrival at Mme de Warens house. "Go wait for me at my house; tell them to give you lunch." To talk our leisure, she kept me for dinner. It was the first meal in my entire life for which I lacked an

---

*Cf. "Randonnée," in *Hermès V. Le passage du Nord-Ouest.*

appetite, and her chambermaid, who was serving us, said too that I was the first traveller of my age and size whom she had ever seen lack an appetite. This remark, which in no way hurt me in the eyes of her mistress, fell right on a big boor who was dining with us and who alone gulped down a meal that could have fed six. The show seemed to me to have been successful. Not eating, not even being hungry, is erasing oneself as a parasite. It is not I; it's he, the big, voracious glutton. This boor replaces me with quality beneath my own, and he thus gets all and gives nothing. In Turin, moreover, he will rob me. The parasite is the enemy. The war, or all against all, is translated in the following way: parasites against parasites. Here: Maman feeds me, feeds her Little One; what else does she do outside her function and her role? Attention: it is not natural, but vicarious. Maman is the Savoyard vicar. And I really believe that the word *vicar* and the word *invited* have the very same root.

Let's change tables and go to Turin, to Mme Basile's house. Pretty, coquettish, and thrilled too by his little chatter. The parasite eats but amuses the host in return. He carries wind in his purse: chatter, talent, payment in words. His misfortune is that he speaks rather badly in public (he doesn't know how to use his good looks to his own advantage), he gets upset, stammers, says whatever comes into his head. And that is the failure of his tactics: he is also contradictory in wanting to become a parasite while staying silent, a gigolo while remaining virtuous and a virgin. Only writing remains, the vicarious partner of conversation. And he will soon pay an abundant share—if a bit late—with this money.

M. Basile, while away, left an Aegisthus by his brunette, who is now beginning to excite our hero—who is not as naive as he looks and whose torrents of virtuous discourse gently veil the usual practice of *picaros*. The triangle is in place, a triangle found everywhere: Claude Anet at Maman's, then the wood-cutter, M. Basile at Madame's, and Aegisthus in his absence—Monsieur's vicar—other living or fantastic doubles, by Heloise. The third man, for now, is the parasite.

Let us not yet close the triangle: someone has a relation to someone or something else. A third arrives who has no relation to the people or the things but who only relates to their relation. He branches onto the channel. He intercepts the relation. He is not mediation but an intermediary. He is not necessarily useful, except of course for his own survival: this relation to the relation allows him to exist. But the danger he is in is immediately visible: he can be excluded by an association grouping the two subjects whose relation he parasites, or by one subject who wants to keep the object exclusively for himself. This risk of exclusion is known to him as soon as he sits down at the table, as soon as he is hungry. A risk of death. He always hears the ringing of the bell for last rites, the bell that scares him, the announcement of the last meal, the interrupted last supper, before his death. He always knew that he was a third; he always knew that he was only in third position; he always knew that the implacable law is that of the excluded third (the excluded middle). He is well aware of exclusion, wandering, outside the city with its closed gates; he is not of this world. He is well aware of persecution: here I am alone on earth, excluded by unanimous agreement. Excluded by a combat, by the general will. Henceforth I have only myself as a resource. Can he survive this way? Can one be auto-parasitic? Reveries: having only myself to feed. No, no, it's impossible. Death comes while he is writing of his vicarious mother, and the last word of his life is the watchword of his life: the help I received. This help is not returnable, never given back, never erased, unpardonable, like a relation without a reciprocal and without a converse. Is it necessary to continue telling the true story of the parasite and the paranoid? Either word works—the essential is the prefix. "The Tiger and the Flea" was not a fable but a parable.*

Let's sit down to eat; we're wasting our time talking theory. It's the Jacobin's dinner. Look at the parasites swarm around the tablecloth: the monk, the confessor, Aegisthus, the spy, and myself, the narrator of the confessions. It is certain that they pay in words. The table was not sufficiently large; it was necessary to add a smaller one, where I had a pleasant conversation with the salesman [commis], who is like a vicar, the lieutenant of the actual seller. The spy is the vicarious husband. Imagine then two levels, the big table and the small one, above and below the salt. The flow of the meal goes from the high table to the low table, in this direction and not in the other. In the conversation with the proxy husband, I lost no attention from the others and no food. I was in the good position and the good direction. There were many plates sent to the little table that were certainly not intended for him. The spy sees the mask(er)s go by—that's the feast. Suddenly, heavens! my husband! Basile comes in making a to-do. The king says: who is this little boy? and makes some demands that show the treachery of the spy. Aegisthus, the parasite of Basile, replaces Rousseau, the parasite of the brunette. The king is higher than the queen, the spy is lower than the innamorato, who, the next day, is outside again. Excluded, expelled, chased. Alone again on earth.

Maybe we should stop reading the right way, and go back to our reading and back to the clearest memories of childhood. If the same situation is often repeated, to the point of becoming law, let us follow its recurrence. In it we should find an archaic model or a primitive diagram.

*Critique, nos. 375–76, pp. 730–41.

Here follows the horrible tragedy, the history of the nut tree on the terrace. My uncle had it planted to have shade. By the way, who gave him such an idea? It is well-known that the shade of the nut tree is deadly. In short, the affair was conducted with some solemnity. But my cousin and I wanted to plant as well, without dividing the glory with anyone else. A cutting of willow did the trick, and it was planted eight or ten steps from the august nut tree. But there was no water to water the cutting. We weren't allowed to run around enough to get some ourselves. Hence the industrious invention of the subterranean aqueduct, made of boxes and planks, which led to the willow, detouring the water destined for the nut tree. This is the good botanical model, and botany, as we shall soon see, is the queen of sciences and of all parasitic detours. The nut tree's basin, now with a hole, communicates with the hollow of the willow, at a low level. The large table and the small table, the high basin and the low hollow, allow an alimentary flow between them. The (weeping?) willow parasites the fruit tree with its shady leaves. Suddenly, tragedy. Heavens! My uncle! Struck by the sight of the division of the nut tree's water between two basins, the uncle took a pick and shattered the aqueduct. There is always someone to surprise the parasite who has branched onto the channel. But the text continues about the glory of this affair. For having invented that, I thought myself better than Caesar: when he visits the Pont du Gard, he is there alone, right in the middle of the aqueduct. No one destroyed that one. Why wasn't I born a Roman?*

The model is slowly becoming finer and clearer; it is becoming fixed as it is constructed. From the large to the small table, Mme Basile's envoys bring good dishes until the husband interrupts the flow. From the high basin, at the foot of the nut tree, toward the hollow one below, at the foot of the willow, water flows to nourish the cutting, until the uncle interrupts it. The parasite is an interrupter. The host interrupts the interruption. We are reasoning, I think, by recursion. Let us go then to the end of the text; we are on the Ile Saint-Pierre. The happiness of being housed, fed, sheltered, and protected by a tax-collector [*receveur*], whose job I think can be analyzed in the same way. Would the best hosts be the best parasites? This logic is unshakable; it is inscribed in language itself. Once again we find the tax farmer, the rats, and the cascade. It's the twelfth book or the fifth promenade. Here is the lake, a round basin enclosing two isles, one large one that is inhabited and cultivated, and a small one, uninhabited and lying fallow. The first is a

---

*The etymology of the verb *supplant* is disputed. You might suspect that my preference is for the idea of planting below, planting at a lower level. Thus M. Lambercier's nut tree is supplanted by the willow.

paradise—I mean a reservoir: plants, animals, fish. Therese and I, he says, enjoyed sharing the gathered fruits and vegetables with the tax-collector's wife and family. The admission is important: I wonder if the hostess thanked him; I assume she gushed her thanks. In short, with as much solemnity as before, during the planting, here, there, is population. Rabbits go on ship from the large to the small isle until the authorities of Bern interrupt this population and chase the herbalist away.

But here suddenly, things are reversed. The small isle will eventually be destroyed by the removal of land from it used to repair damages made by storms and waves to the large isle. It is thus that the water substance is always used for the profit of the powerful. What happened? What kind of circulation? What kind of revolution?

Large table, large isle, august nut tree, the great. The great of this world—the nobility. Of high birth, well-bred, sometimes rich. The citizen is low in breeding, birth, and money, but he is swelled with merit: think of it; he is a philosophy teacher. The reverie, the promenade, imagination, lead us back to the chateau. Remember the carefree, unselfconscious, friendly, and smiling program of the person who admitted to us that he could love only young ladies and never the badly kempt girls of the people: the favorite of the master and mistress, lover of the young lady, friend of the brother, and protector of the neighbors. Julie's lover is about to realize this plan. He has the mother, more or less, the daughter, surely; as the brother is dead, Claire and Milord Edouard are his vicarious proxies; he is loved, adored, coddled by everyone. He becomes Fanchon's and Claude Anet's protector. Everything is in its place, including the haughty refusal of money, which through masterful tactics, ends up with the doubling of the proposed sums.* The little willow was never watered better; a weeping willow was never in a more beautiful garden; the small table was never laden with so many choice pieces; the little island was never so well-populated. One can meditate for a long time on what the wonderful merit of this anonymous person [Saint-Preux] might be to merit such a hubbub around him. Philosophy? That has never happened. Love, love, I tell us, love come from nature and not from conventions, the love that regales, that ignores differences in social level, the love where Marion is as worthy as the young lady. Perhaps, but why can you love only young ladies? Why do you have Marion dismissed? Why does Fanchon remain in her place? Why save her at any cost from this rich gentleman?

Listen: she writes badly. I leave to one side my biases and critical coolness; yes, for such a style, I would give up twenty quarterings of

*La Nouvelle Héloïse, pt. I, letters 15-18.

nobility, chateaus and parks, power and fortune, all the inequalities. Except, perhaps, Margot's bed. The French aristocracy had to have loved language, and placed it above everything else. Just as it should be. It abandons its difference for a packet of letters perfectly written. Yes, the parasite pays in words. But his kingdom for these words. This male thought of great souls, which gives them a special idiom, is a language whose grammar the parasite has. Had I been Julie, Claire, Edouard, old or young, man or woman, king or Fanchon, I too would have been on my knees. Was it necessary for men of letters, Grimm or Voltaire, less noble or ignoble, to have been jealous? I would exchange, these discourses for all inequality, I think, he says, however, nothing but petty things.

Love, I tell you, hidden, secret, subterranean love. And suddenly, the horrible tragedy. Heavens! My father! He sees all; he has understood all, uncovered all; he mistreats his daughter; he hits her; she falls and bleeds. I suppose that she bled so much that she miscarried. Death of the child, expulsion of the child, death of the young willow from the pick's blows, an aqueduct! An aqueduct! The parents discover the exchange of letters or the flow of water. Heavens, my uncle! Heavens, my husband, M. Basile! Heavens, the noble, brutal father. Heavens, the government of Bern. The lover is expelled, the author is expelled, the child is expelled, the parasite. The one who is branched onto the incline, not the one who speaks about inequaltiy, but the one who experiences inequality, who sketches its levels and knows it well enough to make use of it. "As soon as a man needed the help of another, as soon as it became clear that it was useful for one to have the provisions for two, equality disappeared, property was introduced, work became necessary." Who then is this second person who delves into the provisions of the first; what then is this need?

We are reasoning, I think, by recursion. We must reach the limit, the very first moment of life, of which there is no trace. I cost my mother's life. At the moment of expulsion, the one who gives life lost it and the expulser is herself expulsed; the original hostess dies. The one whose birth is weaning itself will never be weaned. He no longer has a home, food, or warmth. The parasite kills its host, as happens sometimes. Hence this interesting genealogy, the tree where the aqueducts are broken. I never had a mother, who was dead since the expulsion. I never had a father, or almost never: expelled from the country for an affair in which a captain's nose bled. I never had a brother, or almost never: libertine and subject to fugues, he fled, disappearing completely. I never had a wife, or almost never: I married the one I called my governess rather late. Thus I did not have, could not have, must not have children.

No father, no mother, no brother, no wife, and hence, no children. No upstream, no downstream; we will destroy the aqueducts. The thing is deducible and necessary. It was not an event in his life but a continuation of its rule. The five children are expulsed, like all the rest, like father and mother, like me, like those must be who might parasite me. They would have lived at my expense, living off me; they would have put me in the position of the august nut tree. I want to remain a willow, watered, weeping, and without shade.

Destroy the aqueduct, destroy the canal, undo genealogical ties, or remove dependence. Insularity can be defined in that way. The paradise of the Ile Saint-Pierre or the people of Corsica, unsullied by legislation, a new people. I am an island. I am unique, no father or mother. My mother died at my birth: nature broke the mold I was made in. My enterprise never had an example, and its execution will have no imitators. General theory of agenesis. *Sine patre, sine matre Melchisedec,* I belong to the number of great messianic figures. In *The Words,* Jean-Paul Sartre repeats the same gesture, the same genealogical cut-off.

And thus, my family is composed only of vicarious members. My mother having disappeared, Mme de Warens is the vicarious mommy; my father, expatriated, my uncle replaces him; my brother on an escapade and I hang around all the hustlers of the world, and everywhere, triangles in abundance that will restitute these inseparables to each other; my wife, unworthy of my equality, is only my servant, and I pay her with the title of governess. Thus I put my children up for adoption. Sophie and Emile will be their vicarious replacements. Family of words, children of paper. The logic of the vicarious is a genealogy of the sacred.

The pen is falling from my hands, caught in the act of stealing an apple with the skewer. Why did I take up my pen now? To confess the story of the ribbon. The sin, admitted here, remains the same. I accused Marion, I said that Marion had given me the ribbon. No, Jean-Jacques didn't lie, for, in a certain sense, one never lies. He put Marion in the position of having been a thief—a predator—to put himself immediately in his usual position, that of the parasite. Marion gave it to me as a present. He admits the real the truth while lying. This shame that has weighed on him throughout his entire life had just been revealed. The desire to be rid of it contributed a lot, he says, to the resolution I made to write my confessions. He takes up his pen and lies. It is now that he lies. It is bizarre, but nonetheless true that my friendship with the girl was the cause of my ignominy. I was thinking of Marion; I wanted to give her the ribbon. And then I accused her. Liar! Did you ever give anything to anyone; did you ever intend to give? I was a chatterer, a liar, and a *gourmand.* I would have stolen, fruit, candy, victuals.

No, I would never have given this ribbon to Marion. What I wanted was to get it from her hands. It is not I, but the Xenophon of the *Symposium* (another meal) who defined philosophy as a procurer or a panderer. As someone who places himself in the middle of a relation of desire to parasite it. Canonic example: one day, at the table, at the very moment she put a morsel in her mouth, I yell that I see a hair: she spits out the food on her plate; I grab it and hungrily swallow it. The model is brought to its most abstract simplicity. Or to its naming: when she offers me a plate [*assiette*], I move my fork to take [*piquer*] a small morsel of what she was offering: parasite, sponger, *pique-assiette*.

Jean-Jacques, Lawmaker's Judge ———————

He is now sixty years old. He lives more or less alone. Every morning he copies music at so much per page. After dinner, he takes walks around Paris alone. Sometimes he writes to affirm that he will not write any more. He is somber, wary, suspicious, thinking himself both good and bad. They say that he is crazy, and history says that he went crazy. Is he really crazy? I think I can resolve this question.

He has all of Europe's great polemicists against him in an era in which they had high-quality venom. He had lived through furtive departures in eary morning hours, with warrants issued for his arrests in Paris, Geneva, the Ile Saint-Pierre in the Lac de Bienne. As soon as he goes to England to seek refuge, people start to talk about his delirium of persecution. But there is an error of view and of time: attacks against established power had not yet become effective means of taking positions and power. The martyr did not only risk losing a promotion. Rousseau really could feel and find himself persecuted. But that is not the main thing.

The main thing can be clearly read in the minutes of a trial during which Rousseau himself is in the position of judging Jean-Jacques. Three hundred pages of feverish writing where a lawyer and the public prosecutor speak, not before the tribunal of the *Confessions* but before a higher court, the king, if possible, otherwise God, the supreme Judge: this is why the author wants to place a copy of his next-to-last book on the altar of Notre-Dame. Since the gate was closed, he found himself excluded once more from these legislatures.

His story again: the misfortune of a man alone faced by all humanity together, unanimous and evil. People smile, look down on him, and put the book on the shelf of the monuments of psychiatry. One moment, I beg you, before you classify it. What is it really a question of, through the pathos, fear, and suspicion, suffering and pretense,

116

side-glances and theatrics? Of what a man can really know of what others think of him. And of what others think in general and what they do together. Before examining the act by which others think or speak, it would be a good idea to examine the act by which the others are the others.

First of all, and quite logically, this individual must be considered independent of all relation. Without that, the others, from his point of view, would not be other. Here then is a description of isolation, of insular singularity. From the happiness on the Ile Saint-Pierre to the tomb on the Ile aux Peupliers at Ermenonville, the island is always present and accounted for in the theory, for the constitution of Corsica. The island is defined by its edges, or, every definition is an island. It is determined by what it denies or refuses, high ground in the water. In his last dialogues Rousseau uses only such words: he is surrounded, circumvented; he finds himself closed in as if by a barrier; he lives in a tight enclosure; he is in a cage. It is not sure that he is unhappy there, since he wants to live in prison, nor is it sure that he is happy there. In any case he sketches out this isolation.

Yet, in what seems to be a unique case since the beginning of the world, all of Paris, all of France, all of Europe, all the world, plotted against one person. One person who has been alone on earth since then.

The thing, I think, is interesting from the simple point of view of logic. There is a well-defined simple unit—me, me alone; there is only one, alone, only me. Outside this unique, isolated case, there are no others; there could not be any others because the others form a well-defined set that is compact and uniform. Who am I? Alone: alone is not the way I am, but my essence. Who are the others? Everyone. Not everyone minus one, but everyone, absolutely speaking. Everyone without exception and alone without remission.

Everyone. The great, authors, men of letters, doctors, the powerful, women, people in good standing, the administration, the government, public opinion, businessmen, idlers, passers-by. Visitors and beggars. Those who write letters and those who send manuscripts. Those who sell me cheaply and those who sell me dearly. Those who are nice are ingratiating; those who are tough insult me. Those who look at me inspect me; those who seem not to look at me scorn me. Always interesting from a logical point of view. Totality comes from the union of a subset and its complement. Those who do this and those who do not do this. Those who think like this and those who don't. Thus, everyone. If you lay your hands on affirmation and negation together, you are always right.

All the public, the whole generation, all humanity.

There are no individual or single entities in this set. It is of no importance that this one is an author, that that one is a doctor or an administrator. This totality is not the aggregate of numerous diverse elements but the sum of forces that can only come from a gathering. Hence the constant use of the terms of league, sect, plot, which through unanimous agreement for their execution, cause everyone to agree to a harmonious movement and universal assent.

Rousseau recognized the existence of a social contract from the outside. He describes *de facto* at the end of his life what he set up *de jure* and abstractly in his exercise of political philosophy. The others, in a block, have a pact together. And this pact comes from general animosity which is the perversion or the derivative of ancient general will. Jean-Jacques and his double rewrite the *Social Contract. Rousseau, Judge of Jean-Jacques* is his second treatise on political law.

He is surrounded by shadows, by a triple ring of shadows. He knows nothing; he cannot know what they want from him, what they accuse him of, what kind of plot his persecutors have formulated. For three hundred pages he constantly asks why and how. When he was writing of the social pact, no contradiction bothered him; everything seemed crystal clear to him. It seemed transparent to go back to a first convention; it seemed evident to him that an act of association would produce a group ego or a public persona. Today, those plotting against me, those in league together, form, he says, an indissoluble body whose members can no longer be separated. In the political sense, they form a republic. Rousseau sees that what he had foreseen is now constituted, but he is outside; he sees a dispersed set form a unit, a unanimous gathering of forces—and it all seems shady to him.

The truth is that he is right; the truth is that he made decided progress in politics; the truth is that his theory was not as clear as he thought; the truth is that no one ever knew and no one knows how a unanimous agreement is formed among separate individuals. The truth is that this question is still dark, black, in the shadows. Rousseau moves down from theory to praxis and from clarity to obscurity. What is the collective? Politics is the set of theatrical discourses of magicians who want us to believe that they know what it is.

However, there is at least one clear answer to the question. And professional politicians usually know it. For unanimity to appear within a group, sometimes all that is necessary is to bring about general animosity toward the one who will be labelled public enemy. All that is necessary is to find an object of hatred and of execration. Best-sellers and landslide elections occur this way. General will is rare and perhaps only theoretical. General hatred is frequent and is part of the practical world.

No, Rousseau is not crazy; he remains a public writer. He moves to experience, from the abstract to the concrete. Not only does he see the
formation of a social pact from the outside, not only does he attest to
the formation of a general will, but he also observes, through thick
shadows, that it is formed only through animosity, that it is formed
only because he is its victim. Why? I don't know; he doesn't know; no
one knows; it's not clear; it may never be clear: it is nonetheless thus.
Union is produced through expulsion. And he is the one who is expelled.

Is he crazy? The answer is simple and easy. The one who suffers
from a delirium of persecution simply mimics a political practice. This
politics needs martyrs and consumes a lot of them; it will never lack for
martyrs, always finding enough volunteers: martyrs, in fact, are only
kings, princes, barely inversed. Failed ambitious men who are going to
succeed. Look at the chapter on the "Legislator" in the *Social Contract*:
even there Rousseau was already judging Jean-Jacques. The superior
man, the wise man, the one who is capable of transforming everyone in
parts into a great whole, is the author, quite obviously, of the *Social
Contract.* He is beyond emotions, yet knows them intimately; he is outside the contract, yet foresees it and formulates it. He is unique, almost
a god, and here he is alone on earth. He would have worked under
Louis XV, and he will flourish under the Convention. Then everything
is turned around, and the inverse is still true. This political praxis mimics
a delirium of the same kind as well. Vigny's Moses, Goethe's Mohammed,
Rousseau's man in need, before him or after him, or Rousseau himself,
is only, when all is said and done, a classic paranoiac. The psychiatric
document and the text of political philosophy are both written with
the same ink and by the same hand. With the same words and the same
meaning. And the words—*crazy* and *political*—no longer have any
proper meaning, since they have the same meaning.

The result of this is both considerable and profound. The men-
tally ill are not all in asylums,* as people seem to think. They abound
in kings' palaces, in high government positions. But we have known this
for a long time; the experience is quite a common one. What we didn't
know, what Rousseau teaches us through his theoretical life and his
lived books, is that a political discourse can be a delirium and *vice versa.*
In other words: since we don't know at all what collective functioning
is, the theory that accounts for it is cruelly delirious. The tortured, the
hungry, the dead, know this or knew it in their very flesh.

Another classification that collapses. The *Contract* is studied in
institutes of political science and the *Dialogues* in schools for psychia-
trists, even though it is a question of only one text. Let's make these

*The French has "Petites-Maisons." —Trans.

good people study together: madmen and politicians form one population of students and subjects for studying. Sudden anguish: it seems to me that the evidence found in Rousseau's work is general. Yes, these diseases are political. Yes, these politics, theories, and behaviors are only diseases.

Noises

We are buried within ourselves; we send out signals, gestures, and sounds indefinitely and uselessly. No one listens to anyone else. Everyone speaks; no one hears; direct or reciprocal communication is blocked. This one here speaks learnedly; he is as boring as the last course he gave; he doesn't care if people hear him. Another, more jovial, plays a strong role that he dearly holds onto: he spreads his good humor through his discourse. The third, an irritable pipsqueak and always on his high horse, terrorizes those around him; they all play their favorite instrument, whose name is their own. All that should produce cacophony; I admit that it makes noise. And Leibniz is right, monads are closed; they neither hear one another nor listen to one another. And yet, sometimes, there is agreement. The most amazing thing in the world is that agreement, understanding, harmony, sometimes exist. Leibniz supposed God for this law-miracle.

He said: here is an orchestra. Each musician plays his instrument as if he were alone in the world. He likes only his English horn, this English horn is he himself in person. He plays his part of the score, and when he has finished, at the very end of the page, he puts down his things and leaves the theater. But only to die. How could the first viola be in harmony with him, for the first viola has never thought of anything but his four strings? Leibniz answered: God created the viola so that at a certain predetermined and well-fixed time, it would produce the note preformed harmonically to that of the English horn. God foresees harmony and God is harmony. History is programmed; everyone has a score. Others say that they are in the same linguistic milieu together. Words have to find each other, since they are part of the same set. And this is the same solution: there is a conductor or a common text to play. Someone or something always precedes.

121

That doesn't resolve the problem but only gives the answer. We give ourselves the answer in the form of a person or a pre-text. The probability of harmony is weak in the multiple distribution of senders and the qualitative weakness of reception. Harmony is not a law; it is not regularity. Harmony is rarity itself. It is, quite precisely, a miracle. I call a miracle a very great improbability. When the miracle occurs, from an improbable accord, it produces a new song, so very rare that it is forbidden for repetition to have ever occurred for as long as the period of time was before the meeting. This agreement is negatively entropic; it is a producer; it is perhaps production itself—its definition and its dynamism.

In any case, repetition is death. It is the fall into the similar, like the fixed identity of the too-well-known. If the only concert(s) in the world came from the already written, the world would quickly become a pale hell where shades floated about. It is often like that, I know. But were truth and reality always prescribed, everything would be transformed into the sepulchral. The always already is only a cemetery where entropy rots matter away. Fortunately, the rare exists, exceptions come about, novelty appears—the improbable miracle. Through this rarity, the world comes into existence, we live, and we think. These three events are improbable but are there nevertheless. The preformed and the ever-repeated are this text of death bearing the disappearance of the real. Another incarnation of thanatogenic philosophy that seeks to transform the world into a pillar of salt or a plain bestrewn with corpses. If there already is a text or a conductor, if there have been enough repetitions (enough practice), then the world is a hell and we are but shades in it. Then death has won the game, aided in its work by philosophy.

Of habitual cacophony. The participants send more or less canonic sounds here, and sometimes they make sense. The sum or the product or the composition of these sources is heard as caricatural, inaudible, unfelt. The meal last night was ordinary. The jovial man spoke loud and recited; the learned man perorated, sufficient unto himself; the man of doctrine screeched the truth and nothing but the truth; the irritable man boomed out about power; the vain man spoke well of himself; the wise man kept quiet, taciturn, waiting for fatigue to set in so he could have the last word. Amidst this chaos, I had the cheese course served. Let us say that I was the host and that the goat cheese [*chavignol*] was delicious. It was divided from hand to hand, but it remained identical to itself until it disappeared. The plate held the stable ready to disappear; the air vibrated with noise and disagreement. It would not have been customary for the jovial man to listen to doctrine or for a vain man to listen to the learned man; it would have been miraculous had agreement been produced. Supposing such an epiphany, we would certainly have been able to resolve some ancient difficulty: a theorem, a text, or even a thing, would suddenly have entered the room, like a wind proper for bending our heads, and would have alit on the table amongst us. When a closed monad hears a shut monad, when a deaf man listens to a mute, together they produce something living that is entirely new, that is never a repetition. This birth is a proof. Our naivete—that is to say, the newborn come to light—is a proof, and a decisive one at that, of the fantastic negative entropy of the plighting of troth. Suddenly, there is production. The only new is naivete. The only new is the miraculous. But this miracle comes from agreement.

If you are naive, you will be the child of novelty. But also, listen, you will have children. Here childbirth has come in beauty, in the middle of the banquet.

We know nothing of composition, of the product, of the sum, of the integral of monads or of individuals, however their society or association is named. We know nothing of the simplest or most direct operations—addition, multiplication, composition, combination—when it has to do with us. Alas, we can only subtract, analyze, kill. The collective is a black box. The set makes noise. Even if each element plays in tune or sends meaning, the set together produces a false, dangerous, senseless clamor. The collective is white noise itself; we do not know what an orchestra is or how a chorus harmonizes. The collective is not a preestablished harmony, or to put it another way, it is not the always already there. Noise comes out of the black box. Noise and shivarees.

The politican pretends to understand, as do the scientist and the theoretician. The religious man pretends to understand, as do the soldier, the inspector, and the militant. Each social function is a known and pinpointed variety of black ignorance intelligently disguised as white expertise. But the reversal of real noise into theatrical harmony, of the killing of meaning and sound into an accord that is at least represented is not the only benefit here. Every social function from the judge to the professor and from the artist to the president, every function that is classified or classifiable in some theory of classes or functions, every function, I say, eats and lives on the aforementioned ignorance. It appears as soon as the black box must be closed. And this operation is paid for rather dearly, so that the holder of the key lives well off it. The one who holds a key does not necessarily have knowledge as well; he can also guard a lock and forbid it to be opened. Each social function is the guardian of a door of the ark, and of a dangerous door, so it would seem.

We understand nothing of the collective nor of the set. We must admit that this ark is full only of shadows and that only an untranslatable noise comes out of it. That there is no site outside the box or the ark from which someone could hear or translate or see. That we are in the ark and if we are outside, we are no longer ourselves. The collective is not an ordinary object, it is not susceptible to definition or to division or to exteriority. Nor is it a subject: who, among us, would be a subject? Who would this "we" be? Who is it? What does it say? Where is it? This set is not a subject; it is not an object; it is thus outside the function of knowledge. We do not know what "we" means nor what constitutes it. We do not know what happens between us and what passes between us. If there is no knowledge, how could there be will? This will is an automorphism, and by that word I mean the projection or the reproduction of what was thought to happen within me in this new mythical subject, the "we." It is a retranslated egology. Who can assure that the "we" has the same attributes and the same faculties as the ego? A thought, an intelligence, a will. Why not desires, appetites, or sexuality? We have made the same error about the collective as about God; we made it in the image of the ego. Of my soul sometimes, when it is given will, intellect, the power of decision, when one goes from the personal *cogito* to the *cogitamus* or from the monadic *volo* to *volumus,* but often of my body: great beast, mystical body, Leviathan, biological models, the Beast. No, we know nothing of the "we" except for what we think we know of the ego, body and soul. In sum, we know nothing, and once more, the collective is black and makes noise.

What is not discussed? What is there no dispute about? What do we immediately agree about?

On a point of law, there is a contract. Law is our rather stable existence; politics is our unstable history (in principle, for in fact the professionals rush to stabilize it for their own profit). The theoretical social contract is written in tatters in law books. Put together, they refer to an unwritten text, that, were it written, would teach us what being together means. But this text is not written and perhaps cannot be. In any case, we are not discussing law, except on the edge of jurisprudence. We are not discussing law because of the policeman. We fear the force on which it is based. We agree somewhat and obey a lot. For we are afraid, afraid of the dark.

Law organizes our concrete life as a group, as a family, as well as relations among peoples. It is full of details and meaning. It varies from one culture to another; specialists seek to connect the differences; all these efforts, differences, and similarities fluctuate according to the circumstances of history. The agreement is lost.

There is, however, a corpus which is agreed on, as if by miracle—the mathematical corpus. It is debated only at its limits, by researchers discussing advanced points. For the rest, there is no disagreement. One can be anti-Darwinian, against general relativity, but no one can put the four rules into doubt unless he wants to leave the community. The scales at a market can be fixed, but neither addition nor subtraction can be falsified; your partner can cheat you in an exchange, but he can't cheat you in giving you your change. Mathematics is an agreement among us. The circle has one center, the ellipse has two; what can you argue with here? In a way mathematics is a "we." It is no longer such in the closed circles of invention but nevertheless remains such as far as it is understood. It is, rather, a new "we," invented by the Greeks, infused by them into history, with great consequences, among which is the act of painting us a common and ideal portrait. Is it illusory? We agree on numbers at least.

The agreement is not related to money but to units and then operations. Money refers to the law text, minted on copper, brass, gold, silver; paper money remains a convention, a contract founded on force and on death. The economy depends, quite obviously, on violence. One can easily see that the agreement on numbers is of a different nature and with other consequences. It is translinguistic and transcultural; nothing can be done about that. It is possible for us to nourish scientists indefinitely in recognition of the fact that they built this fragile bridge among the rest of us, perhaps a unique one, in fact. Only mathematical signals circulate among us. They are the only ones to cross peacefully the thickness of incommunicability that separates us and that is crossed, cruelly, only by armed forces, screaming and deadly.

No, this train of signals was only the second. First of all a train was necessary, as were signals. The condition for agreement on a meaning, for it to be minimal or unequivocal, is, quite simply, perfect agreement. For an accord to be realized, be it about a thing or a word, there must be an accord.

I am alone this morning, as usual, leaning over my work in a white silence. My ears are undoubtedly sensitive to this vague white noise that is indispensible to survival. From a fold of space, as if from a hollow in the word, an audible wave comes to me. It is impure, it yells, it grates, it whines—thus I flee; I curl up in the heart of my attention, in the apex of my solitude. I instinctively look for a high spot that cannot be reached by this attack. I am afraid. I am afraid of the grating noise, of stridulation, of the shivaree. My very skin is horrified: it furrows up and bristles. If the intensity of the burst filling space were to increase, I would soon lose this refuge within myself and lose consciousness.

Maybe the sky will fall on my head; maybe there will be thunder, a volcanic explosion, an earthquake, a tidal wave or a tsunami. I flee. Maybe it is the other who is roaring. I am afraid. I am afraid of the howling, the uproar, the stentor throwing the thunderbolts of God. Hence I flee. Nightingales are afraid of nightingales that sing and who thereby define the extent of their power. We must assume that the melody that enchants us is an inaudible whining for them. Noise separates us, individualizes us, just as fury disperses us. The thick wall that exists between us is built of noises and cacophony. The monad has neither door nor window; we are deaf, and for others, we are dumb because most of the time what arrives at our sensory apparatus that is always open, our hearing, is unbearable.

We are surrounded by noise. And this noise is inextinguishable. It is outside—it is the world itself—and it is inside, produced by our living body. We are in the noises of the world, we cannot close our door to their reception, and we evolve, rolling in this incalculable swell. We are hot, burning with life; and the hearths of this temporary ecstasy send out a truceless tumult from their innumerable functions. If these sources are stilled, death is there in the form of flat waves. Flat for recording, flat for closed ears. In the beginning is the noise; the noise never stops. It is our apperception of chaos, our apprehension of disorder, our only link to the scattered distribution of things. Hearing is our heroic opening to trouble and diffusion; other receptors assure us of order or, if they no longer give or receive, close immediately. None assure us that we are surrounded by fluctuation and that we are full of fluctuation. And it chases us from chaos; by the horror it inspires in us, it brings us back and calls us to order.

The real seems to me to be stochastically regular, like similitude or homogeneity randomly scattered.

The monad has neither door nor window, and this is so so that it can defend itself from deadly malady. If we perceived all the noise of the world, if we suffered our own noise, we would faint and move toward the flat (waves). Thus the monad double-locks its orifices, and finally, it suppresses them entirely because of this physical danger—death by inundation. After all is said and done, it does better to rely entirely on its own resources.

But the Leibnizian solution, through an unexpected paradox, is maximally poor, to minimize the disorder. Order having taken everything over, the mote of the dissonant sevenths still remains facing the flow of harmony. The outlay is not great, but the diversity remains weak. As far as I know, perfect tuning is not the height of art, and perhaps it is only its misery. Might harmony be a somewhat excited variety of flatness? Might it be an antechamber of death? This order from which parasitic dissonance is chased as much as possible, this homogeneity, this similar moving toward identity, this repetition, this straight line that is also the shortest, this flatness—aren't we slipping toward this when we lose acuity, consciousness, life? I fear that harmony is only a heavy fol-de-rol for minds that crave only repetition. The world around us, in us, victoriously defends itself against this stupidity with the miraculous torrent of the unexpected. What remains intelligent in the cursus of the sciences is what is ahead, escaping the law. The best in me turns around; it is not only chased by the noise, chaos, and disorder, but also by the rule, flatness, and death. The best—that is to say, the least cadaverous.

The supreme poverty of the system of harmony becomes known to us not only by the nature of things but also by collective establishments. In Leibniz's scheme, God sets up each monad, and the monad's only singularity is its position. What circulates in the system is a single message, the law, differentially coded by the position of individuals. The only novelty that can intervene in this uniformity, this order, is my situation. The boss does not give orders to the vice-president in the same way that he does to someone in a lowly position. All the horror of a society without hope is there: only one thing is said there, and quickly and without interest, but it is said only by being modulated according to the position of the receiver. I imagine that that describes an animal collectivity. But I only imagine this, for what we know of animals tells us that, relative to us, they are geniuses in politics. The animal metaphor is quite often flattery.

Noise destroys and horrifies. But order and flat repetition are in the vicinity of death. Noise nourishes a new order. Organization, life, and intelligent thought live between order and noise, between disorder and perfect harmony. If there were only order, if we only heard perfect harmonies, our stupidity would soon fall down toward a dreamless sleep; if we were always surrounded by the shivaree, we would lose our breath and our consistency, we would spread out among all the dancing atoms of the universe. We are; we live; we think on the fringe, in the probable fed by the unexpected, in the legal nourished with information. There are two ways to die, two ways to sleep, two ways to be stupid—a head-first dive into chaos or stabilized installation in order and chitin. We are provided with enough senses and instinct to protect us against the danger of explosion, but we do not have enough when faced with death from order or with falling asleep from rules and harmony.

Our chance is on the crest. Our living and inventive path follows the fringed, capricious curve where the simple beach of sand meets the noisy rolling in of the waves. A simple and straight method gives no information; its uselessness and flatness (or platitude) is finally calculable. Intelligence, we knew, remains unexpected, like invention or grace; it does not surpass the surprising to head toward the anything-under-the-sun. Rigor is never in the simple tending toward the identical and would be nothing without uniting and holding together what should not be associated. There is only something new by the injection of chance in the rule, by the introduction of the law at the heart of disorder. An organization is born from circumstances, like Aphrodite rising from the sea.

Music ——————————————————————

It is interesting that the word used in French by musicians to describe their written texts—their scores—is the word *partition*. It is interesting that we have had a rigorous definition of this word since mathematicians chose it. This is not the first encounter between these two groups, these two functions and their language. Without always knowing it, they are always together. They were born under the same sign, at the same moment; they are twins, companions weathering the same storms. Only they know what an agreement is, what fine tuning is and how to accomplish it. To play together, there must be an agreement (tuning up), and there must be an agreement to calculate or deduce together.

They divide a set or collection or any sort of object in parts or subsets separated two by two. None of these parts encroaches on another. And their intersection is empty. No note of the violin can be played on the flute, and so forth. Just as it is for the coat of arms with its separated spaces. What I mean is that the text is adapted to the instrument; no one is permitted to play on the oboe what the cellist has to read. Everything is paradoxical here: to play together as well as possible, the disjunction must be perfect and strict. There is no common text for anyone. Only the conductor has the whole score in front of him.

How and why did Rousseau choose to copy music at so much the page as his job? How and why did this practice fascinate him, to the point of his giving it the longest hours of his life? To the point of counting, at his leisure and for the sheer pleasure, the thousands of pages he had covered with notes. Why and how did he follow the notes this way, almost blindly?

129

I think that Jean-Jacques lived the parasitic relation without seeing it in all its evidence in front of him. The necessity of reviewing his life by confessing it came from having to look for what was missing in the theoretical writings, what the theory was hiding and not showing clearly.

Rousseau progressively constructs (as this book tries to do) the field of human or social sciences. Not the sciences themselves, but their field and its conditions. It is clear enough that it is necessary to begin with a theory of relations, that in this beginning hesitation between a local or global theory is unavoidable, and that this hesitation is integrated into this problem. In a small close group, the garden of Julie, a refined *ménage à trois* castrates the new Abelard; in an even rarer group, attentive raising leaves a green orphan; on the other hand, the *Social Contract* speaks of the general will and traces the face of the legislator. Local, global. The *Dialogues* show the blind view of the difference [*écart*] by exacerbating it: I am alone and there are all of them. The local is minimized to the point of solitude, and the global is maximized toward the quantified universal. I see at last, in the shadows, the aforementioned general will. And the thing is atrocious. Perhaps the legislator is some dangerous madman or some sacrificed innocent person. But at the same time, the *Confessions* obscurely look, in the vicinity of the solitary monad, to see where the relation is going, where it is fixed, and how it is constituted. The relation tends toward zero; it is going to vanish in the isles in the middle of lakes.

Jean-Jacques dies and his last sentence attempts to give to woman the aid he received. His last word confesses that he never returned any aid. Truth from his last drop of ink—perhaps he dies without knowing that he finally discovered what he was looking for. The simple chain—me, my brother, my neighbor, my friend, and my society—demands a linkage and there is none. No there is one; it is the simple arrow, the logical atom, the atom of relation, lived, obscure, in his life at the hostess's house. But as for me, separated from them and from everything, who am I myself? The one who always received and who, *in articulo mortis*, suddenly remembers that he had resolved to give back. The parasite. Detached, yes; I am nothing but a poor madman in the shadows, but my first attachment is derivation, scion and stock, grafting, installation in a small house with my family. Small.

He abandons his children. I don't care about the moral aspect of this affair. What do fault, punishment, guilt, oaths, and true or false reparations matter to me! These viscous adherences are repugnant. Why and with what should I defend Rousseau? Why should I attack him? Are ethics and combat always necessary to create a theater and impassion the spectators? All that is tiring. What does it matter to me if he was good or bad, what does the handful of ashes in an urn in the Pantheon matter? Let's leave this circus, leaving ethics behind. What counts is, almost, the herb garden—I mean the vital symptom, like the sign of the species, biology, natural history. A parasite never nourishes its children. Otherwise it would be in the position of the host. A parasite defends itself from being parasited; the thing is there in all its simplicity. I cost my mother her life; she was my hostess. Symmetrically, I abandoned my children; I am not a possible host. No one can replace me. Welfare is a possible hotel. Look at this animal lay its eggs in a suitable store or an eventual vector; the descendants will develop there, fed and sheltered, and they will die there, like their grandmother. What would have happened if Rousseau's children had been abandoned to the general will instead of to public welfare?

Perhaps I might have liked to say *epiphyte,* this herb garden pushing me too. I don't know what holds me back: undoubtedly movement. The promenade.

Islands of coherence appear that had not been perceived. Theory is less in its designated spots than it is in the obscurity of the confessional texts. Philosophy looks for it there; we must follow its path. It causes the old cultural tradition to emerge again, the one that associates the life of some plants and animals to our abuse values. The hotels found, attachments, the instinctive abandon of children, even botany, sickness—these scattered elements work together, not so much in kind as around a function, or better yet, a relation. The garden of Julie abounds in parasitic plants; it is the herb garden of paradise.

It is easy to run to aid the victory, to see that what is missing from this tradition is in fact this laborious gesture that Rousseau for hours and days on end never stopped doing. Why was he so set on earning his living by copying notes? Answer: because of noise. Answer: he was completing the field of the parasite.

He could have lived from his work. I'll stop for a moment. What is a work? It eats its worker, devouring his flesh and his time; it is slowly substituted for his body. This invasion causes fear. Who am I? This, there, written in black on white, fragile, and this is my body, has taken the place of my body, frail. This is written in my blood; I am bleeding from it, and it will stop only with the last drop. The work parasites the worker; no, soon he no longer exists. He dies of it. And he can do nothing about it. He lives from it. I eat my work and from it; I drink this streaming production daily. I sleep under the tent of its tabernacle in the expanse of its space; I exist in the shade of its volumes-fruits. Who am I? This body, united in its crucible—I would be nothing without this. The work parasites me, and I parasite it. Soon, perhaps, we will be wise fellows together at a dinner. Soon, let us hope, we will be adapted to each other at a joyous banquet, both light and perpetual, where we will share ambrosia. Yes, I know, my life is becoming symbiotic. Close parenthesis; it was not entirely a noise.

He copies clusters of notes when he could be living off his work, being nourished by it. No. He cannot live, like you and me, only from what sustains, for we know on what he has made his life depend. On truth. To live on truth, that's all. But he did not say what is true in the field of economics, in the field of politics, nor in that of education, in the general, contractual conditions of life in society. It is not that he lied. But he proposed things only by abstractions. He comes back, then, to experience; he meditates; he confesses. The compact meaning then emerges—the relational truth so long sought for. I have lived at the table of others; who am I then?

Who am I, assuredly? Here I am alone, without relation. Reduced to myself, I nourish myself from my own matter, for it does not give out; I am sufficient to myself, though I ruminate empty; my dried-up imagination and my extinguished ideas no longer furnish food for my soul. Who am I then? Strictly speaking, a partition. I am not an element of a social set, a family, a group, humanity, for all of them have untied my belonging or inclusion; I have lost all relation. I live in the disjointed; around me intersections remain empty, calm waters, agitated, around the isle. Who am I? A partition.

This meditation, Cartesian in nature, rediscovers, Leibniz's solutions. They are in music as if buried. Harmony conceals the collection of partitions (scores) with no relation. Might as well sit from morning until night in their deafening presence. I write; I've kept watch since dawn, waiting and in order to wait for a fire that will spurt forth one day, the writing of fire, atop the wall, above the banquet that was suddenly interrupted, where the tongues of fire fly over the stiffened necks, finally opening ears. He keeps watch to music from the early morning; he waits for the answer hidden in the jumble of notes and keys, the simple answer to the questions, in their black traces.

I am the partition; here is the partition. What is harmony, what is music? How is this composition established?

He is in the shadows, and we are there with him; we see clearly for having seen that night. The collective is a black box. What can one see of relations and who sees them? Men parasite men, man is a host to man, and that is still a black theorem. The relation parasites the relation; the relation itself is a parasite; this logic is obscure and is overturned, for it is fuzzy. I mustn't look any longer in the transparent epiphany of a poor theory for what remains black in the thickness of the barely observable.

The general will was an abstraction, but general animosity is concrete, lived, and suffered. On the road of conditions we can no longer stop the request.

How did they agree? I don't know. How to agree—not for or against this one or that one; that is henceforth no longer the question—but how to agree, here and now, in any way possible.

During the banality of life, life as it is to be confessed, interceptions come and go. Invitations here and there, at the Marquise's, the vicar's, the lion's, the master's and the rat's, astute branchings, furtive thefts, small noises, the pen, suddenly but seriously, the pen falls from my hands. Small noises and interruptions increase until a crisis or a catastrophe is reached. The ceiling falls on the table. The floodwaters fill the valley. Crackings, noise, chaos.

Outside the room, Simonides. Outside the shipwreck, the old arborescent hosts. They hear the noise; they are the friends of the gods. Or inversely, the catastrophe is Pentecost; the third is alone outside; he brings the wind and the sound. Jean-Jacques is alone outside; he sees the shadows; he hears the chaos. Victory is in the hands of the parasitic noises.

I am speaking plurivocally. Of Rousseau, his work and life, the road he travelled, his conclusion; of all that precedes, the banquets of this book; of the Acts of the Apostles and of Graeco-Roman tales; of Fellini's *Prova d'orchestra (The Rehearsal)* with my text amidst the orchestra in words and images. We must begin again, in the room filled with rubble, in an uneasy obscurity, among the dead and the living, at the risk of noises that will soon come back. Parasites multiply until they reach the level of thunder and fury. The relation of abuse never ceases to rise. The simple arrow goes on; it has no brakes. Until a threshold where noise, abuse, or the arrow are no longer tolerated. Simonides is faced with the dead; Philemon, with the flood; Rousseau, with the night, the third man outside the closed room. What can be done?

What makes us disagree? What interrupts us? The one who eats our bread and prohibits our messages: the parasite. The guest becomes master, and he produces a terrible noise. I am that guest. We must begin with him, with noise, with me. Who am I? The parasite. And I am outside, alone, on the middle of the isle and during the night. Listen. Open your ears. The words give you the solutions. Follow the words. The parasite dis-accords, makes noise. I am a partition. I am alone, isolated, solitary, disjointed. Alone without any relation, or armed with a relation that mixes up messages. Henceforth, I am exceptionally qualified for the study I set for myself. I am an exception to the "we," making this "we" impossible. But this exception is universal. What is it, then, that puts us in accord? The agreement, the tuning up [*accord*] itself.

No theory, I beg you. The note. Follow the note. Music saves us and the notes save us. The notes calm us and music calms us. Grab onto the notes; follow them. Them alone. The *accord*.

The *accord*. On what object, about what? Later, later. But, at least, on a meaning. Later, I tell you. On the sound then, first of all. If you do not make too much noise, I shall try to stop my own; if I sound correctly enough, you will evolve toward that peaceful justice. Before exchanging a single word, before agreeing on the code, we must at least emit a sound together. Here, one can send and receive at the same time. Yes, my signal is the only one in the world, and my voice cries out in the wilderness, in the stony desert of my whinings. Specific, individual pebbles. Let us remove these parasitic stones; by filing down the thorny edges of the sound, we approach each other. Being in tune musically and sonorously, the *accord* is the archaic accord of nuptual agreements [*accordailles*]. Together. A vibration in several voices. Coming together [*jouissance*]. The collective, at the least, is sonorous utopia. Hermes requires translations. Pentecost sings, resounds, and blows; the tongues melt in this fire; music has spoken in tongues. It is free of parasites. The universal language of a buried contract.

Just as a hungry guest is fascinated by the buffet of a feast, Jean-Jacques keeps (to) music. There lies, manifest and under wraps, the solution. This solution includes and excludes him; it includes him as a partition, and it excludes him as a parasite. Who am I? The condition of music, of the *accord,* and its obstacle.

He copies it, writes it, keeps it, watches it, gives it. He exchanges it and sells it. He has always known how to resolve his question: not by what he says, but by what he does, which is clearer than the light of concepts and easier to understand than the doubletalk [*langue de bois*] of philosophy.

And by what he does when he says.

If a pen ever left a rustling noise on the blank silence of its field, if ever someone heard it, to describe in kind celestial voices or the noises of hell, it was the keeper of this music. Free of parasites, free, free, free of itself, absolutely purged of ego. The more I write, the less I am myself. Finally free of this noise.

Each line moves away, runs away from the chance advance of chaos, of volcanic lava, of the cracked earth of an earthquake; it flies above hurricanes; it pacifies roaring beasts, the jaguar or the hungry wolf; it brings back the beloved from hell; it advances courageously in the vicinity of noise, facing it; an accord resounds, not a simple one, not foolish, naive, repeated or beaten in tempo, but at every step, completely new, nourished for a long time on disorder and on the unexpected and placed gently at the limits, on the fringe, the margin where the pure crystal of fountains flows between you and me; let us dance while waiting for the animals to quench their thirst. Language accords us beneath the meaning, and the meaning, often, disperses us.

Write, like him, on the distribution of a card game, on the black, shadowy back of chance; write on the outside that you will show to others while hiding your hand, your partition; don't stop writing on the wrong side of chance, disorder, noise on the wrong side of your own circumstances, and even in their flesh, a small music-harmony, for the other and with him.

Part Three

Fat Cows and Lean Cows

Economy

Salad Meals ———————————————
——— Stercoral Origin of Property Rights

Rousseau was not willing to tell us how the founder of civil
society went about enclosing his land. He staked out a claim or dug a
ditch, it would seem. The dawn of the following day, the stakes were
pulled out or the ditch filled, not by an egalitarian philosopher passing
by, but by those who wanted to put themselves in the property-owner's
place. One of the successors occupies the space so quickly that I think
he was contemporaneous with the first occupant. In the first diggings of
the city walls of Rome, the twins are poorly distinguished from one
another: the one who encloses the terrain and the one who transgresses
the enclosure. They are both first *ex aequo* in this tie of origin. And
they kill each other. It is not too difficult to find simple people to believe you, but to save oneself from their jealousy is a forlorn hope. The
first who, having enclosed a terrain, decided to say, *This is mine,* was a
dead man, for he immediately gave rise to his assassin. In the beginning
was the murder; ancient texts tell us so, and reason shows us. Romulus
only worked to bury Remus deep in the ground.

There are, however, closed things—I mean property. What is the
origin and what is the foundation of property? I never thought that my
peers and I were angels, but we are not stupid enough ever to stop making war, ever to obtain a few moments of peace. The theories of war
without a truce are usually conceived of by rivals of conquest and glory,
full of that *libido dominandi* that makes great men of them. Humanity
would be so peaceful without these great men, be they true or false.
Continuous combat is their strategy and their private pleasure [*jouissance*]. No. Everyone is not like that. To reiterate: those who espouse
this philosophy are so well known, so swelled with power and glory,

that they have placed themselves on the side of the dominators, that they are represented by a dominating class that needs, quite precisely, this philosophy. Go look at the giant billboards where they are painted in red and pink. No. Some of them get other kinds of pleasure: mental and sexual, to be short and sweet. If property were not founded on murder alone, history would not be quite what it is, a river swelling with entreaties, blood, and tears; it would not be, would not exist at all, would have been finished for lack of fighting men, finished since the dawn of time. In war there are cowards, at least the dominators, who have others make war rather than making war themselves. Whence the fact that idle times stop it. There is peace. We would not be here without peace, to be sure.

Private property exists. I seem to remember books that deny its existence. In fact, a careful search, suddenly done by the police in a closed area, quickly reveals the very common nature of what everyone wants to hide as personal property. Every bag holds only public things and underwear is rather banal. Everything was bought in a department store. I learned, in such circumstances, that there is no private language —I mean no private things or words.

This thesis is even more just in that it places at an unfair advantage all the police of the world, all the totalitarian powers, the strengths of money and ideocracy. No one keeps private money, for it is useless and unexchangeable; no one can invent ideas, outside the banal, and if so, he will be put away.

Though it be infinitely just, it would still be necessary to consider it false, by a certain taste for liberty, by a certain horror of falling into the beastly. By taste, by smell. This thesis of the large animal is an idea that has no nose. I shall explain what I mean by answering the question: how do we make the common proper?*

Whoever was a lodger for a long time, and thus in a group even in the most secret acts where the private is never safe, remembers someone who was not willing the divide the salad course. When the salad bowl came, he spat in it, and the greens were his. The salad was all his; no one argued with him. Just like thousands of others, he had resolved Rousseau's problem. He spits in the soup, they say. And thus it is his. A new interrupted meal.

No need for a ditch or for stakes; the spittle distances the starving competition. You will surely hate this man, for you too like salad, but what is equally sure is that you will not touch one leaf of what is

*"Proper," but also "clean." —Trans.

now his. You will kill him, perhaps, but an irrepressible disgust makes you pull your tongue back into your mouth. Private property exists. Suddenly it is stable. As if the jealous twin had disappeared.

A dog that pisses and takes a leak on the root of a tree is said to be marking his territory. From salads we move to the animal's land. The object varies from food to general ecology. But what does not vary is the phenomenon that is used to chase away the neighbor, the twin rival, to transform public into private property, making the common one's own. A process has to be found, originating at one point, that can fill some surrounding space; some sort of expansion has to be created. What is a milieu, my milieu, his milieu, or the animal's? Simply, it is the full extent of the phenomenon, the volume filled by the process. The first, the very first occupation of spots. The expanded must be found. It has to be a sound or an odor. It must hit the open ears or nostrils. These phenomena are common to all receptors that are always open.

Tomorrow, we will remember, with some difficulty, our moving and sonorous world, polluted with the unbreathable, stinking air of motors. Something is dying, in this fog. This noise had conquered space and had even displaced the peace and quiet of the country. In this green valley, this fallow land, this prairie, this stream, this hedge, only war had brought such a commotion. Today, the jet, the bulldozer, and the chain saw pierce your ears just as the dentist's drill attacks the tooth, producing a burst of pain. This war doesn't take place only in Troy, in the city, but is everywhere; we have lost our recluses; we no longer hear the animals splashing in the river; we no longer smell either manure or the odors of summer; bread, milk, peaches, and tomatoes have lost their savor; the motor has taken over the senses of hearing and smell with noise and stink. Ancient powers had a hold on our souls, but this one holds our bodies. Nothing is deeper than the senses. But the thing is dying, in the chaos. The noise of the media has covered it.

The motor was supposed to replace man's labor. But in fact it was only a substitute object of work. When and where has it been a tool? Here and there, we might say, on such-and-such an occasion. But we will have worked with motors as much as and even more than thanks to them. They have just replaced us.

They produced a calculable amount of work. But they made noise as a by-product. It is not certain that noise is a by-product; perhaps it is the direct aim. We will discuss this if it is worth doing so. But in any case, everyone knows that the one who has power is the one who has the source and emission of sound. The one who has the strongest and loudest voice is always right. The stentor who deafens with his commands takes their place. And the one who has the trumpets is followed by the artillery. No one moves more quickly than music. Plato knew this and said so; and the French state, Platonist in nature, keeps its hands on the channels of diffusion of hubbub and shivaree. Who has the power? The one who has the sound, the noise, and who makes others be quiet. He doesn't even need words; all that is necessary is for him to intercept. To say anything at all, but to prevent others from saying. It is enough to thunder. Power is nothing but the occupation of space. There are not many techniques for conquering, for invading space and land. And the first, perhaps, that of the nightingale, the rooster, or the lion, is voice, sound, cry, sonorous shaking. To be at home, from here to there, private space. And from there, to take the most space possible. Power is only a variety of din.

　　　Yes, of course, that is the origin of the supports of discourse. Look at the variety of languages and accents that mottle the globe. Here strangers understand nothing and signals are nothing but parasites for them. The signal proper is noise for a third, who is excluded. Yes, of course, that is the origin of the central point and the centralization of power. Sound, like odor, comes from a point source. When the siren at the town hall replaced the church bell, we learned that the power had not changed. And it is thus when radio replaces the siren. The same goes for matters of taste: your recipes are revolting; ours are delicious. We do not host just anyone. The same waves are sign or hullabaloo; the same substance stinks or smells wonderful; the same food is odious or exquisite. All that defines a reticulated space, which one could call Pascalian, where everyone, for a time, is master of his niche, and where each center, distributed, produces its local power by identification inside, expulsion outside, where every group is found in its place, where the unstable equilibrium of relations of forces fluctuates, where that which turns from, for, to, against, when a thread of the network is crossed is not only a moral precept or a truth value but everything that delights or disgusts the body. Language this side of the Pyrenees, parasite on the other. Sound on this side, din on the other. Their language is only noise, barbaric rumblings. Clarity here, darkness there. Outside Languedoc, oil smells and is considered disgusting, though it is so delicious on garlic bread here. Under this relativity of morals, institutions, and laws lies the diversity of languages, that precedes, it would seem, the very origin of languages, since space is good for both voices and yells, vultures and roosters; there lies the couple message-interference, the night of noise and the sun of meaning; there lies the double response of the senses, taste and disgust, pleasure and pain, welcome and expulsion. It is not very interesting to seek whether the body is impregnated with culture or whether culture emanates from bodies. What is interesting, on the contrary, is to assert that the same situation is found everywhere. That it is in anthropology and in relation: the profane and the sacred occupy the same space, generalized from Pascal. That it is in religion and politics. All the human sciences, all the quasi-sciences, and all praxes recognize such a logic. It is, perhaps, the general condition of all communication.

But this condition is formulated by physics itself. It is the theorem of ambiguity. This, here and now, is information. This, seen, heard from there, placed there (but also: smelled and tasted from there), is a noise. Is only a parasite and must be excluded. I have already given an origin of language based on this principle, crossing the living body from part to part, tracing a path from biophysics to the articulated word.* We find the same occurrence in exercising our senses, in the formation of the collective, in the birth of culture. In our relations to food, excrement, noises, space, and other people. The human sciences know how to build this map. But the exact sciences do the same. The two types of knowledge are in competition here. We speak the same logic in several voices, in this strait between two oceans. The Northwest Passage is open once again.†

The nightingale covers its exclusive niche with its musical voice. No one may enter here without this harmonious geometry. You are from there too; your accent betrays you, O Galilean. Or: I recognize you with your southern drawl [enfant de la Gascogne]. Danger, tranquility.

Privatization begins with the emission of a phenomenon that expands. Then a whole country is tied up by appropriating all the transmitters. Yes, the media replace the motors, proof that noises are not by-products. Space is full of loudspeakers. The system of sound traverses the differences, from West to East. Everywhere, all the time, his master's voice, for the one become a dog.

This mouth is open and emits. Around the source, the space is saturated with what emanates from it. It shows its beautiful voice, they say. No. The atrocious horror of its noise and the stink of its spittle. The volume-niche of the mouth where no one else would eat. And in this area, everything good to eat, fuck, or drink is kept for this mouth. It stinks from cheese. You would have to be a fox to like that. It sings—it swallows. It speaks—it feeds. It spits and gorges itself.

And the parasite appears. It is invited, or not, to the host's house. The hotel, the hostel, the master's house is open to the frozen passer-by. For a while, the private falls into the public domain and the

*Hermès IV. La distribution, pp. 259–72.
†Hermès V. Le passage du Nord-Ouest, preface and passim.

host's own falls into the common passing by. The parasite comes in with this open-door policy. Its immediate activity is to seek to appropriate for itself what is temporarily in common; and so it speaks. It does not even have to speak; it resonates. It makes noise, like the gnawing rats. It produces toxins, inflammations, fever. In short, it excites the milieu. It excites it thermically, making noise and producing a fever. It intervenes in the networks, interrupting messages and parasiting the transmissions. Thus its name is coherent and its act single. The phenomenon of expansion is its proper business and its appropriation.

Parasite. The prefix *para-* means "near," "next to," measures a distance. The *sitos* is the food. In this open mouth that speaks and eats, what is next to eating, its neighboring function, is what emits sound. *Para* measures a difference between a reception and, on the contrary, an expansion. The latter makes one's own what is in common and what will soon be even more one's own, the living body. It already eats space.

It is not the only expansive phenomenon coming from the body. He who spits in the soup does not yell for as much. The mouth speaks, eats, and vomits too. George Dandin, finally, stinks of wine. We are approaching the stercoral, the expansion of odors.

Don't bring your shit to my house any more, a philosophical boss said to me recently when he thought that I was an adult. He was angry and spoke floridly. Burglars, its seems, leave disgusting trails in the apartments they have robbed, trails found among the objects left behind. The privatization of the common and the appropriation of space do not occur only by yelling or spitting; sometimes excrement is enough. The dog took a leak on its niche, where the philosopher would vomit. That is how they mark off their territory. Those who see only public space have no sense of smell. As soon as you soil it, however, it is yours. Thus the dirty is one's own [*propre*].* The first one who, having shit on a terrain, then decided to say, *this is mine,* immediately found people who were disgusted enough to believe him. They distanced themselves from his territory, without war or treaty.

What is one's own [*propre*]? What isn't dirty. What isn't dirty? What is mine [*mon propre*]. *Stercus suum bene olet:* that is the foundation of property, that one's own [*propre*] dung smells good. No, it is not a play on words: one's own [*le propre*] is what is clean [*le propre*], and property is only cleanliness [*la propreté*]. This thing that is horrible for you is mine insofar as I am alone in not finding it execrable or repugnant. You leave; I'll stay, at my place. If you vomit from it, I

*Or, "the dirty is clean." —Trans.

believe that your intention is to reappropriate this space for yourself. The one who vomited on the root of the tree, a few books later, appropriates its genealogy for himself: it was already done. We all know clean people who separate their milieu from their fragrant apartment, who, as hostesses, know how to receive strangers. The stranger enters, is allowed to enter this banalized terrain. Washing is a social act; purifying one's space is an act of welcoming, or a religious, amorous, collective, or hostal act. The more the body is dirty, the more the niche is soiled with feces, the more the person is attached to his property. The host is clean; the parasite is dirty; I mean that it is only clean for itself. The "for itself" stinks. You can eat, sleep, make love, and so on in the deodorized hotel, but you won't sleep a wink or eat a morsel in dirty surroundings. For these surroundings belong to one person. Would you want to eat the ortolans after having chased away the country rat? But the city rat goes back to his activities almost immediately, for he is more at home than the master.

A stroke of genius: money doesn't smell. It is mine; it's a little pile of shit; it doesn't smell; it's everyone's. It is mine, yours, yet it is clean and hence exchangeable. I can thus have everything for money. By working, I water the terrain with my sweat; it is mine. It keeps my odor.

Harmony gathers what noises kept apart. What perfume will unite those who separate odors? Leibniz wrote about the musical *accord* before the social contract, but Rousseau was looking for it when he concerned himself with music. Can such a pre-text be written about aromas?

You shall love the odor of others.

Here then is a stercoral theory that supplies a fundament, as it were, for private property. It is not left, but simply filth. It sketches out a space centered around this locus of emission. Just like, a while back, around the loud speaker. The closer one gets to this spot, the closer one is to the private. Inversely then, the further away one goes. I am meditating on the parasite: the prefix *para-* always measures distance. *Sitos*, in Greek, sometimes means excrement.

Perineal distance, perineal vicinity. The sexual is so private that it is mine, maximally. Nothing is as close to the very spots of excretion. We are not simply born between feces and urine; we love there. A treasure guarded by dragons. The distance is minimal between my privates and what is dirty for others. It wasn't long either for a mouth that eats and speaks, that swallows, that spits and yells. The same organ belongs to relation and rejection. It attracts and repels. It encloses its terrain and invites the stranger. It is host and parasite. No. It is host and guest, clean and own [*propre et propre*]. Inviter, invited, clean for itself and dirty for others. For both the mouth and the sex organs, the prefix *para*-evaluates distances and vicinities between the two times two functions. Both above and below, we are open onto two differential bifurcations.

Barbarians had parasitic loves, confusing sprinkling and fertilizing. They took possession of the terrain and soiled a hostess; she was their private property; they had soiled a hostal space and become its owners. How many customs follow from that. These (s)quitters [*foireux*]* speak loudly, and they love their own dirt; they only come [*jouissent*] by appropriation. They have a clean, quiet female who is self-effacing. Inversely, these females often occupy an unclean space that does not allow penetration.

Humanity will come to these barbarians when they learn about the bifurcation of sex and tongue. The marvel of kept loves, the miracle of free loves and of free speech.

Cancel this distance: love is excretion, food is spittle, vomit, and the woman is a good, like speech. It is the same equivalence and the same exchange system. Has philosophy really been rid of these archaisms? Of this clean/dirty body and of the common dream of appropriation?

The strong theorem of all idealism is written as follows: the world is my representation. This can be translated into: the world is my marked territory; the world is my diarrhea. Among good idealists, the privileged are those that come out of their bodies. Saliva, blood, urine, sweat, vomit, and sperm, other such defecations. These dejecta that mark the terrain with their ink make them imperialist owners. Idealism is stercoral and the stercoral theory discovers idealism.

No. The world is there, without me, before me, after me. I am only my privates—my sex organs and my tongue, homeless fires.

---

*Foireux means both "cowardly" and "affected with diarrhea." —Trans.

Meals of Satire ————————————
Exchange and Money, the Exact and the Fuzzy

He doesn't know how to do anything, and he is demanding.* I shall analyze this sentence with precision and the most faithful exactness. As if it were a question of entomology. Without passion, with a cold eye. But I can't help it if this sentence is a memory that comes back to me. Better yet, it has never left me. It is perhaps my first, original, and fundamental astonishment. I was still young; I was already doing math problems or translations for some well-dressed and well-fed old goats with their shined shoes, nice shirts, and round bellies. They didn't know how to do anything, certainly, but they were of a different sort. The weak already had to be protected, and I was surrounded by them. Everyone knew and I was persuaded of the fact as well that I would always get by—that with a few nuts and a blanket, I could survive without ever failing to give good milk to those around me. My world was made of hard things, of pebbles, pickaxe handles, or the tines of a pitchfork. We travelled the roads together; they were very smooth so that the carriages could move over them smoothly. But they were as deep as tombs beneath and filled with our sweat. The engineers came for an hour or so from time to time to complain. It was never perfect. They didn't know how to do anything but were very demanding. I have always met such old goats, such wimps, such bosses, such strong men. I have always considered them as more astute than I. They always have money, position, honor. Those who are bent under the violent squall of intuition, those whose life is intermittently interrupted by subjection to the tool, never had time for mediation. The one who transforms is

*The French reads: "Il ne sait rien faire et il est exigeant." —Trans.

147

beneath, working under the filling-in of the road. It covers him. And the others run on top, the soles of their feet at ease. I'm able to make my own way; that's enough for me; some paper, a pencil, light, a brasier, I am content; leave me at least a moment of silence. I live in the immediate. With the hard contact with the referent and of metal in the gangue to be transmuted into gold. In the immediate of the world. In the happiness of the immediate. I can't separate myself from it. I am tied to my work more tightly than if by chains. I haven't, no longer have, never had time. I don't have time to run around. They don't know how to do anything, and thus they have time. They walk, see, compare, judge, and know exactly where to find a good meal. They examine, measure, criticize. They are the men of mediation. Of choice and of judgement. They occupy space; they know where to place themselves and where to place another, who in turn is looking for a place. The discourse of place occupies space. It annuls all discourse that designates something. It speaks only of strategy and of the knowledgeable and invading occupation of spots; it is only strategy. The subject of space conquers spaces, occupies spaces, pillages spaces, creates spaces. It parasites the inventive relation to the raw with its noise. The parasite of the mediate parasites all the channels. The noise of those looking for a good meal fills the countryside with its song. It even prevents the worker from producing. Paradox: while some live from its product, it must be hidden so as not to hear all this to-do. Production and invention consist of injecting information into flatness to change it into something rare. How could base lead have been changed into pure gold? By this inventive injection. But this relation cannot come about in this rat race [foire d'empoigne]. The artisan does not leave his stall, whose opening remains a bit dark; he sees, sometimes, to his amazement, the weak pass by. They divide the street, blacken the square, fill the space with their routes, and sit on thrones. They only know how to be demanding. They find all the points where what is important is decided. They have thunder, power, and glory in their hands. They look for the rare and make it their daily bread.

It's true, I admit it. I have never been demanding. I have never stopped being active. I have to know and understand this difference. This difference of existence whose static notion I have made a bit clear around the point of equilibrium. Here the difference is dynamic, since it is written: action.

Never demanding, except about the reality without examples of invention.

He doesn't know how to do anything, and he is demanding. He would die if he ate mediocre food. He is fixed on rarity. He demands something instead of nothing. That is both his existence and his reason.

What does it mean to be demanding, or exacting? To look at the word *exiger,* it is a question of acting plus a distance, a difference toward the exterior. *Exigere* in Latin doesn't have exactly the same meaning. It is more instructive. It means, first of all, "to push out," "to chase," "to exclude." It is true that *agere,* Latin for "to act," has as its first concrete and physical meaning "expulsion." It is not uninteresting to take note of what action was for our immediate ancestors. It was purging, banishment, eviction, rejection, elimination. It is not at all astonishing that the word *action* is now used in the theater. The tragedy with goat's feet expels the scapegoat, the victim that Girard talks about. Tragic action is a more or less sufficient expression. But we, too, know this well: satire, fables, and comedy, around the parasite, speak essentially of exclusion. In the beginning is the action, that is to say, the crime.

But the exacting person is not content simply to act, simply with action. He attains extortion [*exaction*] as well. *Exigere* also means "to make someone pay." *Exactor* is the tax collector as much as he is the one who banishes; *exactio* is banishment and tax revenues. But taxes can be exacted from us too. It is not uninteresting to compare this liability to taxation [*exigibilité*] with extortion [*exaction*] : the violence by which the tax exceeds what is owed. How excess falls back on the norm, how existence winds up tolerating the intolerable difference, how equilibrium in movement recuperates the static balance: these are paradoxical laws that are still ordinary laws. Extortion can be exacted just as excess becomes normal. No, existence is not stable. To exist is already an excess or an exception.

We have moved, perhaps a bit quickly, from purges to taxes, from exclusion to extortion, from space to money. What is pushed outside is not only the sacrificial king or the repudiated wife but also the form of produced and excess merchandise. *Exigere* means to make these products flow, that is to say, sell them. Flowing is nothing else: the flow is directed toward the exterior. Could selling be another form of expulsion? Would one exchange only what is chased? It is true that Joseph, ousted in another time and place, was also sold by his brothers. Are we now at the very origin of exchange? Does one dispose of only what one no longer wants? The fruit will spoil, the grain will rot, the parasites will eat up the stock; we must sell, get rid of it. Chasing, selling, exacting a tax. We are sacrificing our stock, they say. If it is true, money is a substitute for the victim. Money is the trace of the excluded person. Money is the symbol of the banished person. The sign of sacrifice. Money is religious; it is God: Marx says so directly. It is also, as I have shown elsewhere with Freud, the stercoral as such. It is immediately understood as such if it is the substitute for the expelled person. But it would still be nothing if we did not understand that it is exactly the substitute of the parasite and the parasite itself, the expelled one that always returns.

This result is not unexpected. This flow of merchandise or of fruit offered was once devoured during the feast. The guest paid for it with words and signs. The exchange of the logicial for the material is a parasitic invention. The parasitic is there, at the very beginning of exchange and gift-giving, of gift-giving and damages; it switches the changes between what is not equivalent. From the evidence it seems that the logicial and the material are not equivalent. And it makes them equivalent. It is thus the most general equivaluator. It is money itself. The sign at a distance relative to food (para-site), the sign at a distance relative to goods. That is to say, the very mobility of exchange, its flow. Earlier I described the parasite as the power of metamorphosis. It was, in fact, the general equivalent. And it was the parasite that the Latin host could beat (and insult) during the feast.

Not an unexpected result, another way round. Every relation between two instances demands a route. What is already there on this route either facilitates or impedes the relation. Sometimes the screen helps, and the aide sometimes is an obstacle. Love forbids us to love, and words sometimes deafen; the tongue is the best and worst of things; I don't invent the law; I don't invent the fact that there is no law. Between these two poles everything is possible except the excluded third. The third, by nature and function, is the population on the channel. We call it parasite, as is already known. But we have prepared its logic: the algebra of fuzzy subsets. Fuzzy subsets are found exactly on this route, on this canal.

It is well-known that money can be substituted for every relation. Money once again is the third, filling the channel with its liquid cash; it is the channel of liquidities. Money is God, money is the Devil; it is Being and Nothingness; it is what is prized and what is rejected; it is the included and the excluded, inevitable on every path and barring the path from every relation. It is there as the general substitute. I said: the parasite always comes back; if you chase it, it comes back to its place. Dispose of the fruit, sell it; it returns in the form of money. What you exclude, you include by this equivalent. Thus you cannot discourse on money by using a bivalent kind of mathematics. Thus all your models of mathematical economy are disqualified. Marx was wrong, Freud was wrong, Zola was wrong, I am wrong, economists are wrong. The only kind of mathematics applicable to economics is the theory of fuzzy subsets. Fuzzy algebra and fuzzy topology. Inversely, he who speaks this way speaks of money, just as Aesop spoke this language, the best and the worst, and better yet, everything that goes between the best and the worst, between the false and the true, the certain and the nonprobable, the outside and the inside of belonging, between God and the Devil, shit and the valuable, Being and Nothingness. The mathematics of the fuzzy proceeds, in fact, from the same intuition proposed here. What I exchange comes back: does it belong to me or is it outside? The question cannot be answered nor easily divided. It is in fact a spectral question, about the fuzzy theory of flows. It is simple, to the point of being redundant. It is a model only in the old sense of the world: economics, really, imitates it.

All the obstacles of ordinary economics are there as well as the future of economics. I'll return to this when I have some free time and when something other than this relation interests me, this relation I have with someone who refuses money as a substitute. We shall soon speak of love, a few minutes from now. While waiting to love no more, a warning to the specialists: your basic mathematics is fuzzy. Work then; I can very well not come. If I do come to economics, it will be amidst tears, for I will have spent my time loving. Of course, here the tongue functions like money. It is all too clear that every semantic field is a fuzzy subset. The science of meaning has henceforth found its formalism. If I come to linguistics . . .

Where was I? At *exigere*. The Latin word also means "to achieve," "to finish one's work," "to perfect it." And to perfect one's life as well, the work of works. We were using the word *exact*. We must be happy that the exact sciences occupy the spot not far from cost and taxes, from exchange and fuzzy, from expulsion, from violence. Let no one enter the laboratory if he is not a geometer. We know that *exigere* means "measure," "weigh," "examine," "judge," "regulate"; here is the exact measure, the quantitatively precise experiment. This experiment costs— money, energy, information; it increases the entropy of the isolated, closed laboratory. As for the immediate vicinity of exactitude and exaction, it allows us to say a word about the rationalist activity of nuclear physics. What is the work of the thing or the concept here? It is not an actitivy, but rather a small distance from the active or the act that makes it exact. As if something outside of activity was added to work. What is this difference?

The answer is physical and metaphysical at the same time, since physics recently asks itself questions on the difference interpreted by the prefix *meta* (or *meta-* or *para-* or *ex-*). Elsewhere I have said that the reason for existence was the "moreover" [*plutôt*] of its principle, the inclined reason. We find the same difference here in science. Its relation to the real is to find it: exactitude here is existence there.

He doesn't know anything, and he is demanding. That is said of La Fontaine's villager: this *gourmand* needs milk and veal and nuts, while grass is enough for the cow, and soil, for the tree. One needs, and the others have enough. The arrows of relation are not turned in the same direction. One sees immediately that, throughout the world, grass is more frequent than calves or milk, that there is more soil than there are nuts. In other words, primary material exceeds transformed or finished products. The transformer, producer, inventor, delves into the common, which is always in sufficient quantity. The parasite seeks rarity.

To be demanding means to choose. This choice, this filter, implies an elimination, for order and coherence; we are coming back to the first meaning: chase, push outside. The one who examines, separates; the one who judges, excludes; the one who chooses, divides things and populations. In any case, they produce rarity. No, they don't produce it; they select it when it is already there. The producer promotes it, beginning with the common; when it is absent, he gives it back to the parasite. The fire cooks the chestnuts, and Raton, carefully and cautiously, moves the ashes away, taking the best-cooked; behind him Bertrand cracks them.* Between himself and the producer, always the man of the fire, the monkey had placed a gate. The gate of rarity. The spot of sorting. Raton chooses, but Raton doesn't eat; Raton is parasited, Raton at the gate: here is Maxwell's demon. Everything is there: fire, the elements—chestnuts, the choice, and behind, the one who believes in perpetual paradise. In perpetual motion: the more the vase poured, the less it was emptied; Philemon recognized this evident miracle. I've already spoken of the divine feast of Baucis. A servant arrives, and Bertrand and Raton flee. The same as before: they heard a noise at the door of the room. One parasite chases the other; the perpetual motion stops. The demon is exorcised. Chased, pushed outside, removed from the gate. From which one sees that what we call literature is a reserve of science.

The parasite runs through the space and sows the gates. To sample the rarity. Most often it knows how to distribute them in a cascade, for the rarity to be relative, to create more of it, and for there to be history. It places the gates in a structure of order. Hence another illusion of the perpetual.

At the little gate, a population passes by, element by element. One by one. In Greek, this was called *catena*, "the chain." These long

*La Fontaine, "Le Singe et le chat." —Trans.

chains of simple and easy reasons suppose a gate, first of all. They pass through, link after link, for choice, rejection, acceptance: text. The gate can be, must be, maximally narrow. I'll reject everything, etc. Hyperbolically narrow, so as to play immediately the last gate of the all-powerful. Everything is there again: fire, the demon, exorcism, the always of the perpetual, God, etc. Exigency installs gates: exiguous, it goes without saying since the word tells us so. Rarity makes itself even rarer as the gate narrows.

One by one: little is necessary to be assured of the skin of one. But the mimetic passion of rarity pushes the population to the strangling bottleneck in front of the gate, where it is crushed, where its members fight, trample each other, and hate. It is offered, cadaverous, to the blade of a few. That is the genesis of power, the solution to the paradox of La Boétie: how can so few people command the greatest number? I wonder sometimes whether the death, be it deferred or not, of the scapegoat is not a unique variant of this model. Genesis of power, genesis of economy, which also selects rarity. It is not so much that political power is founded in the end on economic function. In fact, the two instances function the same, in a structurally isomorphic manner.

The mad passion of gates assures the emergence of kings and of the elect, of precious good, of what is sought, and, undoubtedly, of scientific exactitude. Of exigency: exact, exiguous, extortion.

While waiting for the spare time to demonstrate all these things at our ease, we can enjoy Juvenal's *Fifth Satire* during the interim. The feast, the rich man's table, that of the great, the king, the master, functions as a gate. But the meal itself is said to be rare, and there is a competition for seats at the table. The ragamuffins try to outdo each other to get the scraps. They are in the lowest position; someone was missing and the hole had to be filled. They fight. At the head of the table, the head fills himself with vintage wine; below, the parasite has only the rotgut. The king drinks a cup of amber seasoned with beryl, protected from robbers by a police-slave; the rotgut goes to waste in a cracked cup. A good, costly servant, with a hangdog look. Moldy, compact flour, soft wheat flower. Monumental fish, little crab. Corsican or Sicilian lamprey, the eel of cloacas. Fine virgin oil, lamp fuel. At the low end, stinking scraps; above the salt, truffles, foie gras, boar, the beautiful scene of the knights trenchant, the envied theater of rarity. The whole question, jealous anguish and spoiled life consist of passing through the gate. How is the rare attained? It is not Hegel but Juvenal who formulates this: how can one become master, or rather, the king of one's master? Not how does the slave become the master of the master, but how does the parasite become the host of his host? You have to have

four hundred thousand sesterces, says Juvenal to the Would-Be Gentleman, and then we will no longer know which is the Turk and which is
ridiculous. You have to have a sterile wife whom you can offer without
risk of a follow-up. Pimp. Parasite and pimp.

Decimus Junius Ethicus proposes a moral. It is simple and naive:
nothing is more frugal than the belly. One never misses the little that is
enough for it. A dock, a bridge, a tattered mat, a loaf of bread, the wise
man is a bum. The bum [clochard] is a good philosopher, and the gate
perverts him. Return to the paths of childhood.

Bergson loved to demonstrate his *élan vital* by using a streaming spray of water as a model. It rises, reaches its acme, falls in a shower
on the sides of the axis of the column that is almost hard—the column
of the spray. Geyser, that old faithful, which promotes an evolution that
breaks and falls in repetition. Where does it come from, what is its living force, what is its spiritual energy? It was perhaps the movement of
God.

I draw the spray the other way. Recently, I drew a flame the
right way.* It was for the information era with its unpredictible, random flakes of fire. I draw a geyser, just as I had done to make Lucretius
clear. Everything falls and goes toward equilibrium. Toward stability.
Toward death. We no longer need the *élan vital*. Here then is the torrential flow that follows the laws of nature.

I have marked the turbulences that festoon the laminar here and
there. These turbulences are fractal, like the world. They are the world.
Today I mark their difference relative to the plane fall and the stops
along the paths, along the interesting paths by which the return to equilibrium is deferred.

The principal axis and laminar generators are static. At a distance,
existence. Something exists rather than nothing. The angle is formed; it
varies; its space is fuzzy. It fluctuates.

All the words used here participate in this distance. Exact and
ex-action (extortion) relative to action (to the least action), abuse relative to use, parasite and parable (or *parole,* "word") relative to the
action of eating or speaking. Everything is deduced from it, as well as
the exchanges. We are carried by the flow and the fuzziness of existence,
its fluctuations and its circumstances, the advance of its production.

Hermès V. Le passage du Nord-Ouest.

Meals among Brothers —————————
————————— *Theory of the Joker*

So he left all that he had in Joseph's
charge; and having him he had no concern
for anything but the food which he ate.

Genesis 39:6*

It seems illogical or even scandalous to throw away food. It is
done nonetheless. What is at a distance from food (*para-site* says so) is
expelled or excluded; it is the excess or surplus [*excédent*]. The first
fruits, sometimes, or the best flower, if it is a question of sacrifice. Chasing out the parasite also means kick out, dispose of what is on the side,
what is next to food. It is not necessarily the being that devours it. It
can be its excess or its surplus. And everything that precedes is necessary as the metaphysics of excess. As usual, the very thing that is excluded returns.

Sacrifice: Joseph's brothers want to kill him. They chase him
out. They show their father a long-sleeved tunic soaked in the blood of
the scapegoat. Joseph is a sacrificial victim. The whole myth is marked
with substitutions. There is no murder but rather expulsion. The expulsion doesn't really occur; the sale replaces it. The tunic full of blood is
a false substitute; the twenty pieces of silver are the true substitute. The
Ishmaelites paid; the money is the presence of Joseph in Canaan and his
first return. In Egypt, having left prison, Joseph interprets the dreams
of Pharaoh: fat cows and thin cows. He will become the Minister of
the Economy and of Finance.

*The French text, erroneously, cites Genesis 29:6. —Trans.

155

This is perhaps the first treatise of political economy. Fat cows: years of abundance; thin cows: harvests of scarcity. When there is an excess harvest, the usual practice is to get rid of this surplus by lifting the bar. And then they die of hunger during the years that the cows are thin and the stalks of wheat are burnt by the wind. What else could be done? We must return to these simple peasant practices from which all of culture came. Here are abundant fruit, vegetables, milk, wine, wheat. The fruit spoils, the milk sours, the wine turns to vinegar, the vegetables rot, the stores of wheat are filled with rats and weevils. Everything ferments; everything rots. Everything changes. Rotting and plague are not only symbols of violence but also real, singular referents that only need themselves to give rise to clearly defined processes. The surplus is gotten rid of because it is perishable. In fact the rotten is expelled, merchandise is disposed of [écouler], because it might start to run [couler]. Exchange is born in that change of state. Exchange is to this change what excess or surplus is to sufficiency, or exaction to action, and so forth. Exchange does not want it to change. It wants to stabilize the flight [fuite]. Contrary to everything thought about exchange, it does not mobilize things; it immobilizes them, it disposes of them, Πάντα ῥεῖ, everything flows, of course, everything dies, everything rots, if it dies it bears much fruit.* What runs [coule] is disposed of [écoule]; what changes is exchanged. The very simple idea of the equilibrium of exchanges is ontological. By the very movement of the exchange, what changes, no longer changes. It might have become rotten, and now it is money. The fact that money is refuse or feces is not at all a symbol or a fantasm. It is exactly the substitute of the expelled rot, the equivalent of disposal by corruption. The stroke of genius, of course, was to go look for the stable in the unstable, or rest in movement, to go look for what is opposed to change in the exchange itself.

Yet this is not the only solution. Surplus can be disposed of or stocked. It can be stocked in the form of money or as itself. Then rot sets in and the parasites are at home. From this point on, we are bound to go to the end of the process of decomposition: wine-making, cheese-making, bread-making. I once drew philosophy from cheese. Here it finds its general nature.

Let us return to Joseph. If Canaan is poor, it is because it does not stock up. If Joseph and Egypt are rich, it is because they do. The two processes face each other.

*John 12:25. "Si le grain ne meurt" is more common in French than is its translation in English. —Trans.

Joseph's brothers, his jealous rivals, decided to get rid of him. Let's kill him, they say at first, and throw him in the cistern. What they will do, in any case, will be to throw him in the cistern. What is a cistern? It is an artificial, man-made spot for conservation. In the Indo-European semantic field, *cista* in Latin is a chest or basket, especially a basket used for sacrifices. Tibullus signs of it as the confidant of the sacred mysteries. The Greek κιστοφόρος, "bearer of sacred baskets," designates a coin of Asia Minor which had such chests drawn on it. A cist is a stone sarcophagus, a tomb or megalith in which the corpse is buried with all his goods. His fortune is there with his body: But in the Semitic semantic field, the Hebrew word used here—more or less a well, a water hole, another sort of cistern—means the hole in which one falls, but especially the hole into which garbage is thrown. The union of these two semantic fields expresses our thesis well: this spot, where a rotting excess is gotten rid of, has to do with the sacred, with death and sacrifice. But is has connections with goods, exchanged treasures, money and coinage. Buried, thrown in the cistern, Joseph is excluded, sacrificed, plague-ridden, but he is also kept, stocked, just like the water he replaces. The cistern regulates the wet and dry years, as the Egyptian granaries will soon regulate the years of fat cows and meager harvests. Joseph in the well—an enigmatic and ambiguous situation: the stock foreseen for the next exchange. He is expelled; he is kept. He is sacrificed; he is sold. The mortuary and sacrificial foundation of exchange. Reuben recommended this solution with the avowed aim of saving his brother and bringing him back to their father. Already the decision to exclude shows some adherences: an eventual return, perhaps a conservation. How can everything be expelled while keeping it; how can it be chased while conserving it; how can everything be allowed to vary while keeping an invariant? This question is an economic one.

The meal begins in the vicinity of the spots where there is action. At the back of the scene a caravan appears. Ishmaelites with their camels bearing gum tragacanth, etc., merchandise from Gilead, bringing it to Egypt. This interruption induces Judah, who, like his brothers, has raised his eyes at this spectacle, to think of selling Joseph. But this sale will be done by intermediaries. There are always substitutes just as there are vicariants. Midianite merchants pass by; they remove Joseph from the cistern and sell him for twenty pieces of silver to the Ishmaelites. But the text says that it was the Midianites who sold him in Egypt. It is necessary to note that Ishmael, the son of Abraham and Hagar, the Egyptian servant, was a brother who was chased out and excluded, just like Midian, the son of Abraham and Keturah. Just when Joseph is expelled, the excluded brothers appear in the background. The excluded brothers have become merchants; they traffic in merchandise. The relation of the excluded to money already appears as the referent of the story. The money circulates rather badly; it doesn't circulate, in fact: Midian sold twice.

Jacob receives the coat stained with the goat's blood. Joseph is the victim and is innocent; he is the victim's substitute and its vicar.

The story of Joseph stops for a moment amidst the tears of his mourning father and abruptly detours to speak of Judah, precisely the one whose idea it was to sell Joseph. He leaves Gilead, for Adullam, where he has three children—Er, Onan, and Shelah—by a woman. Er marries Tamar and dies. Tamar, who has survived, is given to Onan, her brother-in-law. Onan, as we know, let his seed spill on the ground when he was united with Tamar, lest he should give offspring to his brother.

Put the little brother in the cistern, in the basket, not to put him there, to take him out of the cistern.

Unhappy with onanism, Jehovah slays Onan. The last son, Shelah, remains for Tamar. He is too young, and when he is older, he is not destined for Tamar. Tamar is a widow without children; she is forgotten. She puts on a veil and waits. Judah passes by and takes her for a prostitute. She negotiates her price: a kid. She demands a pledge from him. And Judah gives her his signet, his cord, and his staff.

The story of Judah contains the story of Tamar, continued in that of Joseph. A curious exchange is substituted, quite suddenly, for the violent quarrel of the brothers, for murders and exclusions—in short, for the sacrificial. Tamar is promised to the three brothers, who are successively taken from her in different ways: by death, by onanism, by forgetting. She has; she doesn't have. You have; you don't have. Then she is passed to the father through sale and prostitution.

But the equivalent of Joseph sacrificed was a slaughtered goat. The equivalent of Tamar is a kid. Again, that directs us to sacrifice. It is about to occur. When Judah is told, your daughter-in-law is with child by harlotry, he orders her to be pushed out and burnt alive. Thus Tamar is really the victim. As Girard has shown, she is innocent; and, once again, her sons will be twins, rivals from the hour of their birth, just like Jacob and Esau. Rivals for the maternal flow. Now she shows Judah his seal, staff, and cord: you are the father; it is marked. She is righteous, more righteous than I, inasmuch as I did not give her to my son Shelah.

Tamar is the victim, just like Joseph. He is sold, the excluded brother, twenty pieces of silver for excluded brothers, now become merchants. Tamar faces him, in a more or less dual position, as the sexual object of the brothers and father. Of the brothers who are enemies among themselves, since Onan uses his method to prevent giving offspring to his brother. Tamar moves from one to the other, always the same and yet transformed: always a woman, owed and desired, but a widow after having been a wife, but sterile though fecund, because of the practice of Onan, promised and not given, prostitute but virtuous though incestuous, mother in the end, and giving to posterity what she had received—rivals. Metamorphoses and stability. Variations of the invariant or circulation of the equivalent. She is adapted to all the positions and can move from one to another, subject to the laws of circulation. She is perhaps already a general equivalent.

The fact that she is worth a kid marks her as a victim for sacrifice. She is veiled—that is to say, hidden behind a veil. Thus Joseph disappeared far from his coat soaked in blood. The sacrificial is deferred. Joseph is not assassinated; the goat is his substitution, a ritualization of Abraham's sacrifice. Tamar is not burnt, but it will no longer be a question of the kid. The death of the kid is deferred. The token—the seal—is enough, stable writing as a promise. Tomorrow I shall pay. Once again, making stable what is unstable. I am tied by the cord and involved by the seal. The passage to the symbolic is assured by an object that the Greeks called a symbol. A token of recognition. The symbolic is the deferral of killing. Could exchange be a deferral of murder? Tamar already makes clear what will happen in the story of Joseph.

Genealogy of synthetic judgements.
That is something else.

Tamar is a wife; Tamar is a widow; Tamar is forsaken; Tamar is sterile; Tamar is the prostitute of the crossroads; Tamar is the victim; Tamar is a mother; Tamar is righteous. Unveiled, veiled, unveiled. Promised, not given, given. Not fertilized by Onan, fertilized by the father, not marked by Onan, and marked with the seal. Tamar does not have a fixed identity, whereas Judah is Judah and Jacob is Jacob. For a long time, she is not recognized, her justice is not known; it is she who has the misfortune to be united with Onan. United—that is to say, not united. She who sleeps with Onan sleeps with him and does not.

It is not sure either that Joseph is Joseph. He receives the ring and the gold chain from Pharaoh, just as Tamar had the seal and the cord; Pharaoh gives him a name: Joseph is Zaphenath-paneah. He is a slave; he is a majordomo; he is a prisoner; he is the bailiff of the jailer; he is forgotten by the great cup-bearer; he is the minister of Pharaoh and the master of his brothers. Joseph is not fixed in his identity, whereas Reuben is Reuben and Jacob is Jacob. For a long time, he is not recognized, his justice is not known; he is both master and slave.

Tamar and Joseph are sacrificial victims. In the cistern and ready to be burnt at the stake; the goat is the substitute for one and the kid is supplement for the other. Joseph is the goat; Tamar is the kid.

The victim is not killed; the victim is not victim. Faced with murder, the gesture is deferred, as is the decision. The action bifurcates and the tautology starts to predicate; it slips; it jumps to something else. It no longer says: *a* is *a;* it substitutes and begins to say *a* is *b.*

The victim is not fixed in his identity; the victim is anyone: he could be the youngest or the first to arrive. Who is he or she? This one because it is he; that one, because it is she; here and now, Jephtha's daughter, Iphigenia, or Idomeneo's son, perfectly determined; but chosen by chance, randomly picked, totally undetermined. The victim is this one, yet this one is another. May be another.

In this circumstance, a sovereign logic emerges that needs explanation, which is the explanation itself. There is no beginning for reason without a link of the following sort: this is not this; this is something else. This chain breaks away from redundance, identity or repetition. An object has to be found that can be spoken of in this way. Or a subject, it matters little. It is thus a vital experience that the rejected child never be himself. It is also a cultural constraint that a woman must metamorphose. It is a social experience that the one who is sacrificed is anyone. But it is especially a Judaic invention, an explosive novelty in the Fertile Crescent, that the one who is sacrificed is substituted, that suddenly, the victim is something else: a goat, a kid, but also the beginning of a completely other series.

I shall call this object a joker. The joker is often a madman, as we know. He is wild, as they say in English. It is not difficult to see the double of the sacrificial king in him, come from the Celebration of Fools, come from the Saturnalia. This white object, like a white domino,* has no value so as to have every value. It has no identity, but its identity, its unique character, its difference, as they say, is to be, indifferently, this or that unit of a given set. The joker is king or jack, ace or seven, or deuce. Joseph is a joker; Tamar, queen, just, despised, whore, is also a joker. *A* is *b, c, d,* etc. Fuzzy.

That joker is a logical object that is both indispensable and fascinating. Placed in the middle or at the end of a series, a series that has a law of order, it permits it to bifurcate, to take another appearance, another direction, a new order. The only describable difference between a method and *bricolage†* is the joker. The principle of bricolage is to make something by means of something else, a mast with a matchstick,

---

*See my analysis of *Thérèse Raquin.* I suppose that the white domino has the value of a joker; it is not always true in the game of dominoes.

†*Bricolage* has no good English equivalent. It means putting together as if by odds and ends, with bits and pieces, and so forth. —Trans.

a chicken wing with tissue meant for the thigh, and so forth. Just as the most general model of method is game, the good model for what is deceptively called bricolage is the joker.

The joker Tamar makes the series bifurcate so often that, having been incestuous, she goes back to the beginning, the always new fraternal rivalry. The chain of events makes a cycle, a circulation, but with a supplement, toward David and toward the Messiah. The same goes for the joker Joseph, though he is more complex.

Joseph is expelled, not killed. He is excluded. Reuben did not want to—he only put him in the cistern to conserve him, to bring him back to his father. He is put out and put up. In this unique spot, he is both rejected and kept. Joseph is excluded; Joseph is included. As a joker, the excluded is included. The joker, first of all, has two values; the fact that they are contradictory changes nothing here. Or, better yet, it is because he is excluded and included that Joseph becomes a joker. He leaves; he is always there. You rejected him; he is always present in your story. You send him away, by the caravan, into Egypt; you will make a caravan to join him there. He left, but he doesn't leave you; he dogs your steps. He will see his father again; you will come back to him. The movement, the hesitation, the vibration, and the double frenzy of inclusion and exclusion constitute the joker in a multiplicity of fuzzy values, and a multiplicity of situations, in a spectrum of possibilities. It changes; it is there, stable. Perishable merchandise that might have become refuse comes back in the form of money. Money is the most joker of jokers, what has been called the general equivalent. With two values, excluded, included, then a fuzzy multiplicity of values and possibilities. Intuitively, the two sides of a coin should have been constituted in this way, and the head and tail, from the very first, should have been the operators of chance. Inversely, the victim is not chosen by chance; he is head and tail, the coin with two values, the fuzzy spectrum of probability. It is always possible to say of money: this is something else. A new principle: the association of the included and excluded third.

The joker changes; it is a token of exchange; it is multivalent, and bivalent at first. Tamar and Joseph change, and they are exchanged. Subject, indifferently, and object of the exchange, Tamar, the kid, the victim, and finally, the seal, the payment. And Joseph, twenty pieces of silver. The money from the wheat of Egypt is put into bags of wheat destined for Palestine. The brothers left the money, but the money doesn't leave them. Excluded, included. The money is always there, in the exchange.

This is something else. I dreamt of a sheaf of wheat, of the sun, and of eleven stars. This sheaf is not a sheaf, yet it remains a sheaf, and you are the sheaf. The moon is your mother; the stars are your brothers. The wheat bends like a moon; the sun places its forehead on the earth, in the wheat field. This is something else. I am a star and a sheaf of wheat; you are a sheaf and the sun; in the beginning is hatred.

This is again something else. You dreamt of a vinestock with three branches, and of three baskets of cakes on your head. And I say to the bailiff and to the butler: the baskets are days, the cakes are your flesh and body, the branches are days; the days are branches and they are baskets. Here is the meaning: this is something else. In the middle, servitude, life, and death.

This is yet something else. Pharaoh dreamt of cows and wheat; the thin cows ate the fat cows; the thin and wind-burnt wheat covered wheat that was ripe and in abundance. I shall tell him the meaning; this is yet something else. The cows are years; the wheat sheaves are years; time is a cow; it is divided into clusters of grain, just as it was divided into branches or baskets. If the sheaf were a sheaf, if the star were a star and the cow a cow, there would have been no meaning, no key, no explanation, no interpreter. No rhyme or reason. This has to be something else. Finally a logic of light; we will finally eat to stop our hunger. We shall send caravans of grain and fruit toward the Promised Land.

All these chains of words abound with jokers. Given some series whose links are well identified, where there is a law, an explicit one. The same is diffused the length of the differences, constituting the axis, be it rigid or supple. Suddenly, a joker. Can I read it? Certainly. It is enough to recognize the upstream law and the downstream laws. The joker, in the position of bifurcation, makes it possible by the confluence of values that it insures. It is both what has been said and what will be said. It is bi-, tri-, or poly-valent, according to the complexity of the connection. The ramification of the network depends on the number of jokers. But I suspect that there is a limit for this number. When there are too many, we are lost as if in a labyrinth. What would a series be like where there were only jokers? What could be said of it?

Dream logic seems to me to be of this nature. Multivalent because of jokers. Connections *ad libitum*. Time is the cow; time is the sheaf; time is the branch and the basket. The cow is a sheaf; this is something else. The cow is a joker; the basket, the sheaf, other jokers. Beyond a certain density, or a certain number of multivalent elements, the series cannot be known. The question is not so much finding one or two or three or *n* keys, but of speaking a language that takes jokers into account. Joseph and Daniel give the meaning, the key; they determine the indeterminate series; they harden the soft logic. Freud, on the contrary, discovered a language with a general equivalent. It is understandable that Popper takes him to task; Popper would be right if the dream weren't woven of series of jokers. Freud translates, into his poor language, a fact of great simplicity, a fact reproduced in five or six other spots of culture: polyvalence. For a long time I had confidence in Popper; but henceforth I think that Freud comes off well, faced with the criterion of exteriority. The proof for that is the following: try to make money falsifiable. In spots populated by jokers, there can only be counterfeiters. Marx and Freud, quite simply, passed by that point. They constantly manipulate multivalent contents; they write in languages with general equivalents. It is true that they never thought to suspect the risk of the matter and Popper is right to impose the criterion. But it cannot be doubted that they discovered general equivalents and Popper did not see this. It is not because a theory is always true that it should be repudiated. It always works for another reason; it is in the realm of general equivalence. It is outside the true, outside the false; it indicates contents that are jokers. *La cosa*, as the Italian algebrists of the Renaissance used to say, *la cosa*, the thing said to be unknown, the unknown = x, multivalent, of which it can always be said that it takes all values. This is something else. You have seen a new Northwest Passage.

　　And that is why the story of Joseph, our first treatise of economics, is also a treatise on the interpretation of dreams. Cistern-capital and cistern-unconscious.

　　The distribution of jokers.
　　Given the universe of discourse. This universe can be organized according to the distribution of jokers. If there are a few in a cut of the cards or in a sequence, the determination is strong and there is constraint; it is rather near monosemy. A discourse with no jokers is even conceivable. This universe would reduce to this identity principle. Thus the universe in question is undervalued by $a \equiv a$. If you increase the number of jokers or their percentage in a series, a cut, or a sequence, and go to the maximum, the saturation point, polysemy overtakes the space with multivalence and equivocity. Near the end is the world of dreams, completely filled with polyvalence. At the limits of the dream, at the limits of the universe, the discourse composed exclusively of jokers is money. When there are only jokers, that's capital, a bank account, the general equivalent. They overvalue the world.

　　A curious universe, though a logical one, where dreams adhere to finance, where gold is near dreams.

　　As for the distribution of jokers in the universe of discourse: the identity principle and the principle of indiscernables are undervalued, and the circulation of money, right near dreams, is overvalued.

This universe has the form of a cornucopia. From a narrow, unique point to the wide mouth of equivalence (wide and narrow can change positions here). The universe of discourse is a horn of plenty.

Parasites, noises and grub(s), swarm around this horn.

Judas is innocent. In praise of Judas.

This is something else. Tamar: this kid is my body. Tamar: this cord is my body, the cord, the staff, and the seal. The joker is no longer in the dream; it circulates in our exchanges. The object that changes and is exchanged is the body. That of Tamar, the daughter-in-law, of Tamar, the prostitute. Joseph is freed from his cistern; twenty pieces of silver, this is his body.

Judas is innocent of the blood for that reason. This is something else, and this, this bread, is my body, this sheaf, this wheat, and this flour. This is something else, and this is my blood, the fruit of the vine and the branch. Judas sees another joker being formed. He understands that it is the substitute for sacrifice. He is a Jew, and thus he understands what he must understand in his milieu and his culture, that the sacrifice must be stopped, that there must be a substitute, that there must be a joker. And thus he does what Reuben does, what Judah, his ancestor, does. He changes the victim into money. He simply makes the founding motion of exchanges. Selling Joseph is not sacrificing him, not killing him; it is a way of saving him from death so as to be able to bring him back to the father one day. Judas is innocent; he must now finally be praised for Jews and Christians to be reconciled forevermore, to pull up the deepest anti-Semitic roots, those dwelling in ignorance. Judas reasoned correctly—he made the fatal series bifurcate; he reoriented the murder, changing it into something else and thereby avoiding it: Judas was a wise man. Accusing him, scorning him, is a denial of justice; it is already a text of persecution. Judas is innocent just as Oedipus was. Hence his despair when he sees that the sale failed, that it contributed to the sacrifice and that the sacrifice was not at all avoided. And he is the victim, the other victim.

Meals of Chestnuts ──────────────

────────────── *The Sun and the Sign*

Bertrand the monkey and Raton the cat dine together, says La Fontaine. They dine together on the meal they made for themselves, but they are also noxious parasites of the same host and the same master: robbers and destroyers, everything is lost, everything spoils, everything runs around them. We will soon see about this dining together.

One word removes doubt, if there still is any: the cat lets the mice go if there is cheese left for him. He becomes a predator only if he can no longer parasite someone. Everyone knows that: in order for a cat to be a rat-catcher, he must be starved. Preying and hunting need more energy and finesse than sponging. Thus the latter is more probable. This could also be translated: the more widespread, the more natural or the more native. If these translations repel us, high probability is enough. It is the figure of equilibrium.

If the researcher is in his niche, if he has his method, his cup of tea, his pressure group, he stops producing and starts reproducing. He no longer goes out; he no longer heads toward the pitch-black attic; his whiskers no longer twitch at imperceptible signs; he falls asleep in the cradle of the same. Do you want to discover? Forget about the cheese.

Bertrand and Raton enjoy their niche. Today's story assays relations, as in assaying. We measured it for hunting. It is only the starved distance from parasitism. As soon as possible, it comes back to the figure of equilibrium.

Let us try to describe this dining together, this commensality. It is an egalitarian relation in which each gives and receives in turn. The parasitic relation works on the principle of the lion's share: the one who takes does not give; the one who gives never receives anything. What,

165

then, is the figure of equilibrium? Let's look at Bertrand and Raton. They look at the fire where the chestnuts are roasting. Both of them are far from cheating their common master, which would have been expected from equal commensals; they place themselves in a series and parasite each other. Raton pulls out the chestnuts from the fire and chooses them; Bertrand immediately eats them. The figure of equilibrium of the relation is still the same. It is not I but the fable-writer who is making a point today, not a political comparison, but one about the genesis of this power. The first word of this text is *monkey*, the last word is *king*. It is a question of a prince who scalds himself for the profit of the king. The most monkey-like monkey is the last link of the parasitic series; the king, without any power above him, is the first link of the series of power and glory. It must be thought, since it is true, that the two series are the same. The height of power is the bottom of the attractive well in this equilibrium of relations. The quest for power and the struggle for power are only series or cascades; they are the parasitic fall without end. And like every repetitive law, it doesn't produce information.

The figure of the pyramid is remarkably deceptive. We think we see groups of people assault it and knock themselves out trying to climb to the top, where only the strongest arrives, after having sent his rivals down into the abyss. The figure must be turned inside out. As Thom would say, it would more likely be a well of potential, as Plato would say, a cave. Mice? No, cheese. Chestnuts? No, Raton. Struggle with the rats? Struggle with the fire? Rivalry with Raton? No. The law of the relation is to place oneself below another, so that the chestnuts fall unimpeded. Below, deeper, further down in the well, or further downstream. The one downstream is the one who wins. The one who is at the mouth—a good word—will be king. At the bottom of his den where the animals come in, he eats them all and none escape. Bertrand and Raton are not dining together. They are not in league against the host. They do not argue over the chestnuts. They are not equals. They are not rivals. They are not face to face, each on a bank of the stream. For the law of current, the law of potential energy, the law of gravity, makes them immediately fall. Were they commensals, were they rivals, they would need a great deal of energy; there would be an excited state, perhaps a murder, and undoubtedly a division. The simplest is to move down, so that the chestnuts roll down to the lowest point, all together. The one who reaches the downstream position is the one who eats. And the wolf knows this well, for he tells the lamb that it is disturbing the pure waves upstream from the wolf.* The one who plays the predator, the one who

*La Fontaine, "Le Loup et l'agneau." —Trans.

plays the predator, the one who would play the rival just as well, first justifies his action by the iron law of wages of his parasitism.

Rivalry is only a spectacle; it is the state of appearance. Equilibrium is phenomenal, and the distance is real. The law of opposition belongs to phenomenology; the law of irreversibility or of falling downstream is real. Behind all representation.

Again the rats' meal. They hear a noise at the door and flee; the parasitic cascade collapses and breaks. The parasite-noise chases out the parasite-animal; I believe the first to be more fundamental, lower, further down in the well. The less meaning there is to discourse, the closer it is to power. Behind the mouth, the largest, all-swallowing mouth, there is nothing but the immense noise of the ocean. Chaos, noise, disorder. The base of existence. This parasite chases out all the others. Behind power, behind the ultimate power, behind the universal appetite, in their vicinity, on their edge, noise spills out into space. The bottom of the well is black; the back of the cave is dark; the pure wave is bitter. Every relation, figure on ground, is only inscribed onto disorder. Here then is the pure theory of relation: it follows in an ordered fashion, the river flowing down; it is irreversible; it does not return on itself. It is the first relation, the relation of order. Behind it, as its (back)ground, noise. Disorder. At the end of the stream, the sea. This parasite is fundamental. It falls from simple arrows in the noise of a waterfall.

The rats return to the feast when the noise stops. We are not told if the servant who intervenes goes back to bed. The cat will not come back, we say to ourselves. He's been scalded, it seems. But the country rat was scalded as well. The monkey and the cat mark progress: the two rats are really commensals. Sooner or later, their relation would have had the figure of a series. The country cousin leaves for the reason. He suddenly sees that the city lives on chestnuts that the peasants pull from their trees, that the city will always eat even until the death of the farmers. The two rats are no longer commensals; they will be in a series just like the monkey and the cat. Raton is not happy; the peasant goes home forever. Behind him, humanity feasts; he nourishes humanity; humanity kills him. He was once afraid and with good reason. Today we live out the universal event announced by the fable—not only the flight of the rustic man but also his murder. Agriculture, old primary parasitism, is eliminated by parasites of a superior level, accustomed to noise, the parasites of the megalopolis. The city rats have eaten the country rats. Just as the thin cows eat the fat cows. Without guessing, fools that they are, what will happen when all the rustics have disappeared.

The equilibrium of a living being in its environment resembles the one that the host and parasite finally realize and sometimes arrive at. After a good deal of bother, sicknesses, deaths, and catastrophes, one favors, for example, the intestinal transit of the first, who nourishes it in return. When everything is added up, the parasite would do well not to kill the host on whom it feeds. We need the word, others, and objects.

Thus, at first the relation is an abuse, but sometimes it winds up being a common habit [*usage*]. It is a simple arrow and stops being such only very rarely. It starts with the irreversible and stays oriented that way. The simple irreversible arrow is the atom or element of the relation. This local atom can be linked to others to form a local river, a flow of blood, tears, and murders. The thin cows eat the fat cows and thus make the Nile flow; the wolf eats the lamb and makes the bloodied wave of the stream flow. In the direction of history. The relation makes life and kills; someone is maintained by the survival of another. The parasite lives on the host, by him, with him, and in him, *per ipsum et cum ipso et in ipso;* it makes him its house, its tent, its tabernacle; it reproduces in him and increases until the inevitable point when the host dies. The host becomes the Host of the Eucharist, victim; and the guests of the meal are deadly enemies. That is said in several languages, from natural history to the history of religions, to history as such. Everything begins with what I call abuse value. The first economic relation is of abuse. But when the arrow does not kill, when abuse does not pass the point of no return, the relation can evolve toward another equilibrium. This is as rare as an equilibrium that would pass or change into another equilibrium, in a shallower well. Rivers usually remain in their beds; they rarely look for a valley that is higher than their thalweg. Distances and fluctuations are needed. That is rather rare, but it winds up happening. The acquired information is remarkable. This rarity is sometimes called justice. A difficult effort, an exceptional, miraculous, human one.

Birth of an exchange. The parasite adopts a functional role; the host survives the parasite's abuses of him—he even survives in the literal sense of the word; his life finds a reinforced equilibrium, like a sur-equilibrium. A kind of reversibility is seen on a ground of irreversibility. Use succeeds abuse, and exchange follows use. A contract can be imagined. The contract is not found at the origin; it is a newly obtained equilibrium that is fragile because it is more highly placed, because it is rarer than abuse, and more exceptional and richer in information. Contrary to the usual models, power runs to the bottom of the thalweg and justice moves away from it; power goes down the course of abuse, but the contract fluctuates toward another equilibrium. These two forces are completely different. He who wants to take power to increase justice lies or fools himself or fools us. He only accelerates the abuse values. He resembles the one who rushed to go down the river in order to climb the hills around it better. In the torrential flow of the irreversible and the abusive, contractual equilibrium is unique. It is only human history to want to create it. It is rare enough for us to be only human in the rarity of our actions.

Several series of double arrows can be conceived of. At least three. A physical contract between us and our equilibrium. New, unthought-of. A social contract among us. The senseless hope for the end of parasitism. A gnoseological contract between the subject, on one hand, and the object, on the other: until now, only a simple arrow united them.

The theory of relations slowly emerges. We now know the series. The parasitic series is an irreversible chain, going down the slope, like the river, like a marble on the wall of the well. We know the law of the series, of the chain, of the stream, or of the well. We can state it; we can describe it. We know the end of the process—disorder, noise, chaos, the sea.

I would like to climb back up the series toward its source. The fables hide from me both this path of ascension and its markers. Behind the door of the room, it hides the one leaving, after having come. Who is there? Sometimes they say that it is death itself who arrives on the scene. I'm afraid to get up to go see, for it is pitch black. If it were only the servant. If it were the servant? Yet, I do get up. I climb up the chain of the monkey and the cat. In front of Bertrand, Raton; in front of Raton, the chestnuts; in front of the chestnuts, the dancing flames. Can one go beyond the curtain of fire?

The blackness of the door, the red fire. Going back up is scary. What surpasses fear—the black box and the blaze of the cave—must necessarily open up some day in the sun. The producer is the one whose leftovers we eat—the chestnuts. He is in front. He is a local fire. And he is a signal. There is only human production by fire and sign. By energy and information. Matter is energy; its form is information. Production needs a local sun and a matrix, a topology of form with its highs and lows marked out. Thus, every production is energy, of large and small magnitudes. The large for the force, the small for rarity. Thus, production is both solar and rare.

The more I climb back up the parasitic chain, the more the irreversible river is troubled. I head toward the sun of local fires; I jump over the high flames where the crouching chestnut-eaters are being grilled; I open the black doors of the boxes of rarity. The red of energy, the black of the improbable sign, chromatism of the producer—these are the colors of the work. Light flames in black boxes when a new, explosive intuition appears, when the new object leaves the hands that open it. And solitude increases, in a naked world that is ever more simple, where little suffices and where one's former needs are left far down-stream. Here rarity multiplies ideas under the path of the sun. The chain is simple; it goes from the sun to the sea.

Around the sun and the blackness of the surrounding space, those of fire and signs are at work; why not call them archangels? They hide; we hardly see them; we can look for them in broad daylight with a lantern. They make no noise. But it is certain that the series is being formed behind each one of them, to the last one—the king with his noisy glory and full powers. Throughout the series, the noise increases and becomes extensive under the feet of the king, in the vicinity of the pure sea of noises. The river becomes more and more troubled until the mouth is reached, full of sand and mud. The king, knee-deep in silt and mud swarming with parasites and noises. The sun at the head of the line is the physical beginning, and the sea at the end is a physical end. The chain of living beings has the sea as its end, and it is as irreversible as the sea. And it goes from the producers of novelty to the refuse-eaters.

In Bergson's theories, or in those of his recent parasites, through those of Thomas Kuhn, the new comes from the outside. The outside is not necessarily negative. Novelty is not necessarily the opposite of what the father says, as some worthy sons have thought. The negative is only redundant here, poorly distinguished from what it repeats. The new cannot be foreseen. It is outside, with the madman, the genius, the hero, the saint. How is it possible for them to be there?

Whoever lives inside enclosures survives, eats the stock, para-sites what justifies the closure of the system. It is closed for and by the parasites. Whoever is excluded from it is not provided for with food; he has no larder, no pantry. He must make do with what he finds, seeking his fortune in the world. Or else he dies or he goes mad. Or else he be-comes mad as a hatter or follows the paths of genius. And becomes a producer. With what he gathers on the ground that had never gotten anyone's attention, with the remains of divisions and cells, with the refuse found in the garbage dump, with the crumbs from the masters' dinner, he succeeds in creating a work. Or he dies. For him, the work is a question of life and death. He becomes a producer by putting his whole life into this primary material. I have called him an archangel be-cause he bears information, news, and novelty, and because he is necessarily at the head of the line in relation to the parasitic chain. Head of the series or outside the closure—it is the same image in one or two dimensions. His novelty is having injected his life into the produced object, instead of drawing his life from the chosen object. The only novelty is my improbable life.

Exclusion is no small matter. We are the children of a couple excluded from paradise. This paradise lost is that of parasitism. All animals and vegetables that were good to eat were there for the taking. Outside, it is necessary to produce, to die or to produce, to die and to produce, to die and to work, to invent something new, history for example, outside the stability of this first garden. Soon, to invent a garden, to dwell in the promised land, where parasitism will once more take hold in the milk and honey.

When the one who was excluded has produced, the enclosure sheltering the parasites opens, sending out pseudopodia to include this work, new blood that helps perpetuate the enclosure. Inside it, everything is sleeping. Production is impossible, since all activity there is either judgement or demand, an activity of ticket-takers. This activity produces exclusion; the excluded are the dead, and rarely, producers. From whom the process begins anew.

We have just suddenly moved to collective parasitism and to social parasitic structures. It is not astonishing that Bergson discovered a model of this sort by passing through the religious, coming from the living and going toward the collective and the historical. Modernity, with its various types of specialized history, including the history of science, has only parasited this discovery.

What is capital? It is the reservoir above the dam, an iron mine or a coal, manganese, or tungsten mine; a gold mine. An oil well. It is a stock of energy and of primary material; it is an island of negative entropy. Elsewhere I called this capital a reservoir. This is an optimistic name: conserve, preserve what can re-serve. In fact, the reservoir or the reserve is a pocket of time. It is matter but it is only time. Geological time, the long period needed to amass it; technical time, the explosive moment that is sufficient to use it up; technical time, the short time needed to build the dam; and finally, the long time needed for its exploitation. Be it renewable or not, the reservoir is a conceivable function of time.

What is capital? A city, a class, a group, a nation. Us.

What is capital? A treasure, a wad of bills, a bank. That used to be called money. Money [argent] nowadays is hardly ever gold or silver [argent]. More and more it tends toward being a sign: paper money, checks, credit cards—that is to say, an engraved number (stamped or written magnetically) on a rectangle of plastic, that is to say, information.

Could capital be a number, a very large number? Large enough for a pile, a stockpile, for accumulation, for the reservoir, the city, fortune, lake or quarry, compact crowd, and a well-supplied account, but also large enough to be able to designate an individual: every object has its register; every subject has several. Everything has its spectrum in black and white; we have returned to the dawn of philosophy; we have become Pythagoreans once again; all things are numbers. Although the ideology drawn from that tends toward the side of masses or atoms, or matter and social or individual, it remains nonetheless true that it is always a question of a large number. It is the same where information is concerned. Look here at the reason that antagonistic sites resemble each other. The large number is mass, but an individual needs a large number.

What is capital? It is a store of writings. The old standard of precious metal, having become banal, tends to disappear. What remains is the number, the register of the individual (or of the society) to which a certain amount of legal tender is attributed. It is a question of electronic money, signals exchanged between computer terminals. Now capital is in the memory banks. Henceforth, money is only a particular case, for there are other writings in the memory banks: those of books and libraries, of lists and registers, of headings and directories, of annals and court records, of obituaries and criminal records, of codes and quotas. The encyclopedia is enriched and is miniaturized at the same time. The old encyclopedias would not have printed the post office's hours, the fluctuations of the stock market, nor the state of cyclones today on the Aegean Sea. The individual and the circumstantial enter along with the general into this new bank. The bank of givens—this is the new capital where money is only a subset of signs. Henceforth, the general equivalent is the given in general, written in the reservoir of signs.

The professor and the scientist, the priest and the artist, the praetor and the banker, the underwriter and the politician, the adman and the journalist, the administrator, the judge, the singer, the dancer, and the policeman—all these professionals brought by the code to one language, brought by the number to the same memory bank, brought to the bank, around the same capital, reorganize themselves in the same function.

We have known for three thousand years that they all did the same job. The Jupiterian function is the function of the sign. The technology of data processing finally brings us a data bank. This is less progress than simply the revealing of the truth of our systems. The only thing discovered, the only thing built, is the stock of stocks, that is to say, the "common stock" of everything that pertains to libraries, surveys, and lists. And the group of groups appears, the Jupiter common to the circulation of signs. Quite curiously, the world of tomorrow is already readable as primitive with our sophisticated technology. That proves that we never speak except of our own. Nothing new, nothing new under the sun, under the sun of the sign.

We are moving toward a data bank.

Let us return to the first capital: lake, mine, oil deposit, functions of time. The dam holds the water that comes from glaciers and from snow, from wind, clouds, heat, and cold. Coke, gas, or water power is stored heat in any case. A while back, the collection of capitals was converging on the rock made of signatures; these resources also head together toward one spot: the sun whence they come and to which they go. These reservoirs are only subsuns. Their source, far upstream, is the sun. The real, ultimate capital is the sun. Subcapitals are time functions, but our time is that of the sun. Our cosmological, astronomic, energetic, entropic, informational times, all cyclic and reversible, as well as the irreversible times of disorder and death, of life and order randomly invented—all of these intertwine in the sun. In matter of energy and of matter, only the sun creates and transforms. All kinds of materialism, and especially those that seek to account for real movement and its excess, join together with various energetics and perhaps idealisms here —they are, when all is said and done, all subcults of the sun.

And thus our knowledge and our ingenious praxes are set today on the reproduction of the sun. When a dam was built, when oil was drilled for, it was not yet clear that it was already a question of the sun. The water was too cold, though it was high; the coal was too black, though it was explosive; the oil was too heavy, though it was inflammable. Shadows. In the magnetic reactor space of fusion, where the star seems to levitate outside, the burst of light no longer blinds our intuition: our inventive works have never done anything but imitate the sun, or imitate the imitations of the sun; henceforth we build it faithfully, in the secret centers of its flame. Finally, the epiphany of the oldest idea in the world. The old Platonic hyperbole comes out of its metaphor, the old cave of the (robber) metaphysicians; today it is fabricated. We are still a bit aside of this hyperbole; we have not entered the great beyond of essence. Not only do we look directly at the sun, not only do we merely represent it; we also produce it. Alas, it is not the marvelous transcendence that we expected: it is simply the end of a story. Metaphysics descends, losing its prefix.

In a month, in three days, in twenty years, we will have brought the sun down to earth, we will have established it here, we will have set it up, we will have set up a place for it. It still escapes us a bit; it moves; it blinks. We will have annulled its distance and recaptured its time, having reduced its transcendence. What will we call this revolution? I don't know. It will be a new one—a successor to Galileo and Copernicus will give it its name—yet it will not be new. For our paths have long been leading there. Reserve above, ultimately the source, for the functioning of our motors. There are pieces of earth which were suns already.

We have put into orbit and will continue to put into orbit communications satellites coupled with data banks, so that our informational motors function without a hitch. I do not know what this revolution, again an astronomical one, will be called. One of Ptolemy's successors will give it his name. It will and won't be new.

We will have completed a trip on a known path. The mastery and manipulation of these suns and these satellites—of these two capitals —fires and signals—of this new system of our ancient world, will express our virtuosity with high- and low-level energy, with transformable material, with understandable languages. Our world was one of production and translation. It made two philosophies fight in order to be established on their common agreement.

A chapter in the book of reason is about to close. But we already know that end; we know its consequences. Arriving at the capital-sun or at the data bank, at the two concentrated reservoirs of fires and signals, at the concrete universal of projects of production and paths of translation, is only extrapolating from the system in place, going to the end of its tendencies, having confidence in its extensions, placing novelty in conservation. And thus completing it, almost causing its birth, causing it to appear in its purified perfection. We used to believe in a double progress, like a double revolution: it is only a kind of growth. It shows us in its pure state that which our sciences, performances, struggles, history, and time imply from their inception. The system is born under our eyes; it was already there: the mammoth of the world, the gigantic dinosaur whose finished enormities are preliminaries, Leviathan, the great beast, already known and named, well-nourished with abundant energy and with normally directed information. The old kind of philosophy is applied anew. Henceforth, we know how to construct this model, since we have the solar force and the data in our bank account.

What more can the largest animal do than a very large animal can? Can we conceive of an animal larger than this beast-world, a sun surrounded with planets of signs? I guess that the system must be rather fragile, all varieties of this size moving toward extinction and death. Once again, is it the end of the great dinosaurs, the end of the great empires? Is there a threshold or a limit to the endless chain of struggle, force, and immenseness, to the relation of order of the strongest, the best, or the largest?

Living eaters of the living, we shall survive, more or less well, in the torrent come from the sun. Noisy intercepters of signals, we shall survive in the torrent that flows toward the lake of data. Good speakers, invited guests at the world's table, we shall try to exchange light signals for the sun's objects.

Will this feast of injustice and mortality be interrupted some day?

The Cows Come out of the River ————
———————————————————— Stocks

> Pharaoh dreamed that he was standing by
> the Nile, and behold, there came up out
> of the Nile seven cows sleek and fat.
>
> Genesis 41:1-2

The Yellow River is seen from bottom to top, starting from the plain, whereas almost all the rivers of the world flow in ,a hollow bed. From the beginning of our time, since the farmer began to alter the surface of the earth, since they needed to irrigate the rice paddies, the Chinese peasants have been there, under the river, in the shadow of the river, drinking the water of the Hwang Ho, defending themselves until death against the waters of the Hwang Ho. Source of life and major peril of destruction.

The Yellow River is an enormous geological transformer. It tears through its heights, rather violently, sometimes capturing tributaries of a neighboring river basin; it is so energetic and so inventive that it can leave its homeorrhetic equilibria to look for falls and slopes outside its own slope; it devours the ground; it eats the land in relief; it carries away melted mountains; further downstream, it lets them go, returning the stolen loess; it engulfs its lower parts, thickening the bottom of its bed to the point of losing its banks; if this occurs, the river wanders randomly through the plain. From the upstream water down to the sea, by its fluctuating energy, and quite often outside the constraints of the currents, it redesigns its bed. Superb model of a methodical path that is more laden with information than it is redundant, a complex model of a path taken [randonnée].

For a long time it has risen, terrifyingly, over the plain. It is a furrow, like all rivers; it is a wall of high banks and dizzying embankments. It not only overflows, like the Garonne; it breaks. It is a suspended canal; it is a river and a bridge, a river and a dike. What is subterranean for us is aboveground for the Chinese of the plain; it has risen, as if in levitation, and flows through the air. And the waters rushing through are already the waters of heaven. The whole course of the lower river is a dam; the Chinese peasants live and sleep under its wall at the mercy of a crack. With the smallest crack, the cascade is stirred into a cataract, and the flood comes.

Travelling at random through the plain, it irrigates all alone; it is only necessary to wait for it. But one can die from such waiting. It doesn't come; it comes, enormous, unexpected; it drowns instead of fertilizing. It is better, then, to channel it, regulating it, constructing a network of trenches around the major artery. The genius of civil engineering is seen in cuts and fills, dredgings and subsidence. Rationalization of chances or normalization of the stochastic—the Chinese became masters and possessors of nature. They controlled a reservoir, but at the same they suspended a heavy sword over their heads. Every week, the Hwang Ho deposited tons of loess among the slopes and rose. More embankments, slopes, and banks were built. And so forth. What else could be done? Once again the model is superb. And terrifying. When you raise a wall, the water increases behind the wall; so you raise it even further and you raise it even more. The solution to one question raises ten problems, and the trouble begins anew.

Work without end and with diminishing returns. It is not the labor of Hercules; Hercules' labors were optimistic. When the Greek hero had chased out the parasites, the monsters, or cleaned the Augean stables, the space was finally purified. As far as I know, mythology did not consider the return of the parasites. The return of the chicken-pox virus as shingles, fifty years later. The Augean stables are cleaned; the river's loess accumulates.

Our sciences, our technologies, our Western culture: work at the base of the Hwang Ho or the detouring of the path of the Alpheus?

In Mesopotamia, in Egypt, or elsewhere—by the Yellow River, for example—agriculture opened up a new universe in the Neolithic Era, a universe of which we are the descendants. How could the cultivation of the earth have begun?

Gathering precedes cultivation, so they say. We don't know how to do anything, and already, we are demanding. We choose. We refuse, in that choice, other vegetable species. We eliminate them. The motion of exclusion or expulsion is there already at the gate.

Suddenly, I think it is radical—rigorously, literally radical.

We usually excluded weeds and separated the wheat from the chaff. But that is not possible when the wheat is growing. Thus the purge, the sacralization of a given space, of a *templum*, of a garden, begins by the total and radical expulsion of all species. And not only of the hare. Agriculture could not have begun before the complete denuding of certain areas of ground. Before they served as a clear spot or a *tabula rasa* for their covering of vegetables. The field is first of all a spot from which everything is removed. A battlefield: everything has left the camp, uprooted. And when I say radical, I mean that the very roots have been eradicated, that the ploughshare has been pushed deep enough to destroy everything, even the rootlets of the ejected species. It wasn't a question of fertilizing and fecundating the earth through labor but rather of extirpating, suppressing, and banishing. Of destroying. The blade of the plough is a sacrificial blade, killing all the plants to make a clean space. Everything that grows here is excluded. Not only weeds, but everything. Cleaning by emptying out. That is certainly the first act of religion, and by chance, it is an agricultural one as well. The same action, the same work, the same upset. The same appropriation: propriety or property.

The ploughshare is a sacrificial knife frenetically manipulated at the height of murdering fury. The knife kills a man or an animal. Abel or the lamb, Isaac or the scapegoat. It is a cut-throat. It slices. It does not decide but slices. Not in two, but in three. It cuts up space. It marks a closed line: inside, the sacred; outside, the profane; inside, the temple; outside, the vague area filled with evil. Inside, the city, surrounded by walls, and the country outside. The ploughshare founded the city, and in the hollow of a furrow, a brother killed his twin. The ploughshare is the knife that sacrifices the brother. It cut his throat; it cut up space and earth. This knife or blade does not stop. Why would it stop? It continues madly, cutting everything, going beyond the mastery of the sorcerer's apprentice. Not a continuous and firm furrow, but one furrow, two furrows, three, ten thousand, so that the whole earth is cut, so that space everywhere is sliced up, so that nothing resists its mad movement, no weed, no plant, no root, nothing that is there. When the fury of this knife is appeased, everything has been worked into a fine powder. Harrowed. Reduced to its elements. Analysis.

The first work is a frenetic murder, continued until atoms are obtained. Until no more cutting is possible. Assassination, until the victim is cut into small pieces.

Thus agriculture is born.

It got a denuded space, a white domino.

It was necessary to wait for a random occurrence, a grain. And its death, naturally.

But labor was then not possible. This denudation occurred alone at the banks of the rising river. Inundation uproots everything in its path—trees, bushes, plants, moss, roots. It purifies everything—it performs the expected cultural movement—but it does so naturally. From this meeting or improbable short-circuit, agriculture was born on the banks of the Nile, the Tigris, the Euphrates, or the Hwang Ho. Agriculture is born of the Alpheus that cleans and purifies all the shit of the kings.

There remains then a square of denuded earth, from which all the vegetable covering has disappeared. That is rather a great distance from the equilibrium of living beings. Through this fault can pass, through this fault passes, the vertical proliferation of a given species sown there by chance. The problem, thus resolved, requires for its solution only the simple, elementary operation of expulsion.

One parasite chases out all the others. Men chase out life from a given location. The inundation was not wished for, the labor was not executed in order to irrigate or to sow; everything was done for cleaning. Hence this tear, this catastrophe, through which the multiplication of wheat, rice, or corn could pass, depending on the location, chance, and circumstances.

Suddenly there is another inundation: a windfall—stocks of unexpected food.

The human parasite multiplies as well through this fault, this distance from equilibrium, this catastrophe. In turn, he was to inundate the world. Growth against growth, the inundation of rice struggled by the walls against the inundation by the waters of the Hwang Ho. Epidemics against epidemics, logics of sets.

The invention of an empty space, its discovery under floodwaters or its constitution by the sweat of our brow, open a gap in the world's tissue, produce a catastrophe, a distance, a fault through which rush, not the excluded multiplicity, but rather the mad multiplication of the most random or the best adapted single unit. The previous equilibrium was sewn with differences. But in the local whiteness that we produce, homogeneity appears. Swelling of the waters. Stock.

We usually think that these appropriated, arranged, and well-defined squares where nothing but rich alluvial land appears are recent productions of a learned, civilized type of agriculture. I believe that it would be advantageous to think the opposite. The founding of the naked, empty field, virgin once more, is the oldest work of the human world.

The first one who, having enclosed a field or bit of land, decided to exclude everything there, was the true founder of the following historical era.

Agriculture and culture have the same origin or the same foundation, a white spot that realizes a rupture of equilibrium, a clean spot constituted through expulsion. A spot of propriety or cleanliness, a spot of belonging.

The joker is changed into a white domino.

It is fitting to understand this white spot that appears in the ancestral savannahs, this rent in the middle of their fluctuating stability. Have we ever produced other objects during the moments that history suddenly bifurcates?

Once again I understand the origin of geometry; once again, I understand the stories told about it. The flooding of the Nile overflows the river's banks and wreaks havoc in the surrounding fields. The harpedonapts, priests, or philosophers, the wise men, the agricultural surveyors, redistribute the parcels of land to the peasants or property owners, for the inundation has just erased the boundaries. The interpretation of this traditional statement exactly measures the agrarian culture of our grandparents. The harpedonapts, they said, are the first geometers because the Egyptians decided to use those who knew how to find area through measurement as the judges of their disputes of boundary lines. They had the cord, the unit, the measure, writing, and prestige. Thus, here is the expert geometer sought in public offices when one's sneaky neighbor has moved the boundary stones or has gone beyond them. Let us not laugh too hastily, for everything is there under our noses. Not the expert, but the priest. The priest, that is to say, the one who makes the motion of expulsion, of cutting up of the *templum*. The farmer makes the same motion. The river and its swelling waters are not opposed to the joint actions of the priest and the farmer, but help them in their business, do even better than help them: they act on their behalf and in their stead. It is not only the boundary that the river erases through the excess of its swell; it is the entire population of things that existed in this space or in this field. Everything in it is torn up, expelled; the space is white, homogeneous, and covered with silt. This smooth square appears as the waters abate: who will come to limit it? The farmer, the priest, and the geometer. Three origins in three persons in one motion at the same moment. The field, the temple, and measured space. Democritus and my ancestors said it right; it was necessary only to listen to them. The space discovered by the Nile, the Tigris, the Garonne, or the Hwang Ho is the white domino, the virgin spot of the excluded thirds, the difference from equilibrium. This expanse, because it is empty, is homogeneous, isotropic, and measurable. It is the field of agriculture in the valley, the *templum* spoken of by Mircea Eliade, in both its etymological and sacred meanings; but at the same time it is the abstract space of geometry. The abstract space from which everything was subtracted, from which everything was uprooted, from which everything was taken away, from which everything was extracted. Read attentively Plato's texts where he wants to define the space or the figure: they are all negative, or more exactly, apophatic. The philosopher acts like the priest or the farmer; he removes from there everything that might reappear, including color. He gets, once again, a white domino. Thus there is a rent in culture; thus there is the mad proliferation of one variety that has never stopped increasing, even today. And that is the same solution as my first one, that of the excluded third. The latter was dialectical; it did not appropriate a space. The two must be united to stay with the Greeks. Everywhere else that agriculture was born, only the geometry of agricultural surveyors was born. That is to say everything, except science.

Several white dominoes tear the vegetable covering here and there, especially in the deltas and the rivers' mouths. Several white dominoes tear language into what was called idealities, the realities of the intelligible. The classical age appears to be a founder to us only by having taken up and performed this same motion elsewhere. The Cartesian meditation eliminates, expels, banishes everything, hyperbolically. Once again, a clean slate and a clear spot in the religious major mode, and this slate and this spot are the extent of which I am the master and possessor of my thought. The thinking ego chases the parasites out, chases out in prosopopoeia the most cunning of all who return, who might return at any moment and anywhere, thus chases everything out, speaking absolutely; it discovers, elsewhere, the world, the white of our dominance. Virgin wax. In the tear thus constituted, simple and easy chains of reason constantly pass and the simple and single multiply, as do the rational and the technological. History bifurcates again; this cannot be doubted. Mastery and possession begin.

The constitution of a virgin space bathed in light, not as an ideality, but as an object-world, makes such a considerable rupture in the cultural equilibrium that through the fault of this gap will hurtle the modern rational, the proliferating multiplication of a certain type of sameness. At every apparition of this white, an outgrowth of singularity replaces the former multiplicity of complexes. At every apparition of this white, reproduction explodes.

Wheat, rice. Men. Mathematics. Technicality, rationalization of the world. Men, once more. History, supple, follows these white spots and these geysers.

The multiplication of the parasitic species that produces them jumps immediately after the flow that comes from these white spaces.

The question of origin constantly winds up at deceiving solutions because there is nothing at the origin but this white and empty spot. The origin is always this empty set. As they say, we'll start from scratch [*zéro*]. History is like the series of numbers, and dating is essential.

But the whole question is producing zero. By total exclusion in a given spot. History would begin with the Flood, if the Flood hadn't left some remains: Noah, the ark, and its animals that escaped the inundation. What remains is the motor of history that follows a state without remains. And thus, from the first verses of Genesis with the spirit of God over the waters, it was the first flood, the total inundation from which creation *ex nihilo* had to follow. The work of limitation and division begins, and soon waters are separated from waters. Everything—by that I mean the world—comes from the first inundation, the first operation that suppresses everything and leaves nothing behind.

We begin to understand the meaning, seemingly so mysterious, of this creation from nothing, *ex nihilo*. Not even a little spot on the seed, the hylum, not even that from which a blade of grass could grow. Nothing, nothing remains after the swelling of the waters; nothing remains in the field; nothing remains in the intelligible space where meanings could hang on; nothing remains after the test of doubt, the work of the negative finished before all beginnings. Discourse of radical origin, very improbable and therefore the bearer of overflowing information.

The cows, one after the other, come out of the swelling Nile. Each of them is a swell, a stock, a fecundity, an abundance, and each nourishes those who will pullulate from the bifurcation it announces. The priest, and in turn, the farmer, the protogeometer, the master and possessor of nature, the philosopher of radical discourse.

Dizzying eradication that comes from this chain. The cows come from the Nile, as do our stocks, our chances, and our history. From the Nile: is it the Alpheus or the Hwang Ho? With something left or without, that is the question. The hero creates the void, and everything begins or it remains silt, quicksand, mud, or loess indefinitely. I don't know which one is the path.

I cannot believe that the animal that devastated a part of space knew ahead of time what the final product of his action or exaction would be—overkill—and that he purified or cleaned this spot with this aim in mind. This worked beyond expectations (when he succeeded) for completely different reasons from his motives. Nothing changes when we go from praxes to theory.

This (hi)story would have no end if it went from local square to local square. But its very logic, the logic of eradication, brings about, necessarily, a global without remains, doesn't it?

Cows Eat Cows
Theory of the Line

The chain of parasitism is a simple relation of order, irreversible like the flow of the river. One feeds on another and gives nothing in return. Asymmetry is local on a chain and is propagated globally the length of a series, through transitivity. They make a line. In reality, the matter is more complex. And the theory of lines, as we know, goes much further. For the moment, we will remain at the level of the elements of the relation. For parasitism is an elementary relation; it is, in fact, the elements of the relation.

The relation upsets equilibrium, making it deviate. If some equilibrium exists or ever existed somewhere, somehow, the introduction of a parasite in the system immediately provokes a difference, a disequilibrium. Immediately, the system changes; time has begun.

Change comes from a rupture in equilibrated exchanges. Change is the disequilibrium of exchanges.

A microscopic parasite can be introduced into an equilibrated pathological environment, or a good-sized parasite into an economically stable system, or a noisy parasite into a dialogical message; in any case a

182

(hi)story will follow. For a long time it was believed that these (hi)stories were different.

The questions alluded to above are more or less questions of origin. All of them were resolved by the parasite. The solution was an easy one, since, without a parasite—that is to say, without asymmetry or disequilibrium—there is no irreversible, no chain emerges, and time is unknown.

In the strict sense of the word, commensality is eternal. The Greeks were not wrong in showing us the immortals constantly feasting, drinking ambrosia, and laughing endlessly. We all know perfectly well what ambrosia is composed of, what the ingredients of nectar, the drink of immortality, are. We all know perfectly well where paradise is and how to produce the absence of history. We know that it is enough to break the asymmetric chain, the series of abuses; we know that it is enough not to eat the one who precedes us in the order. We know that it is enough to exchange food back and forth to escape from change, time, and history. To sit at the feast and be commensals dining together. To annul all distance from the *sitos,* or to chase out the parasite in us. Paradise then is there.

Ambrosia is found among the Hindus as much as it is here; it is the brew that saved the human populations of the Fertile Crescent, and from even further East of Eden, from certain infectious diseases found in the lakes and backwaters. Beer, wine, and bread, foods of fermentation, of bubbling, foods of decay, appeared as safeguards against death. These were our first great victories over parasites, our rivals, obtained, as might be expected, for reasons and intentions that were completely different from those that made them triumph *de facto.* From the Olympians to the Last Supper, we have celebrated the victory to which we owe our life, the eternity of phylogenesis, and we celebrate it in its natural spot, the table.

Here the question discovers its model. I shall no longer die from eating bread; my son will no longer die from drinking the wine or the brew of the gods. The chain that was eating us has been abolished. Take this line literally: your ancestors drank water from Jacob's well, and they died. They died from it, as the water was no longer potable. Drink the water changed into wine and the wine changed into the brew of immortality; you will be free of parasites. Of mortal, deadly putrefaction. We must then pass from the model to the system. We are not different from the animals that were eating us, the small animals that were killing us. We eat ourselves; we kill each other. When the cows come out of the Nile, they line up next to each other along the bank of the river, and they eat each other in order, following the Nile, and according to the law of order, just like the rest of us. Let's seat ourselves around the table and pass the food; let us practice a perfect exchange; let us become commensals. That is immortal equilibrium.

Of course, it is not so easy. Throughout the whole Indo-European realm, a stranger, a robber, steals the ambrosia; the system has a hole. And in the Semite realm, at the same feast, someone is eaten; the system has a hole. Just the same, the logicial is transformed into the material.

Even before history, time began by the deviation of systems. We shall come back to this, but we have already spoken of it, with Lucretius, and with ancient and modern physics.

A given parasite is said to be a miracle of evolution because of the complexity of its performances and the sophistication of its cycle. It is also sometimes said that our activity begins to weigh heavily in and on this evolution. Suddenly I wonder whether evolution itself is not the work of parasites, from a certain point of view. Whether, between evolution and parasitism, there might not be cycles of causes and effects, in open circuits with feedback. Evolution would produce the parasite, which would produce evolution. Suddenly I wonder whether the study —not local and unique this time, but global, formal, and pertaining to the mode of operation of the parasitic function—would not be somewhat displaced, on the side, somewhat reflexive vis-à-vis the exact sciences, both the natural and human sciences, like a passageway where they could not be dissociated.

The theory of evolution can be reduced to two terms: mutation and selection. We know on what set the first acts. It is not entirely a metaphoric expression when we say that it has to do with a message written on a base. Part of this message is changed by mutation, by absence, substitution, or difference of elements. It is not entirely a metaphoric expression when we claim that it has to do with the intervention of a noise in the message. Noise in the sense of disorder, and thus chance, but noise also in the sense of interception, an interception that changes the order and thus the meaning, if we can speak of meaning. But that changes the order above all. The interception is a parasite; we could have guessed as much. The new order appears by the parasite troubling the message. It disconcerts the ancient series, order, and message; and then composes [concerte] new ones.

The introduction of a parasite in a system is equivalent to the introduction of a noise. In Lucretius' work, the order of the world, a result of declination in a laminar field, is an order by fluctuation. This fluctuation is a noise; it is a parasite. Time does not begin without its intervention. Irreversibility never appears without this factor of asymmetry. The order in the sense of the order of things and the order in the sense of structures of order cannot emerge without this element of relation of order. The parasite is an element of relation; it is the atom of relation, the directional atom. It is the arrow flying at random in broad daylight. It is the appearance of meaning.

The theory of being, ontology, brings us to atoms. The theory of relations brings us to the parasite.

The introduction of a parasite in a system is equivalent to the introduction of a noise. First example. I am speaking polyphonically. The message is surrounded by nonsense, pure noise, disorder; the system crumbles and everything dies. The plague decimates a population. Mutation makes the fetus abort. And with that, the parasite—the assassin—commits suicide. The sponger falls back into the stream after having ruined his host. From information theory to anthropology, from signals to life, be it unique or numerous, the dynamics are stable and unchanging, always bringing about the same results.

The entrance of Tartuffe or the Abbé Faujas in a quiet family setting produces comedy, tragedy, sound and fury, violence, prison, murder, arson, a story. How does the system move and why? In Zola's work, everything finishes in fire, ashes, flow of blood. The arrival of Tartuffe induces the placement of new messages in circulation. There is disorder, a free-for-all. No one can speak but Mme Pernelle; the circulation goes from her to the others and does not return. The guest returns and asks for only one thing. Tartuffe is a parasite in the material sense of the feast; he makes the flow of food move toward his mouth, the "and Tartuffe" is a parasite in the logicial sense of a message; he makes the flow of meaning [sens] move in only one direction [sens]. He breaks the dialogue, interrupts it, straightens it out [redresse]; he functions as a righter of wrongs [redresseur]. This noise, this particular noise, straightens out the meaning [redresse le sens] and makes it circulate in one direction [sens]. The sender is not troubled by the parasite, though the receiver is. Thus the second example appears. Suddenly the system is oriented. Suddenly the system starts to decline. Suddenly the system has a meaning. That noise is a straightener, filtering a meaning, creating a meaning. We now see why the system moves and where it is going. If you introduce an impurity in a crystal, you will have produced a transistor. A semiconductor.

Selection can now be understood. The parasite straightens things out, creating an irreversible circulation, a meaning, making meaning. As we have seen above, it constructs gates to fit its demands. A gate, as far as I know, is also a semiconductor. Selection is also semiconduction. The activity of the parasite is parallel to the function of selection. They are two operators on the same structure. It is interesting to look at the operators alone. For this we will not need a far-reaching teleonomy. A direction is created to favor a parasitic life locally. The numerous and different orientations are produced, and that is that. The global pressure of selection is the global composition of these locally created directions, the integration of exigencies.

Evolution has a parasitic structure. It would not favor parasites as much as it does if it were not more or less favored by them. An order, a structure of order, a movement emerges with it, by the noise and the selective gate, by the noise that straightens out and the gate that does the same, by the righting that is itself a relation of order, a difference or an asymmetry. If evolution is an order, the parasite is certainly its element. It interrupts a repetition and makes the series of sameness bifurcate.

We cannot think of evolution without thinking, aside from evolutionary forms and the permutations of the coding, aside from the two mechanisms of mutation and selection, of irreversible time, the basic flow that is slow and asymmetrical, this global meaning that we turn away from thinking about. We must try to think about this time.

Elsewhere I said that living organisms are bouquets or blades of time, that they are exchangers of time. That life, certainly, is nothing but time, but that this proposition is not simple. And that we know three kinds of time, so different that they can be said to be contradictory: the reversible one, datable by the long equilibria of the world, and the two irreversible ones, those of entropy and of Darwinian evolution. The first one protects us and defines our niche; the second makes us die a more or less lasting death, and the last perpetuates us, placing hope in the genius of our daughters and the beauty of our sons. Life would be the intertwining of these three separable chronies.* I leave a free piece floating around, the inconsolable hope in the transparency of the work we leave to posterity.

Their intertwining remains to be understood. If the reversible exists, the repeated and redundance exist. Redundance is there in the system of the world—eclipses and the return of syzygys are indistinguishable *de jure;* it is there in the profound stability of a message that never throws sexual reproduction outside its species. No one ever saw a man and a woman engender a jaguar. No one ever saw an ice crystal turn into a green emerald. There is redundance. There is $a \equiv a$, for as long as the time as this identity gives rises to. Nothing new under the blinding sun of sameness. Logicial redundance, mechanical equilibria, genetic invariants, material stabilities.

*"L'Origine du langage," in *Hermes IV. La distribution;* "Espaces et temps," in *Hermes V. Le passage du Nord-Ouest.*

We have returned to the white fall or to laminar redundance. Nothing is distinguishable in such a universe; everything is reversible and exchangeable. We would like to talk about this immobile mobility. The two laugh and toast in the fixed space of eclipses and syzygys; they laugh without speaking; they toast for the noise; the ambrosia is endless, in eternal return. The more that came out of the vase, the less it emptied.

Irreversible time begins with the parasitic noise, with fluctuation, with the *clinamen*; it flows in one direction. Irreversible time would not have begun without the sowing of disorder in redundance. In the white space I spoke of above, an atom of disorder, an atom of relation, is enough for the movement to start. Everything emerges from this white space, given this quark of noise.

The irreversible time of live begins with parasitic life in its double activity of noise and demand. It intercepts and channels. This double operation is in fact single; it is a question of setting aright, of producing the unity of one meaning and one direction. The distance from equilibrium is in place; the interweaving of the redundant and the irreversible is seized at its point of bifurcation. This declination, this angle, of which only the geometric appearance was known—we now recognize its function.

We don't understand very well how the two chronies or irreversible times intertwine in turn. How one goes down toward death and destruction, while the other constantly produces differences and novelties. The parasite permits us to understand this maximal divergence. Its excessive demands make it always move further down, by the constitution of successive gates; the law of its life is never to allow itself to be supplanted. In this capacity, it exposes every system to ruin, it tends to exhaust reservoirs; it can kill everything it meets. But at the same time it multiplies the complexity which can be either suffocation or novelty; it excites production; it exalts and accelerates the exchanges of its hosts. It is Boltzmannian and Darwinian at the same time. It is dangerous; it is so dangerous that it can eradicate everything around it (and by this power of eradication, we recognize that we are parasites, from labor to philosophy), but it raises up, here and there, productive multiplications. It leads the operation of radical novelty and that of destruction by eradication.

This unexpected result was not foreseeable. We have known for a while that parasitic intervention in the middle of a channel can help and block at the same time. That the parasite is an included third. That it is in the third position in a relation and that it enters into it. That it is concerned that other parasites not enter, that it avoids or does not avoid the relation. That it obeys two kinds of logic: that of the excluded third and that of the included third. And that it crosses the spectrum of the fuzzy. That it is thus a producer and inducer, not of a meaning, as I have just said, but exactly of a direction, excluding others, including the meaning/direction that leads to the collapse of the system and to its perpetual renewal. The same direction brings disorder and high complexity; sometimes high complexity makes disorder; sometimes disorder makes complexity. The stakes of polemics on the second principle are vague, and the polemics are those of the included third. Darwin and Boltzmann hold the two ends of a chain, but the chain is unique: it is the parasitic chain.

The parasite is the active operator and the logical operation of evolution, of the irreversible time of life.

Irreversible physical time begins with a parasite sown in a redundance. With a noise or a disorder, randomly come into a white space that itself had undoubtedly appeared by chance. This noise and this parasite produce a slope, a difference, a disequilibrium, and the slope produces noise; the process, if kept up, will no longer stop immediately. It goes to seek its fortune in the world. It can be immense or mediocre or nonexistent. Local disorder pulls local order toward asymmetry. The parasite is an operator; it is a generalized *clinamen*.

Irreversible living time begins with the introduction of a parasite. In the common vicinity of what is called inert and what is called living, a virus reproduces in a parasitic fashion. It is not uninteresting that it has been called a phage. Throughout classification and throughout evolution, the parasite is there, protozoan, metazoan, present as if to keep up the continuity of the course of life. The cows that eat each other, lined up along the bank of the Nile, make the Nile flow. And the rivers of Babylon. They pull time further along, further down. Times for feast or famine.

Irreversible historical time begins with the introduction of parasitic man, at least since agriculture and animal husbandry started. Perhaps even before, among the trees; no one knows. Historical time began as soon as a parasitic species (parasitic in the sense of evolution) started to intercept messages and became a parasite in the logicial sense; then the meaning of the word is complete; then the animal eats at the *table d'hôte*, inventing the exchange with his host of the logicial for the material. When man becomes a man to be a talky flea, a loquacious rat, or a babbling phage.

Let us return to the white fall. To the wind of the voice, to the yell, to the open, sonorous flow of vowels. Call or complaint, united flow, laminar breath. Articulated language begins with the sowing of consonants. But consonants are interruptions of the voice. Rupture, stopping, bifurcation of this flow. Yes, consonants are parasitic. They block the breath, cut it off, forbid it, close it, propel it, help it, modulate it. They are obstacles and aides, like ordinary parasites. They multiply the inclinations and angles in the course of the voice; they multiply the dams and the deflectors; they encode the white layer; they multiply directions and suddenly produce meaning. Articulated languages are parasited breaths. As was said in the classical era, the vowel is a soul—that is to say, wind—and the consonant is a body—that is, a limit and the temporal prison of the soul.

The vowel is open; the consonant, mute, is closed. We must look at the topology of the canal. Whatever the form, the passage is free for the first, constrained or blocked for the second. The voice is imprisoned in a complicated bureaucracy of networks and gates. Articulation is a set of strangulations; consonants strangle voices. They squeeze them [Elles les serrent].

The parasite forms a line, a chain. It is the element of some chain. And now it operates drop by drop. Στράγξ, the drop, the strangled flow. The στραγγεῖον is a lancet used for taking blood, for intercepting it, for interrupting a flow, for capturing it. The drop is the phoneme. The somewhat viscous flow is detoured, constrained by deflectors, valves, semiconductors with temporarily closed valves or narrow light paths; and by these twists, turns, inclinations, and strangulations, the flow is distilled. As if the phoneme-drop were a unit of strangulation. A double bell of empty anguish, strict at both ends. Tight [serrée].

Consonants make the progression of voices peristaltic. Articulation is the set of the knots of temporary prohibitions where breath pushes. Each language distributes them its own way. Each language is a unique sowing and an original distribution of parasites. It is enough to chase them away—at least in our dreams—to obtain the universal language; that is why the voice of the Paraclete is only a sound or a wind. The vowel of the firebird.

Sometimes winds, breaths, composed together incline toward each other without the intervention of valves or consonants. Oui is a coil, a tress of voice. A bit free, a bit loose, undone, without the anguish of strangulation. Oui without the swarming parasites. Oui in the wind of the Paraclete. Oui in the turbulent tresses of the river. Oui finally works itself loose [se desserre].

The Best Definition

The parasite is a thermal exciter.

He aims to please at the *table d'hôte;* he is invited with this aim in mind. The convivial climate is changed by his movements, his stammering and his looks; he makes others laugh; he takes, gives, takes again, directs speech, communicates a small, warm shudder to the others that assures us that we are together. Without him, the feast is only a cold meal. His role is to animate the event. His is a social role and thus, theatrical. Sometimes professorial, sometimes pastoral. A clerk at the table, a good raconteur, made the others guess where Tartuffe had come from and why he was named Tartuffe. When the parasites abound, in ever-increasing numbers if the food is good, they insure the splendor of the euergetes or of the generous donors. The rich man pays legions with wine for them to sing his glory. Birth of advertising, ring out, clarions of renown. Their applause, with their thin hands, make the masques and leaders successful. Because of them, the play is not a flop. It is true that without them there were no great men. And it is thus that they sometimes become great men, for having been experts in this strategy.

It enters the body and infests it. Its infectious power is measured by its capability to adapt itself to one or several hosts. This capability fluctuates, and its virulence varies along with its production of toxic substances. They lie dormant, rise up, lose wind, are lost for a long time.

How and why? We don't know in general; our knowledge is distributed over cases of species. Parasitology is both a growing and compartmentalized field of knowledge, like its objects, a local knowledge that is specific, I was going to say historical, at least in the old sense of natural history, where the global, it must be said, is deceiving. There remains much to be discovered, for the conceptual syntheses are still awkward. Perhaps it is a science that is more medical than biological, moving along a path toward biology. We know about parasites, their distribution, their cycle, their effects; sometimes they can be effectively fought; do we know what a parasite is in general? What is, in general, its fluctuating and variable action?

Yet it can change the course of history. It has been shown, at least vaguely. Men-parasites do not invade America without having been preceded by those they carry. The fact occurs often enough for a protocol to appear. Human actions and relations are seen in a different light. We now recognize the first elements of a theory of transformations.

The parasite is an exciter. Far from transforming a system, changing its nature, its form, its elements, its relations and its pathways (but who accomplishes this act, what set, what force succeeds? What does "transform the world" mean concretely? What is work, really?), the parasite makes it change states differentially. It inclines it. It makes the equilibrium of the energetic distribution fluctuate. It dopes it. It irritates it. It inflames it. Often this inclination has no effect. But it can produce gigantic ones by chain reactions or reproduction. Immunity of epidemic crisis.

Excitation, inclination—I change the meaning of the prefix, into more or less, right or left, cold or hot, a measured distance—the prefix *para*-. The parasite intervenes, enters the system as an element of fluctuation. It excites it or incites it; it puts it into motion, or it paralyzes it. It changes its state, changes its energetic state, its displacements and condensations. By despoiling actions, like ascarid worms or leeches; by toxic actions, like ticks or fleas; by trauma, like bilharzia or trichina worms; by infection, like dysenteric amoebas; by obstruction, like the filaria of elephantiasis; by compression, like those that form cysts; by irritations, inflammations, itching; by rashes (my two parasites together eat [*manger*] and are scratched [*se démanger*]).

The parasite brings us into the vicinity of the simplest and most general operator on the variability of systems. It makes them fluctuate by their differential distances. It immunizes them or blocks them, makes them adapt or kills them, selects them and destroys them. It is necessary to say of the parasite, generalizing Claude Bernard's expression from his first lesson on toxic agents: the veritable reagents of life? The parasite brings us near the fine equilibria of living systems and near their energetic equilibria. It is their fluctuation, their moving back and forth, their test and training. Is the parasite the element of metamorphosis (and by that old word I mean the transforming movement of life itself)? This movement begins with the phage; it seems to me that I still see it in the very history of man.

Homeostasis makes the returns to equilibrium understandable. Homeorrhesis makes these returns understandable in their very movements. We should say *parastasis,* circumstance, for the set of fluctuations that move systems away from their rest states; we should say *pararrhesis* for the improbable, chance, complex, fragmented, bursting movement, dancing like a wall of fire, that life shows.

The noise of the cheers warms the auditorium; the flashes of wit of the good raconteur revive the warm flow of air. This is not necessarily simply a manner of speaking. Applause doesn't reproduce too badly the noise of thermal agitation, the noise produced by excited molecules. Supposing that the molecules are very excited, the noise they make very easily covers a passing message. The parasite, the mixer of meanings or voices, the dissolution of signals in the fog of noise, is thus this very same excitation, or the one who gets it. The parasite is always an exciter.

It is not uninteresting to have a single operator. It warms the room, gives a fever, increases agitation and thermal disorder. Given a system in general—in this case a social one but it could be living, inert or material, men together, an organism, molecules in a canal—the operator excites the system.

The rats invite themselves to dinner, and that makes noise. I leave it to you to think about the row they kick up. The host, who was sleeping, wakes up; or, he wasn't there, and he comes; his body changes phase and position; he moves forward and pushes open the door. The door or the floor creaks, the pleasurable meal is interrupted, the conversation stops; they keep quiet. Several figures, to be sure, but one parasite and the end of one state.

The thermal excitation is minimal; it is differential. This business seems to occur at night in the dark and in silence. Everything is very small there: scratching interrupting the quiet, a small consciousness upon waking, a small creak, a short run to safety and then immediate return. The parasite produces small oscillations of the system, small differences: parastases or circumstances.

The invitation of friends or relatives to dinner occurs as a supplement to a balance of exchange. It can be said that it is nothing in this balance and that it is the balance itself. It does not make the balance move much, but it shows a deep, direct end to the exchange. Many stories tell that the guests are gods who save us from a great danger when we know how to recognize them, when the meal is prepared, cooked, offered, and placed on the table. They are also dangerous passers-by. They change the state of the collective that invites them in.

They do not transform the collective system as such, but they change its state. No, it is not a revolution, not even a reform; it is a little difference, a minimal action. Philemon and Baucis will love each other even more, as will Alcestis and Admetus after having been generous hosts. But the neighbors of the temple will be drowned in the flood, and the good hostess is brought back from the underworld. Minimal excitation, with a barely perceptible effect—they always loved each other that much. Minimal and reversed excitation, for catastrophic effects. Attention: this logic is very important. We always forget it and understand nothing. We must learn to modulate the weight of causes and that of effects. Without that, no history. The differential change of state insures the group in its equilibrium. Yes, it is no more than a shudder, as if the whole trembled around its stability. If the parasite is of the mind [*spirituel*], it makes us aware that we are we, good together—we were, well, forgetting this. Perhaps we were going to die from forgetting. The little reheating of the system reinsures the state, or, on the contrary, announces a complete change, a bit like the way that, in a stable or unstable equilibrium, a difference is promptly annulled or is increased astronomically. Hence the fear of the difference: a bit of happiness or a catastrophe, conservation or radical change, stability or adventure. Yes, this mouth really does blow hot and cold; I have finally understood that this was worth explaining. By small packets of energy, by this information that comes from the mouth, the system will reinforce its equilibrium or will be transformed from top to bottom. Such is the business of Tartuffe.

These logics shifting around minimal angles are at work in other systems as well. Parasitology, as we shall soon realize, uses the vocabulary of the host: hostility or hospitality. First of all, the parasite is always small; it never exceeds the size of insects or arthropods. In fact, the most numerous are protozoa or bacteria or viruses. Their small effects are usually well-tolerated by the organisms, which quickly rediscover their health, that is to say, their silence (at least relatively). This equilibrium that is well taken care of, thanks to the defense systems, is more solid than the preceding one. With the expulsion of Tartuffe, Orgon's family is vaccinated against the next devout man. In vaccination, poison can be a cure, and this logic with two entry points becomes a strategy, a care, a cure. The parasite gives the host the means to be safe from the parasite. The organism reinforces its resistance and increases its adaptability. It is moved a bit away from its equilibrium and it is then even more strongly at equilibrium. The generous hosts are therefore stronger than the bodies without visits; generation increases resistance right in the middle of endemic diseases. Thus parasitism contributes to the formation of adapted species from the point of view of evolution. At the same time it causes the disappearance, by terrifying epidemics, of unadapted species; the story of these disappearances can even be written. A small difference and a return to a reinforced stability; a small difference and there is unbelievable multiplication and uncountable destruction. Plague and flood. Endemic and epidemic diseases; variations of virulence, always small causes for either almost nonexistent or immense effects, on the left or on the right. The third that is excluded, when such logics are excluded, is quite simply history.

It multiplies wildly with its smallness; it occupies space with its imperceptibility.

A wire does not have to be heated very much for noise to increase. This excitement stops the message from passing. But sometimes it allows the message to pass, a message that cannot cross an unexcited channel. I shall not go into detail about the techniques of doping. White noise is the condition for passing (for meaning, sound, and even noise), and the noise is its prohibitor or its interception. Noise, or again, the parasite, is at the three points of the triangle: sending, reception, transmission. Heat a little, I hear, I send, I pass; heat a little more, everything collapses. The smallest increase, in one direction or another, can transform the entire communications system from top to bottom.

The theory of the parasite brings us to miniscule evaluations of changes of state. It installs unexpected chains where small causes or very tiny differences are followed by zero effects or by effects of return and better resistance or by immense catastrophic effects. Where enormous relations of force can be followed by barely perceptible effects if they get bogged down in the channel.

It is then easy to conceive of transformations of systems where the phenomena produced can change scale in the realm of the observable. This thing is very simple. An informational inclination, sown circumstantially, can sometimes produce gigantic effects on the entropic scale. It is difficult to think of the change in the inert, in life, or in history without being helped by this idea. Yet we didn't have it. In the human sciences, at least, the old mechanical model still dominates, even among those whose discourse talks of rejecting it.

There is no war.

He eats at the house of a great man—the greatest possible. In return, he feeds his greatness. He enjoys belonging. He lives in a sect; he shares an opinion, an ideology or a rule. Truth surrounds him like a shield; he no longer fears nocturnal terrors. He has finally become specialized; he has a method. He will wage war no longer. Surrounded by friends who are stubborn like him, who eat the same gruel from the same spoon, his enemies are only the enemies of his kind and of his difference; but they are rather far and their only function is to insure the existence of the pressure group or of the specialization. The division of work, parties, ideas, science, religions, and even countries, or of all space in general, produces little local kings who have open house where those who militate with drawn-out thoughts eat but never fight. Inversely, the partition into islands, closed classes or spheres, or disciplines is produced, quite simply, by the pressure of those who refuse to fight. It changes the outside into the inside. It is the network of minimum risk. It is rather stable. Sclerosis.

It is generally specific. To an animal, an organism or even an organ. During its cycle it can be carried from one vector to another, but the path taken, which is rather improbable and well-selected, remains constant; thus it is the path that is specific. It lives sheltered in the body of its host (or on his surface) that is its environment. The outside for it is the inside of another. Its outside is an inside. Thus the parasite has few enemies, for the simple reason that it rarely meets any. To avoid the hostility of the host, it sometimes copies some of the cells of the surrounding tissue. Thus it minimizes its risks by lightly transforming its own body, changing hostility into hospitality, exchanging outside for inside. Outside it meets challengers; it can be destroyed by the climate that is variable, by history that is improbable; it can die from the absence of hosts, be they intermediate or definitive. The set of these constraints—deadly ones—winds up pushing it into another type of relation. It thrives and develops by leaving the battle. It invents a life with minimal risk. Rather stable.

What is the good of opposing word to word, article to article and antithesis to thesis, sound to sound or idea to meaning, if by slipping into the channel, one can perturb the sound, meaning, thesis, and system at will? No trouble and no risk. Elsewhere I said that the circumspect strategist is not a dynamist; he doesn't care about forces; he is a topologist; he knows the paths, the channels, the lay of the land. In short, he is a geographer. Let the enemy come with one hundred divisions, armored tanks, and artillery if he will; I will make him go through the swamp; he'll get stuck and drown. The parasite of networks no longer wages war; no message is important, for it is lost among all the noise. The noise is distributed where meaning is rare, low chaotic waves from which the message emerges. Nothing is easier to produce than these little waves; nothing is more stable to conserve. The old kind of combat and the two fighters disappear in this fog.

When the fog clears, the two of them can be seen, now friends, associated and tied together; their only enemy is the bog.

The parasite has put down his arms. It has thus won the struggle for life. The theater of operations has changed locations.

The parasite is a differential operator of change. It excites the state of the system: its state of equilibrium (homeostasis), the present state of its exchanges and circulations, the equilibrium of its evolution (homeorrhesis), its thermal state, and its informational state. The difference produced is rather weak, and it usually does not allow for the prediction of a transformation nor what kind of transformation. The excitation fluctuates, as does the determination.

When a subject of this operation exists, its risk is weak and its expense, minimal. Its risk increases with transformation, if and when it takes place.

The excited molecules start to circulate more quickly. When warm, they are rapid; when cold, they are slow. They spin around.

The excited organism reacts. The flows accelerate; the ganglia swell; the defensive system is mobilized; the fever goes up. The organs' silence stops with this troubled health.

The evening spent around the table is rather warm and friendly; tongues are loosened and move quickly, each in turn; the conversation becomes general, witty, even a bit dizzying.

Heat, noises, whirlwinds.

The parasite was inevitable. I came from fire, from thermodynamic questions. I came from waters and turbulences, from fluid fluencies. The parasite is an inclination toward trouble, to the change of phase of a system.

It is a little troublemaker.

It was there, necessary, on my path. How can the state of things themselves be transformed?

Of Sickness in General

A tradition that merits reexamination called health the silence of organs. The silent body, so light that it floats in air, inspires, it is true, an angelic ecstasy. It might have first been believed that health was only the silence of the medical sciences, all astir from speaking of pathology. The normal does not say much, if anything at all; the norm is a line perpendicular to the horizon, the orthogonal, standing up straight, casts no shadow, as little as that of the sun at high noon. What can be said, then, of the right angle and of its force, except that its efficacy is at its highest point? The normal, like many of our concepts, is a crest, an optimum concept: maximum force and minimum discourse. We speak only of shadows.

Let us return to the sick man; let us forget medical discourse. Sickness is a noise. We called it a shadow. Are these metaphors? Not at all. This noise—is it pain that produces the complaint; is it fear, anguish, or strangulation that make madmen scream or rant? Yes and no. Sickness, of whatever variety, intercepts a function; it is a noise that mixes up messages in the circuits of the organism, parasiting their ordinary circulation. I doubt that a more general definition can be given. It is as good for cancer as for neurosis, for myocardial infarctions as for multiple sclerosis. Interceptions can take place along chains of neurons, or in the circulation of blood, or in synaptic spaces, or between the membranes of neighboring cells, or on the chain of the genetic code, and so forth. Sickness, in general, is parasitic. And the parasite intervenes at a given level. I do not doubt that pain and complaint, anguish and screaming, are various translations of these numerous noises. Language is another translation that associates, at its source, the voicings of pleasure induced by silent health. Sickness is a parasitic noise. And the doctor eats by translating this noise.

It happens, in particular, that an infectious disease is provoked by the arrival of a parasite, a virus, a protozoan, a metazoan, or a fungus. Introduced either permanently or temporarily in the organism of its host that is henceforth its environment, it intercepts flows, sometimes accelerating them, turning them in its favor at every level. This one is specific—in the digestive tract—for the oral cavity or for intestinal movement; that one is specific for the circulation of blood; a third is specific for the sebaceous glands; I shall stop this enumeration, which would last for volumes on end. The sum or a synopsis of these living creatures and their activities would tell us, I guess, that there are no channels, paths, or flows, that, at least in principle, do not have their intercepters. Each one has its niche, and few niches remain unoccupied. And inversely, he who has a niche is a parasite.

We usually name as parasites those beings that survive and multiply according to this mode alone, and we name as infectious the diseases induced in this manner. We never think to relate the interception of noise and this activity of these diseases because, in one case, living beings are at work, and in the other, a relation must be imagined. If the vector is different, the operation is nonetheless the same. Living systems are communicational systems in general; in any case, it is a question of the local decline of a flow.

Leriche says: sickness no longer appears to us to be a parasite living on man and living off the man it wears out. We see there the result of a *deviation,* minimal at first, in the physiological order. In sum, it is a new physiological order; thermapeutics must adapt the sick man to this new order. Admirable.

Following Paul Scheurer, let us call "derevolution" those simple and global discoveries that make one thought derive from another when one of the two is new in relation to the other. The history of the sciences is full of these derevolutions. The quarrels are produced by blinders.

What is a parasite? An operator, a relation. This simple arrow intercepts. It intercepts organic messages in a living system. Noise, perhaps, but language as well, often living. All doctors have the same profession, as we see. Let them speak, cut, give injections . . . they live and eat from the same profession. What is a parasite? A deviation, minimal to begin with, that can remain so until it disappears or that can grow until it transforms a physiological order into a new order.

All sickness, all medicine, is parasitic in this new way. Q.E.D.

Part Four

Midnight Suppers

Society

Impostor's Meals ————————————
————————— Analyze, Paralyze, Catalyze

Comic relief during the work. Molière, speaking through the character of Valère, says of Tartuffe: "The swindler who was able to impose* on you for so long." The word *impose* is well chosen. Tartuffe is an impostor; that is the subtitle of the play. It is usually understood as cheating, the swindler imposing himself. But the same word and the same meaning would teach us that he keeps, collects, or intercepts a tax [*impôt*]. The hypocrite imposes taxes on us to impose on us. To intercept the daughter and the wife, the money-box, the inheritance, the signature, and the deposit. To take, as is customary, the words, women, and goods. Tartuffe—"truffle" in Italian, tubercule, underground mushroom—is a parasite; he detours and captures. He is even the canonic example and the excellent model of the parasite. What is astonishing is that he has come to be the personification of a hypocrite. And the matter is so astonishing that it makes a problem. In other words, the imposture was eminently successful. For the term *imposture* has permitted us to forget its link with tax-collection [*perception d'impôt*], with the exaction of money. Imposture draws attention toward swindling, toward religious cant, and covers up the economic operation of diverting funds. Yet religion is not essential here. If it were necessary to rewrite *Tartuffe* today, he would be an ideologue, a political moralist, an intellectual of the avant-garde who fills his pockets and gets power by defending the rights of man or in playing the role of the sacrificed victim. If *Tartuffe* were told to me, I would make him an economist or a specialist in finance and in tax collection [*imposition*]. Oh! I have

Imposer means both "to impose" and "to tax." —Trans.

201

nothing to do with that, he says of all kinds of monetary impositions and exactions, it is because of growth, money, or productivity. Heaven has simply moved; the strategy hasn't changed. A Tartuffe always hides his local exaction behind a global theory.

Tartuffe entered empty-handed in a tranquil home, where he prospers; his conduct is parasitic: he diverts the will in his favor as well as the wife and the money; he chases everyone out so that he can be the master of the house. He imposes the following dilemma: exclude or be excluded. Hypocrisy only comes later: it is a means and a method. What is hypocrisy?

To avoid the unavoidable reactions of rejection, exclusion, a (biological) parasite makes or secretes tissue identical to that of its host at the location of contact points with the host's body. The parasited, abused, cheated body no longer reacts; it accepts; it acts as if the visitor were its own organ. It consents to maintain it; it bends to its demands. The parasite plays a game of mimicry. It does not play at being another; it plays at being the same.

I don't know if mimicry is entirely parasitic, but it is a necessary trick for the robber, the stranger, the guest; it is a disguise, a camouflage in local colors, when the locale is a host, an other. To feast at the wedding of the master, it is suitable to put on the wedding dress so as not to be thrown to the outside shadows amidst yells and chomping teeth. To begin with, I am starting with mimetic action in the sense of a chameleon, of a polar bear or a polar hare in the Arctic snows, of a butterfly that becomes a flower, of a walking stick, or of the black truffle in the earth—I don't know what it copies. Our group, this black box. It is an erasure of individuality and its dissolution in the environment; it is a good means of protection in both defense and attack. I am a bird; look at my wings, I am a mouse; long live rats. I am an other, *a* and *b,* once again a synthetic judgement and the birth of the joker and the white domino. We are now returning to the former logic. I am another. Ulysses is a sheep when he leaves Polyphemus's cave. Who will say what the Cartesian ego would have become if the demon of Descartes [*le malin génie*] had suddenly shown itself to be deadly and dangerous. It is no longer a question of the animal and its world—that is to say, of the chameleon in the grass—but of the animal and the other, of the parasite and the host-other. At this point it does not disappear on the horizon but into the milieu that is the other. It is thus the brother, the twin, the alter ego, the other finger of a single hand, the similar, and sometimes even more perfect than the original. Tartuffe is not only the pharmakon of the family, the one who will finally be expelled from their home, sacrificed by the prince and finally unmasked, for the happiness of the son and for the collective of the group; he is also—and especially—Orgon's narcosis, his narcissistic and twin homologue. And it is because of that that Orgon realizes nothing. Hypocrisy is only a moral concept, degraded in relation to mimetic action, which is itself an ordinary strategy in relation to the guest/host in its parasitic relation. Yes, my brother, I am . . . But the host speaks, he is a man. The human parasite will speak like him or will be silent. During two acts, no Tartuffe. He wanders about; he is there; he takes hold; he is silent. Under the crisis, under the decisive threshold.

In passing I mention the fact that the ray mentioned in the *Meno* to qualify Socrates' question is a fish whose name is that of the action of putting to sleep, narcosis (numbfish). The pharmakon is to the pharmacy what the narkon is to narcotics. One is of the collective, the other of the individual. The amazing effect of the fish is a drug among drugs. Let us admire the Greeks for having shown the intuition of seeing a pharmaceutical action behind an effect of magnetism or electricity of which they were not unaware. Let us admire their language, moreover, for having associated these physical phenomena that are quasi-medical or quasi-chemical with the myth of Narcissus, the proper noun for these common nouns. The Greeks already knew about the Northwest Passage, just as the Basque fishermen were aware of America, long before Columbus officially discovered it for history and for kings. The question of Socrates wakes us as the image of Narcissus reveals us. But narcosis puts us to sleep. Tartuffe is Orgon's narcotic; he puts him to sleep and then sucks him like a vampire (he puts him to sleep as Socrates puts everyone to sleep at the banquet in the *Symposium,* from which he leaves knowing himself); he reveals him as his double and him; he finally wakes him in the vicinity of death. Tartuffe is a truffle, and Orgon is an ogre. Predator or parasite—that is no longer the question. Twins like Narcissus? Who will eat whom? The question, I think, goes beyond the play.

At the same time—this is a mark of genius—the strategy of mimicry doubles the scenic action. Who can know that the parasite is a parasite, despite or by mimicry? The outside observers. And they are on stage. They are the spectators of the comedy played by Orgon and Tartuffe together. The audience is on stage.

Orgon comes back in; listen, now, to this burst of genius. The three meanings of the word *parasite*—physical noise (static), living animal, and human relation—suddenly start to beat time together to the same rhythm and with the same sounds.

Tartuffe is the guest here, imposing on Orgon, the third meaning. But a host, attacked by the animal, second meaning, usually winds up with a swelling or a toxic reaction. Thus, the hostess was feverish the day before yesterday, with a headache that is difficult to pin down. No one saw where her sickness might have come from.

Noise: and Tartuffe? First meaning. The parasite here straightens out the dialogue, like a semiconductor. The function of this righter is foreseen by Molière: whom the heavens, says Mme Pernelle of the animal, have sent here to right your wayward spirit. For he controls everything, Dorine had said of him. Tartuffe, director, conducts the flows on the paths: the metaphor runs throughout the dialogues. It describes from close up an intercepter on the paths. And that is the single meaning of the three meanings—one person in three functions. And it is always asymmetry, the asymmetrical operator.

The "and Tartuffe?" straightens things out, and the righter fulfills his function, the person like his name, the name as signal. The parasite-animal straightens the flows in his favor; the parasite-signal straightens the channel to point it in one direction, and the religious Tartuffe straightens out sinners, setting them on the road to heaven. But suddenly, and without being seen, the righter answers the question. Where does Elmire's illness come from? The hostess is feverish from the introduction of the parasite-animal.

An animal, we are told, who is in excellent health, plump, with vermilion lips. *Vermilion* is a marvelous word. It is the color of blood sucked by the mouth; but this blood-red color is that of a worm, the cochineal worm that gives scarlet. Tartuffe, a bit of a vampire, has a red mouth. He is big and fat like a worm [*ver*]. Vermilion.

Again, the imposture has succeeded; the parasite is well hidden behind his mimicry, behind his representation. The operation of collection vanished behind the activity of simulation. Everyone sees the hypocrite and sees the blindness of the host. Everyone is blind for seeing only the hypocrisy, for seeing only the mimicry. No one else understands what makes Dorine understand—that Elmire is sick, quite simply, from Tartuffe. That he is a worm, that he is a fungus in Madame's organism.*

"And Tartuffe?" is a noise that cancels reception and that goes back to the sending; it is the means of turning the dialogue toward asymmetry and toward one-directional movement. Dorine closes the circulation; she restitutes the other direction. She is the operator of symmetry. The parasite steals; she is the gift. She knows the laws of gift-giving and of exchange and cannot be fooled either by the theft or by the change. She is the gift; Dorine is quite properly her name.

Thus Madame, disgusted, cannot touch anything. The parasite

*We don't really know if this black truffle is symbiotic, commensal, or really parasitic.

eats two partridges, in whom you will recognize Madame and Mademoi-
selle. Fuck the mother and marry the daughter. You remember Rousseau: favorite of the master and his lady, lover of the young girl, etc., I
was happy. He can be.

She doesn't sleep; he sleeps. She allows herself to undergo a
bleeding. To restore this blood, he drinks four glasses of wine. The
question is resolved: what one loses, the second wins, and that's the law.

But suddenly the law says something else. In the balance of exchange, or in the one-way flow, the hostess loses blood and Tartuffe
gets wine. The vermilion mouth doesn't get exactly what the organism
gave up. Between blood and wine, between wine and blood, a new
process appears that tradition calls transsubstantiation.

The question of Tartuffe is suddenly turned over as it already
had been: what is religion doing here in the parasitic relation? Religion
is not the subject of the play; it is the problem of this comedy.

The end of the play is said to be botched, awkward, and artificial, and the intervention of the king is felt to be as absurd and arbitrary as that of a *deus ex machina.* The host is thought to be done for,
and the officer who comes to execute an order assigns the opposite
order, all of a sudden. His mouth blows hot and cold. Yet he is the
officer of a M. Loyal. We would like to think him thus. Absurd; what is
there to say?

The whole question of the play is the parasitic question. Two
commensals or two symbiotes live together, sharing their goods. Here
the movement is irreversible; everything goes from the master to the
impostor, and nothing is returned. As Orgon is not infinite, the process
approaches an end. And this end is emptiness. The more the vase
poured, the emptier it got; today, despite the prayers, there will be no
miracle. No more money, no more daughter, no more strongbox,
emptiness, cleaning out by emptiness. Tartuffe absorbs everything, including the owner. Outside. What is amazing about the parasite is that
perhaps it is infinite. The whole question of the play is there: who will
leave? Who will get out? Who empties? In other words, who is excluded?

He occupies space, not *de facto,* but *de jure.* By civil, political,
martial law. He has won. His nest is the nest of another. Let's not have
any noise, I beg you. Let's get out of here without a fuss. You must immediately leave the house. You have to leave, you who were speaking as
the master. The house belongs to me, and I have enough to punish the
imposture and to make those repent who speak of having me leave.
Who empties whom and who empties the area?

And the answer is obvious: the host. The host is always excluded.

Who is the host today? Certainly Orgon, and Tartuffe as well, both together at the same time, and I think, with the same relation. The mouth of the officer really blows hot and cold, like that of the guest of the satyr. Stay and leave. Everyone here is the host of his host; that does not simplify the opposition of the master and slave. Someone is mimetic; go see whom. The officer coming on stage, like Loyal himself, I think has decided to expulse the guest. And he falls into a situation of exact mimicry where language itself has decided not to decide. Hot or cold, tragedy, comedy? What will happen?

A while back I called the parasite the third. The purely logical question returns, the question of the excluded third. It is a question of principle. It is a question fo exclusion, which is not purely logical. It is the question of absurdity, here at the end of the play. The absurd, as we know, consists in the third not being excluded. Here, then, is one question in three parts, to be answered all at once. Tartuffe, parasite, is introduced into the house, and there is immediately a crisis: the fever rises; everyone talks loudly—a house misruled. From the beginning, the grandmother goes out; she frees herself from the family in crisis. Fever, disorder, noise, and expulsion as the curtain goes up; problem and solution are exposed together. The denouement is already there. But the expulsion of Pernelle is nothing, for the crisis and the noise continue.

Who, then, is always put in the third position, including in family or private life? We no longer have a place to argue in freedom without being observed. Tartuffe, parasite, is introduced into the house; that means that he is in the third position everywhere. He attacks relations more than beings. He is, first of all, the third between the grandmother and her family; he cuts off their dialogue; he is the third between husband and wife, between father and daughter, between mother and son, between Valère and his fiancée Mariane, between the master and his trustee. He is third in secrets of love and of the State. Draw the elementary relations of this kinship and you will not find one where he is not playing the third position. It is in that that you recognize that the action is finished and that the exaction—or extortion—is finished. It is the logic of epidemics: the virus multiplies; it goes everywhere. The action of the parasite is to go to the relation. It instinctively goes to the mediations, occupying them all. It intrigues. This third, it must be said, is included. It is included by the master in his own house; it is distributively included in every relation. It intercepts all the relations between all the locations. It captures all the flows. It is the included third.

That is absurd; that is absurdity itself, and nevertheless it is so. Like the denouement. At the height of the action. Tartuffe is everything everywhere. He is the brother of the father; he is his heir; he is the husband of the wife and the lover of the daughter; he is the owner.

Name all the characters—he has substituted himself for every one. When one controls relations it is certain that one controls men as well. His mimicry is more than just hypocrisy: it is nothing at all to say that he plays at being devout, since he also plays at being the father, the brother, the son, and the lover. He is the joker, placed everywhere at once, at the same time, and with the same relations. Who is Tartuffe, black truffle, black box? Does he even have an identity? Can it be said that it is a question of the explosion of the principle of individuation? Who is Tartuffe who is so many different metamorphoses at the same time? Is he the actor? Is he the actor, the one who plays such-and-such a character? The parasite, the madman, the joker, and the actor—how are they varieties of impostors? He is a and not only a; he is b as well; he can be the inverse, the opposite, the contradictory. A is b, Q.E.D. This is the very logic of the denouement. It was not possible; well, look, it is possible. We were warm.

Hypocrisy means subdetermination, what is under the decision.

After the turning point, Tartuffe is no longer the only one in the positions of interception. Mimicry is reciprocal and always wins more than we think. After playing (on) others, others wind up playing the game. The parasite is supplanted. He is in the third position in the relation of Orgon to Elmire, and suddenly the cuckold cuckolds the cuckolder. The cuckold puts himself in the third position in the relation of Elmire to Tartuffe. He goes under the table, where he listens. Damis, the son, in the dark cabinet, also captured messages not destined for him. The parasite is mimetic, yes, but the host starts to imitate the guest. One only becomes free of these parasites by parasiting them in turn. The whole thing, from this point on, is demonstrated. The host is the guest of the guest. That does not arrange human relations nor does the decision of the officer. That is all quite absurd; what is there to do?

If the parasite excludes the host, he immediately commits suicide. Where can he live and on whom? That is the paradox and the absurdity of epidemics that do not stop for lack of microbes but for lack of hosts. The death of hosts is the death of parasites. They are completely stupid, suicidal, in their juggernaut-like logic. That is what the tragic is. Increasing, unending escalation, blind to its consequences. It always ends up with an empty stage, a clean one, cleaned by emptiness, where the dead pile up to the very end. The tragic is the flood and the blank plain.

If, on the contrary, Orgon excludes Tartuffe, he will have been taxed enough for the comedy and his family will save its own skin. They will eat at the wedding feast, where there will be new wine and perhaps some ambrosia.

Decision on the level of the meta-question. Did you pay for the tragedy or the comedy? On the razor's edge, where the thirds are included, where everything is still possible, I think the prince winks to the audience and decides, that evening, for comedy. There is comedy when people still remain on stage at the end. The story is not over.

It was only a sickness; it wasn't death. An eruption, a fever. Bleeding was cure enough. The parasite with his vermilion mouth fled from under the knife.

The canonic character of comedy is the sick person. He makes the audience laugh, for he is wearing his bedclothes and his nightcap, and his bed is a mess. Yes, tomorrow, he will be up and about.

The Proper Name of the Host ————
———————————— Masters and Slaves

Molière did not talk just about the devout. He noted, wounded by nocturnal activity, works of animals that we fear to be alive. He touched on the collective and its composition, the collective as a complex of relations, the collective as a simplex. The invading progression of Tartuffe in the family follows the logic of epidemics. As if by multiplying, the parasite reaches all the possible relations between the members in order to intercept them. Thus it paralyzes the simplex. Logic of epidemics for its growth, logic of paralysis for the symptoms.

Tartuffe brings about a crisis in the family, as does every parasite. But perhaps the relations were shaky to start with. Perhaps it was already uncomfortable before he came. Perhaps he is only evening out what is already there. Perhaps the sound and the fury had already been announced by a noise. Perhaps his ejection contributes to the reconstitution of a group in the process of falling apart. Positioned as the third on every relation, Tartuffe is the observer and analyst. Introduced at first, included everywhere, withdrawn or excluded at the end, he is in the position of a catalyst. He paralyzes, analyzes, catalyzes. He is the included third; he is the excluded third. He is well-grounded in the logic of analysts.

An observer must enter the black box or the closed system and get some information for himself or for his knowledge/science: not for me, an individual, a person, says Tartuffe, but for heaven. All that is necessary is to change heaven to understand the positions that generalize one of them. From this point on, he can only destroy the existing equilibrium or increase an already formed distance. He introduces a new asymmetry, a new flow, another capture. He disorganizes the

209

box; he transforms it; it is something else when he leaves. He analyzes, he catalyzes, and sometimes he paralyzes.

The experiment introduces a noise in the message of the box, a parasitic noise. There is no intervention without interception. The experiment withdraws and captures some of the information of the box; it parasites the box. It is understandable that the global entropy of the laboratory increases at the end of operations. Suddenly I'm speaking of epistemology.

Tartuffe is no longer, as he just was, the hero of an action that the family sees, as do we. Everything is overturned; he is the observer. The spectators are no longer on stage to enjoy, like us, the twin movements of the ogre and the truffle, the game of who will eat whom. Everything is overturned. Tartuffe observes, as do we through his eyes—the game of the collective and its metamorphoses. He is not a joker; he is Molière's emissary. He is perhaps Molière himself. Masked, so as not to be seen. But what is the joker, if not a pile of masks?

Theoretically, observation costs nothing. Just a bit of light. The limelight, lighting the work of Maxwell's demon. But the experiment costs something: energy and information. Knowledge is paid for. Of course, it is positive, favorable, and asymmetric; otherwise everything would be blank; there would be no science. But something must be put on another level. Tartuffe, they say, makes the error of loving Elmire— that is an error, a trap, an investment, an experimental rigor. Nothing would have happened without this love, this heat, this fire, that comes by and suddenly flares up. Without this light, we would perhaps have seen nothing. The black box would have stayed black.

I am once again on the razor's edge, if there is a razor. I am once again in the Northwest Passage. The same epistemology speaks in two voices for the physical sciences and for the human sciences. Observation and experiments suppose interceptions, one-way flows, asymmetric balances—in short, branchings and parasitic operations. Knowledge parasites the world, parasites objects, systems, black boxes, and laboratories. It is a general undertaking of pumping out and capturing of information. If, one day, the parasite invented the exchange of material for logicial at his host's table, and vice versa, he also invented science and theory the same day. What would all knowledge be without this asymmetrical, crossed exchange? This irreversible capture.

From this point of view sciences, both human and physical, are united. I shall show it. Tartuffe is a hypocrite, they say. What does that mean? Introduced into a collective, he gives rise to crises. Hypocrisy, assuredly, means nothing else: sliding under the crisis. But the crisis itself is a state of transition between two phases that can be pinpointed, where a transformation will be decided, where it has not yet been decided. The crisis is the state of the swinging of the balance beam, before the judgement is made. Bergson said: dichotomy and double frenzy. Criticism is exactly the court where one decides, chooses, judges, divides. Better yet, where one cuts. At the end of *Tartuffe* we saw how the denouement, the officer of the court, and literary criticism balance each other. There is nothing more coherent or more rigorous: it is a question of the height of hypocrisy, of its apex, its acme. It is under the crisis; it is this under the decision. It would be better to say that hypocrisy is the art of not deciding. Have you ever seen a hypocrite decide? But the human and social sciences that have to do only with fuzzy subsets are immediately hypocritical. They are engulfed in unstable states. There is thus an easy way to slide under Kant, and to get him at his own game. Hypocrisy of fuzzy reason. The word *subdetermination* translates into Latin what *hypocrisy* says in Greek; or, better yet, it says in epistemological language what we wanted to say in moral discourse. But physical theory is obviously subdetermined. Its history would otherwise be closed. It can be falsified by the experiment and observation of the day after tomorrow. Or by something observable remaining unobserved. Better yet, it is subdetermined by all or any possible observation. It can be said to have hypocritical status. It is always in the fuzzy denouement of *Tartuffe*. Very little literature strays far from science, and much brings us back to science. Very little science strays far from literature, and much brings us back to literature. Logic and anthropology are found in the same strait(s); subdetermination has to do with all knowledge.

Every parasite that is a bit gifted, at the table of a somewhat sumptuous host, soon transforms the table into a theater. Thus comedy is first of all a feast. One eats, speaks, speaks of eating, stops eating to speak, all amid the noise. Thus the passage from the material to the logical occurs. The court jester, in a representation, well-fed with a full meal, starts, rather unwisely, to tell the truth, to precipitate crises, withdraws at the moment of rupture, and tries to save his neck when the global balance is being drawn up. Thus the satire is first a meal. Interrupted and ridiculous. Nothing could be understood of the stable presence of the banquet in the middle of these cultural institutions of language if it were not a question of the speaking subject, of the transformation of vital, material, and living energy into verbal, disordered, or linguistic information. The parasite is the location and the subject of the transformation.

The collective, at the table, makes noise. The collective, finally, can be unanimous starting with this noise.

If Tartuffe had not loved, he might have gotten out without a loss. Today, like many others, he would be rich, listened to, he would be a representative or a cabinet secretary [*ministre*]. He loves, takes a risk, succumbs. He should have stuck to language. But he is not caught entirely because of this *faux pas*. He is not protected by the king. Molière goes further in his criticism, and there is the threat of a scheme. He takes a risk and does not succumb. His glory remains immortal today, and in his own time, the Sun-King liked him. Molière sends Tartuffe up front: it is not I, says the author, who observes, analyzes, paralyzes, it is not I, it is he, my character, my emissary, my lieutenant, my mask. It is he who is my pawn, pulling out the truffle from the fire, and it is I who eat the black diamond. Tartuffe is the advanced observatory of Molière, his licensed experimenter, his spy. The powers always deny their secret services. The author can now only condemn the character, and he is then safe. Not seen, not taken, we can begin again, and so we shall. Who is the parasite here? Who, in the end, sweeps the board?

There are many portraits in the parasite gallery. How small energies carry away big ones, how words win over things, and lies over love, and small change over substantial sums, and non-sense over meaning. The less one is involved, the more one wins; the less one invests, the less one risks. This one will not go bankrupt; he does not risk his money; he is not docked for striking; his job does not depend on the fluctuations of the market; he describes prosperity with a pen that is as cold and objective as when he evaluates the possibility of a crisis; he is an economist, and thus, prince or senator. And if he is in grave error, he shall be awarded the highest power. There is no sanction for an error of language. There is no fall in the logicial. It evolves in serenity. The logos cannot be trapped in material traps. Not because it lies, but because it is wind. The dangers of life are too big for its light rustle. The more one is up-to-date [*dans le vent*] and up-to-date on what is up-to-date [*dans le vent du vent*], the more one is in the text and in the glossing of the text [*l'explication de texte*], and in the theory of this glossing, the less probable the sanction. And that is why they all look so good on the portraits. They can't be wrong, and they can't fool us. The gallery will soon occupy the museum; the museum will soon cover the whole city. The Tartuffes multiply much more quickly than truffles.

Science develops its theory via observation and experimentation. It also changes the material for the logicial; that is its technique and its method. No one accomplishes this sublimation with more control and security than the scientist. He has even tried to eliminate lying along the way. Science collects as much information on the state of things as it can, and if it can, all information available. Experimentation and observation suppose parasitic branchings and balances that are always in favor of those who intercept. In this sense, the scientist is not very different from the farmer or the animal breeder. In fact, he generalizes their movements. Instead of drawing subsistence from some variety of flora or fauna, he draws it from some division [*découpage*] of the object in general. In the end, he has an incredible store of information. It is impossible for this one-way flow that comes from or is drawn from the states of things not to finish by making them deviate. The very existence of the sciences changes the world from which they came, changes the world into which they go, through which they pass, and from which they come. Application is not only a return of information onto the observable from which it comes. It is the changing of things by the very presence and activity of knowledge. The great theoreticians like to withdraw their responsibility for virtual or actual catastrophes that come from their inventions or discoveries. They discharge that responsibility onto the engineer, the technician, the politician. Like Molière with Tartuffe. The one who implements the information gets burnt by the fire of the furnace or of his love for Elmire. He is disclaimed, disavowed. But I think that everything begins with the pure activity of observation or collection as such. The application is already there. It drives a wedge into the system and makes it deviate. Generally, only very small energies come into play, too small to make the process perceptible. But sometimes it is, and this happens more and more. Knowledge, yes, analyzes, paralyzes, catalyzes. And thus it is a parasitic activity that transforms milieu and society.

I think that the battle of *Tartuffe* forced Molière to take extreme positions. A full year, in his somewhat isolated retreat at Auteuil, where he sees only a few friends, La Fontaine or Boileau, he reads Plautus and writes *Amphitryon*. These extreme positions are not stubborn; I mean that it is not at all a question of opinions about the devout, about religion, or about other touchy subjects that critics of the previous generation had fed on so often. They are, I think, logical positions, like a theatrical or anthropological strategy, in the three cases of the elements of theory, theorems. *Tartuffe* certainly was the theory of the parasite, of the parasite who hides to live better at the expense of his host and household. If we went to the limit? If we imagined a parasite who was gifted with all powers of mimicry and transformation and who, far from speaking of the sky, came from it instead? If we imagined Tartuffe happy with Elmire? Today then, the parasite is god; he is Jupiter, god of gods, which suggests that at the maximal level of his power, the king, the all-powerful, is a parasite. He comes down from his supreme glory, and in order to enter into everything that pleases him, he completely leaves himself, and it is no longer Jupiter who appears. He changes into anything, not just the human form: bull, snake, swan, for Europa, Leda, and so forth. The perfect joker. Zeus in a white domino.

This passage to the limit of mimetic power is meaningful. Since
the Platonic apologia on Gyges' ring,* we know that the power to become invisible is an important selective advantage for getting into
people's houses. To rob the neighbor, to fuck the neighbor's wife, to
guess secrets, to play the spy, and to become king. The story of Gyges
is round, like his ring; it can be read in every direction. If you can be invisible, you will become king, and if you are king, you have as much
power as the invisible. Power is invisible; it is the white domino. It is
the joker, multivalency.

Gyges replaces the king and marries the queen. Jupiter is substituted for the king and sleeps with the queen. One reduces his presence
to zero; the other makes himself identical to the other. Henceforth,
Tartuffe is nothing more than a mediocre artisan. We have attained great
logic. Given the principle of identity, a is a, the shepherd is the shepherd, and I am who I am. This principle starts to vary. The variation
goes from zero, Gyges, who is nothing more than a wisp if he wishes, to
this multiplicity that is virtually infinite: Jupiter is a bull, a shower of
gold, Amphitryon, a snake, anyone, anything, the one whose place he
takes, or the one whom he chases from his place, or anything that can
be used to get into the other's house. It could be said then that this
"whatever" is equivalent to zero or that the something in general is
equivalent here to zero. That the white domino, supreme dominator, is
that indeterminate nothing that is worth everything in general and anything in particular. But it is not so simple. Jupiter is identified with
others or with animals. When he becomes a thing, I have never heard it
said that he changes into anything but gold. The present theory of the
general equivalent thus generalizes the classical theory, since the latter
is included as a specific case of the former. Zeus is a shower of gold when
the obstacles are really hard to overcome: Danae is in a bronze strongbox buried in the ground, yet the money mixes in through the cracks.
The ordinary theory of the general equivalent explains the omnipotence
of money by its power of metamorphosis. What remains to be explained
is why the power is changeable, why the change is power itself. Why?
Because an element, a being, a relation, a thing—whatever—suddenly invades space and time. It grows from the local to the universal. It is
everywhere. It is ubiquity. The eye is in the tomb and the shower of
gold in the bronze enclosure. Nothing in the world is a black box for it.
Night falls for everyone but for this white/blank dominator. And it is
thus that Hermes, his emissary, his son, speaks with Night in the pro-
logue to the comedy. Stop your chariot, he says; the invisible will aid

*For the story of Gyges, see Plato, *Republic*, 359D–360D and 612B, as
well as Herodotus, I, 8–13. —Trans.

the gods who see in the dark. Power is the passage from the local to the global.

Metamorphosis is omnipotence. It occupies space by crossing black boxes; it occupies time by transformations. No, it is not that; yes, it is always that. It reconciles the wisdom of Solomon and the abundant multiplicity of the discernable. The invariant under variations, or the incarnations of the mind under the variety of figures. God—that is to say, Nature, universal synthetic judgement. Here is the dawn and it is God; here is the tree, it is God; here is the jaguar, it is God; you are here, you are God and I love you. Here then is the infinite of God, His infinite intelligence and the infinite space He occupies. But if time is only this yes under the no, this persistence abraded away, this third that is always being included or excluded, nothing has changed, humanity begs history, its last discourse of pantheistic theology.

Here then is what Tartuffe has become. He is God, he succeeds in perfecting his metamorphoses, the night bends to him, and Hermes, discourse, is his son. That is the extreme position, the maximal logical strategy. Yes, the battle of Tartuffe is nearing an end, and with what a victory! The only thing left is to make the comedy of the parasite; it is done and finished. The term *impostor* will appear here much more often than in *Tartuffe; or The Impostor.*

But the comedy of the host has yet to be written. I still have to say who can be the host. The one who eats is always spoken of, but never the one who is eaten. In any case, since then, *Amphitryon* has become the proper name for "host," and almost its common name as well. The true Amphitryon is the Amphitryon at whose house one eats. This principle of decision is useful and effective. The comedy, for once entitled with the same proper and common noun, doesn't need its subtitle: the host.

The king has left his palace to fight the enemy far away. Out of sight, out of mind. The king has gone a-hunting and lost his place. I have long maintained that hunting is a mistake, for it immediately makes parasitism possible. Someone fills the empty space. Here it is the hunter himself, since Jupiter is Amphitryon.

The host is far away; he is not the host. But in the palace, another Penelope is waiting—Alcmene—whom the king of the gods gathers at home and then consumes on the spot, in her own bed. If the host is not host, the hostess is always there; she doesn't move.

The host here is a woman. The woman is the universal hostess. She is conceived thus and she conceives thus.

Amphitryon is away with the Teleboeans, really far away. She waits. She is first of all the host of the guest. And as the parasite changes

into Amphitryon, even the host is a parasite relative to her. The woman
is a host relative to whom every other host, even the greatest of the gods,
can and must be judged to be a parasite. As if parasitic logic stopped at
her door and involuted in her uterus.

She receives the universal parasite, Jupiter. She receives all the
power of metamorphoses in herself. She envelops the transformation.
She carries the formation. She is the universal hostess of the universal
parasite. The twin, or rather the complement, of the white domino.

Is mammalian reproduction an endoparasitic cycle? What is an
animal that can reproduce only by another animal, inside it? What is a
little animal that grows and feeds inside another? It seems to me that
it is a parasite, the one who finds a milieu of reproduction and develop-
ment in another animal, though this other be the same.

Alcmene will bear a man and a demigod.

The woman, the universal hostess, is the χώρα, the smooth
space, the wax tablet, on which everything can be written. The χώρα is
a topological space before all measure and mastery. It is even deeper
still. It is the space or the box relative to which inclusion and exclusion
are thinkable.* The included third and the excluded third require a terrain where one can come and go, a referent for these operations: here it
is. The universal hostess is the transcendental of these logics, the matrix
for thinking.

The host does not speak much and is not understood; his logic
is paradoxal. It is fuzzy; it is our own. His parasites are eating him up,
and their noise covers his voice. Who is the host first? Before everything,
an object. The old distinction between subject and object is another
reinstallation of the parasitic arrow. The simple arrow goes between
them. The subject takes and gives nothing; the object gives and receives
nothing. As we have no theory of relations, we are still astonished by
the poles and the stations, the substances, the names, and we believe we
have said it all when we understand relations as couplings or combinations. No. The arrow is between; it puts the centers in parentheses; hence
this book of metamorphoses: fox, lion, philosopher, impostor, what
does it matter? Subjects, as they say. That is the advantage of the fable.
The simple arrow thus fills space, pulling everything from above (upstream) and running irreversibly. The further we go down, the more we
speak, the more noise there is. Moving back up, the space is more
hospitable, and calmer, peaceful, tranquil, silent.

*See Plato, *Timaeus*, 52B. —Trans.

I go back up the arrow toward the object. The naked object there such as it is. Science and knowledge always get the lion's share; they always win, as I've said before. I am aiming for an epistemology, a rare and secret one. Is it conceivable to reverse the arrow for a moment? Can we conceive of the earth enjoying us? The supernatural beauty of Tuscany and Umbria, the flowering of space under the sweat of the peasants' brows. Beyond the flame of Los Alamos, the Nevada desert did not exactly flow with milk and honey; beyond the bright mushroom cloud of Nagasaki, the ruins blackened in their otherworldliness. If our work and sciences were exchanges, they would leave masterpieces in the world at the height and splendor of their intelligence.

Can the rights of the world and of things themselves be written? The host speaks; the host-object demands the snake, the cow, the tree, the steer; for once, ask. The woman. Ingrate, they say. Must a right of objects be written? I must write at least the right of men and of groups to refuse to be studied. To refuse if they want. The right of texts to be read, in their simple form and not swollen by stiffening or toxic effects. I shall write this new right starting tomorrow. It is urgent.

Cuckoldry produces an included third. Being a cuckold is being a logical being. That is something. The jealous person excludes the third. He invents the excluded third. Being jealous is being a logical being as well. Molière is a logician; he is an epistemologist. And if he is a sociologist, he is, unwillingly, a sociologist of science. There is much exclusion there, and not only in logical operations.

The parasite cuckolds, the host is a cuckold, and the worm is the hostess. This is a great configuration; it made the greatest minds meditate in the age of great classicism.

How does the parasite usually take hold? He tries to become invisible. We must speak of invisibility again.

He becomes invisible by becoming very small. Bacterium, worm, virus, bacillus, phage—seldom if ever larger than the size of an insect. It passes, sticks, enters; it is small and inside now. Animal parasitism is the work of invertebrates; it stops with the mollusks and the arthropods. It took man millions of years to baffle the traps of this smallness. And we have not yet finished protecting ourselves.

He becomes invisible by hiding. Gyges disappears; Jupiter is transformed into the same. Power is disguised in ideology and the persecutor in a benefactor, the enemy in an organ and the voracious person as an austere one, the military soldier as a militant for peace. The host is determined only by the space where the feast is, and it is simple economy that decides. Molière didn't see things too badly.

He becomes invisible by making, on the contrary, a lot of noise. One can hide by being too visible or too perceptible. The parasite hides behind the noise and to-do of the devout.

He becomes invisible by being impossible. Impossible, absurd, outside reason and logic. That is what is interesting; that is the point; that is what must be thought about. He becomes invisible in the inconceivable.

Absurdity is the third included in the world where the excluded third dominates.

What is he doing there, the one who isn't, since he shouldn't be there? That is all absurd. More than invisible, more than blind, deaf, the one who does not perceive him. The parasite is invisible, and it is impossible. And the host is a receptacle. He is the location relative to which the included and the excluded will define themselves.

A first mimetic square shows Jupiter, god of masters and master of the gods, Mercury, god, but the son of the preceding and his temporary slave, Amphitryon, Theban general, victorious strategist, and Sosie, the valet or the slave. The twin doubling produces unexpected relations.

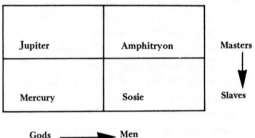

The couple Zeus-Hermes is divine, and thus the master of the couple Amphitryon-Sosie and cheats it, beats it, and cuckolds it. The couple Zeus-Amphitryon is magisterial, dominating the servile couple Mercury-Sosie. Thus the masters are gods for the slaves.

Jupiter is the master of Amphitryon; he is the master of the master. But he is also the master of Mercury and the master of the slave. Amphitryon is the master of Sosie, and he is the master of the slave, but he is the slave of Zeus; he is thus the slave of the master. Mercury is the slave of Zeus; he is thus the slave of the master; he is the master of Sosie, and he is the master of the slave. Sosie is the slave of Amphitryon; he is thus the slave of the master; he is the slave of Mercury; he is the slave of the slave.

Zeus	Master of the master	Master of the slave	Amphitryon
	Master of the slave	Slave of the master	
Hermes	Slave of the master	Slave of the master	Sosie
	Master of the slave	Slave of the slave	

Everything seems to resemble everything else, but this is not so. Everything seems to be symmetrical, balanced, not resolvable, absurd; the die is cast though, and the parts have already been given out behind the scenes.

Everything seems to lead to combat; everything seems to lead to war, to rivalry; everything comes from it, so it seems, and everything goes to it, as we know; everything passes by it, as we see: the general arrives, still smoking from the battlefield, glorious from his victory and from the death of Pterelas, the Teleboean rival; Alcmene gives birth to Herakles, who, from his first day, in Plautus' work, smothers two serpents, and will never stop filling a world infested with monsters, with corpses, and with carnage with the monsters infesting it; that is the genealogy of Hercules; everything occurs here on stage: Mercury thrashes his Sosie; Amphitryon, rival of the sovereign of the gods, pulls out his sword, brings to the rescue several rough-and-tough old soldiers; everything stays cold though. Sosie doesn't fight, nor does Jupiter. They are at the end of the chain and know so. Mercury and the general do not fight; they fight someone or talk swaggeringly. There is no war. Or there is only a war when the result is certain. There is a murder but not war. There is no equality. There is no face-to-face. There are never any twins. Zeus takes everything and gives nothing; he transforms himself when he wants and flies upward when violence erupts. Sosie gets nothing and gives everything; he gets only orders and blows to sustain him, and he is excluded from the table. The hierarchy dominates the stage rivalries—those of appearance.

Everyone carries a local square for himself that strongly resembles the global square, in their asymmetry.

MM   SM   MS   SM
MS   MS   SM   SS

The misfortune of asymmetry and of the world itself never permit the slave to become the master of the master nor the master to become the slave of the slave. There are always crowds of Hermes between the god and the servant to intercept the whole affair. Basically, there are more resemblances between Amphitryon and Mercury, who have only crossed relations, than between those who seem to resemble each other on stage, those who are made up for appearance. The transformations do not form a closed circle; they multiply the mediations monotonously. There is no war between Jupiter and Sosie; there is no question of that; it never took place nor will it ever take place. This fundamental war—avoided—decomposes into conflicts and mimicries that are regulated beforehand. The master wants to resemble a master and struggle with him; the god wants to be the master of a god; in both cases it is to laugh. The mediations are always there to replace the war and to multiply. A master of the slaves of the master can be imagined; he is frequently met on the roads of mastery. And so forth. The chain doubles inside; there is branching out and not closure.

The logic of battles is that of the excluded third. Only time, says Leibniz, the order of successions, can make contradictions appear in the state of things. Hegel, reversing the definition, makes contradictions the motor of time—and a logical mistake. A long night is needed for divine (pro)creation, and the sun comes up on that of man. Night and day, we must decide. Amphitryon or Jupiter. One husband or a single lover. In front of the house, in front of Alcmene's bed, at the door of time sleeping between her legs, the two masters, swords in hand, or thunder, want the other to be excluded from this spot of pleasure [*jouissance*]. Night or day—man is a stranger to the dawn. The masters' logic is a logic of breaks and cuts.

It is not Alcmene's logic; it does not even appear in the square of the inscriptions. At night, she receives Jupiter in her bed; and after the dawn, when the gods flee, she opens her bed to the mortal to appease his violent desires of the morning. The bed, the breast, the house, boxes where the third is included. It is not Alcmene's logic, whose uterus holds Herakles, Zeus' son, Iphicles, Amphitryon's son, born respectively at ten months and at seven months, at the dawn of the long night during which she was fertilized by God. The third included again, two twin sons yet not twins, of father who were twins and not twins; yes and no are possible, in space and time under the same, yet different, relations. Herakles is Hera's glory, the glory of the wife of the lover; everything is included that is excluded. Iphicles is the glory of the force, while the force is, in fact, in Herakles. There are no exceptions to the working of this other logic, the logic of superfetation, the logic of the receptacle.

The logic of the battle is the logic of decision: one strikes, cuts, or hits. Sosie, gourmand, wants to enter the banquet. No, says Hermes, I want to go in, I, your twin, and I shall exclude you from the wedding feast. The dining room is still a box from which he must be excluded or in which he must be included. Henceforth, we shall say the box in general—bed, house, uterus, or simply dining room. That is precisely the spot of the parasite. That is precisely the hostelry. That is precisely the host's space, the χώρα where the parasite wants to feed, sleep, survive, and multiply. The spot where the host is both the local man and the stranger, that of the interior and the exterior, of the inside and outside, of the included and the excluded. Here, logic and anthropology speak together with one voice, the voice of George Dandin, for example. And of so many others as well.

Only Sosie will enter the banquet. The matter is far from being undecidable: it is always the gods who enter the banquet; the poor never go in; the law is immutable. Mercury prevents Sosie from entering. The latter then proposes his logic, that of Alcmene, or that of the slave. The name we both bear; we can both have it under the same master. Everywhere I am taken for Sosie; I allow you to be Sosie; allow me to be him as well. Let's leave the two Amphitryons to their jealousy; and amidst their squabbling, let us peacefully let the two Sosies live. No, no division, no. I shall be the younger; you shall be the elder. No, I want to be an only child. At least allow me to be your shadow. Never. Neither younger, nor little, nor wispy like a somewhat dark trail. The law is immutable. The parasite is more at ease if his likeness is invisible, hidden, small, impossible. Then he supplants him. And thus the law is immutable; if you have the audacity to go in there again, you will be beaten. Sosie, yesterday, today, and tomorrow; Sosie is always chased away from here. He is the third; he is the excluded third who announces and pronounces the logic of the included third, that of the host.

Jupiter, Amphitryon, Mercury, somewhat master, somewhat god, god and master, are on the side of the excluded third. They hold the thunderbolts, the sword, the stick. They decide; they cut; they strike. The three squares of the large square function to exclude. Only the last square keeps the included third: I accept you as equal; allow me to be your brother. But the large square is only an illusion; it is only a hierarchic order with Jupiter at the head and Sosie at the end. The included third is only a local singularity in the order, a rarity of slavery. The immutable law is universal; local singularity is an exception. Being a brother, being an equal, being at peace, are very rare miracles. The monotonous universal law is the law of thunder.

Theorem. This law excludes Sosies; it chases out the thirds from here. Metatheorem. This law excludes all other laws. This logic chases out other logics. The logic of the excluded third is produced to occupy the stage; it excludes the logic of the included third. Who no longer has anything to say; the best is to say nothing. That is the end of the comedy.

No, it is not violence; no, it is not resemblance. It is only comedy. In Plautus, a third is still included—it is tragicomedy. It is representation. If twins appear, the world is turned around. If two men start to fight, everything stops. Theater begins. Stop me, I tell you, or I will create misfortune. The chorus is there, restraining the hero. Dialectics is the logic of phenomenology. Of the discourse of the phenomenon. That is to say, of appearance. We must begin to take all that seriously. Dialectics is the logic of appearance. The logic of opposition is the logic of appearances. War makes believe. There is no conflict. No one risks his life against an equal force, except perhaps to laugh, except on stage, except in the theater, hold me back, then, I beg you. *Tragediante, comediante.* No twin in front, except for the scenery and the false window. Open your eyes and look at them fight asymmetrically. Here is real logic, hidden behind grimaces, behind Captain Matamore's rodomontades. The Germans, speculative or specular, I don't know any more, took this comedy from Italy seriously. Blusterers, bullies, braggarts, swashbucklers, swaggerers, and daredevils have left the stage to figure in sublime philosophy. They dance around and tell of their incarnations. Historians applaud the histrionics. Everything occurs in the realm of appearances; we never leave the theater. And the citizens are deceived.

No, Jupiter leaves as soon as the earth starts to flare up a bit. Amphitryon, about to fight, immediately leaves. To come back with a lot of men. Zeus is willing to fight, with thunderbolts in his hand, if no one else has any thunderbolts. The general draws his sword, but he is the only one. Mercury hits with the stick, but Sosie has no stick. He would be a twin; he would be a perfect double [*sosie*] if he were equally armed. Amphitryon does not have sovereign power either, like the one who copies him. He does not have the power to change into Jupiter. Sosie cannot transform himself in another Mercury. Everything is asymmetrical, and the die is cast. The egalitarian mimicry and opposition in hand-to-hand combat with the slave against the master in a closed field, fairly, each with his means and with the grace of God—that never happens. Has never happened, will never happen. Except on stage, to entertain and make believe, to write history. To give more importance to the professionals of power. Murder, yes; war, never. Too risky. He who loves power is always a coward. Always afraid. Always a capon, a coward, a chicken-shit. He is always behind, behind the one who sticks his hand into the fire. The lover of power is a weakling. And we protect the strong from the weak. The weak play the comedy of the strong. They play the bully as long as there is no danger. They surround themselves with arms, weapons, nuclear warheads. They have four lackeys and never go anywhere without a whole police squadron. Always absent from battles, but they gather the benefits of the conflicts without being in the conflict. Assassination, yes; war, never. Too risky. Even here, especially here, the abuse value is the immutable law. The contract is not there, even, especially, in the opposition. No one ever waged war without having been sure of winning it. Except in sports, a glorious uncertainty, or in painting, George and the dragon, on a mass of cut-up corpses, or in the movies, in comedy, where the dead rise up to salute, in politics, in the theater. Antithesis is appearance; opposition is a grimace; struggle is a semblance. Crime, yes; war, no.

——— *Theory of the Quasi-Object* ———

Hoc memorabile est; ego tu sum, tu es
ego; uni animi sumus.

Plautus, *Stichus*, v. 731

What living together is. What is the collective? This question fascinates us now.

The problem with the preceding meditations is that they do not say distinctly enough whether they are a philosophy of being or of relation. Being or relating, that is the whole question. It is undoubtedly not an exclusive one. I still shall not decide whether the parasite is relational or real, whether it is an operator or a monad.

I want to think that this noise I constantly hear at the door is produced by a being whom I would like to know. I can also think that the one who eats my food or who eats with me as my companion, drinking my wine, is only a useful figure for thinking about adulthood, my fatigue at the end of the day, explosions, losses, hidden power, and the degradations or bursts of messages in the networks. This good and bad Hermes is a god, the god who has prepared my old age and who has not been substituted for the one who made my youth joyful, a god like love, the son of fortune and passivity, a god, yes, that is to say: a being or a relation? The true God, in classical theology, is The One in whom relation produces being, in whom love produces the body, in whom the word, the logos, the relation was made flesh.

I have not said enough whether the parasite is being or relation. It is, first of all, the elementary relation.

What then, once again, is living together? What is the collective? I don't know, and I doubt that anyone does. I have never read anything

224

that taught it to me. I have sometimes lived through certain events that make a little light in this dark. And sometimes, next to a dinner companion. This black category of collective, group, class, caste, whatever, is it a being in turn, or a cluster of relations?

The ferret [*furet*] * smells a bit; it smells like a skunk, with which it is often crossbred. It thus occupies space. We return to property. It is the vampire of the rabbit, following it into its warren; it throws itself on the rabbit, biting its nose or neck, sucking its blood. We have domesticated the ferret and no longer know about the wild variety. We make it run for us, like the buzzard, like the kestrel; we parasite them. We muzzle the ferret before introducing it into the system of the burrow; the crazed rabbit leaves through another hole and is trapped in the net. Once more, a nice diversion of flows in a network.

We have all played the game of hunt-the-slipper or button, button, who's got the button. The one who is caught with the *furet* has to pay a forfeit. The furet points him out. One person is marked with the sign of the furet. Condemned, he goes to the center; he's "it"; he sees, he looks.

What is the furet?

This quasi-object is not an object, but it is one nevertheless, since it is not a subject, since it is in the world; it is also a quasi-subject, since it marks or designates a subject who, without it, would not be a subject. He who is not discovered with the furet in his hand is anonymous, part of a monotonous chain where he remains undistinguished. He is not an individual; he is not recognized, discovered, cut; he is of the chain and in the chain. He runs, like the furet, in the collective. The thread in his hands is our simple relation, the absence of the furet; its path makes our indivision. Who are we? Those who pass the furet; those who don't have it. This quasi-object, when being passed, makes the collective, if it stops, it makes the individual. If he is discovered, he is "it" [*mort*]. Who is the subject, who is an "I," or who am I? The moving furet weaves the "we," the collective; if it stops, it marks the "I."

A ball is not an ordinary object, for it is what it is only if a subject holds it. Over there, on the ground, it is nothing; it is stupid; it has no meaning, no function, and no value. Ball isn't played alone. Those who do, those who hog the ball, are bad players and are soon excluded from the game. They are said to be selfish [*personnels*]. The collective

---

*The *furet* is the animal, the ferret, as well as the marker in a game somewhat like hunt-the-slipper or button, button, who's got the button? —Trans.

game doesn't need persons, people out for themselves. Let us consider the one who holds it. If he makes it move around him, he is awkward, a bad player. The ball isn't there for the body; the exact contrary is true: the body is the object of the ball; the subject moves around this sun. Skill with the ball is recognized in the player who follows the ball and serves it instead of making it follow him and using it. It is the subject of the body, subject of bodies, and like a subject of subjects. Playing is nothing else but making oneself the attribute of the ball as a substance. The laws are written for it, defined relative to it, and we bend to these laws. Skill with the ball supposes a Ptolemaic revolution of which few theoreticians are capable, since they are accustomed to being subjects in a Copernican world where objects are slaves.

The ball circulates just like the furet. The better the team, the quicker the ball is passed. Sometimes the ball is said to be a hot coal that burns one's fingers so badly that one must get rid of the ball as quickly as possible. Let us appreciate the metaphor, used by Kipling: the red flower scares tigers, and the golden bough is not far. The ball is the subject of circulation; the players are only the stations and relays. The ball can be transformed into the witness of relays. In Greek, the word for "witness" is *martyr*.

In most games, the man with the ball is on offense; the whole defense is organized relative to him and his position. The ball is the center of the referential, for the moving game. With few exceptions— like American football, for example—the only one who can be tackled is the one who has the ball. This quasi-object, designates him. He is marked with the sign of the ball. Let him beware.

The member of the offense, the one carrying the ball, is marked as the victim. He holds the witness, and he is the martyr. Here and now, precisely on him, everything occurs. The sky falls on his head. The set of speeds, forces, angles, shocks, and strategic thoughts is woven here and now. But, suddenly, it is no longer true; what was supposed to be decided isn't; the knot comes undone. History and attention bifurcate. The witness is no longer there; the furet moves and starts chasing another rabbit in the network of passageways; the ball is outside the park; there is no sacrifice—it is deferred until later; the martyr is not this one—it is another, and again another, and why not another one again. Everyone. The game is this vicariance. It is the graph of substitutions. Priests, victims, dressed in blue, red, or green? No. Strictly vicars. Vicars by the mobility of the substitutions and by their speed. Sacrificer now and very soon a victim, soon neutralized, quickly changing by the moving ball, in the playing field, marked off as the temple once was. The sacrificed person can, through skill or strategy, send his neighbor into the shooting gallery instead of him, and the neighbor can do the same. Thus, with the ball, we are all possible victims; we all expose ourselves to this danger and we escape it; the more the ball is passed, the more the vicariance changes, the more the crowd waits breathlessly. The ball shuttles back and forth like the furet, weaving the collective, virtually putting to death each individual. The reason that the victim appeases the crisis is that uncapturable knowledge that we all bear, under the voice that says "I"; we know that this victim can be "I" as well. The ball is the quasi-object and quasi-subject by which I am a subject, that is to say, sub-mitted. Fallen, put beneath, trampled, tackled, thrown about, subjugated, exposed, then substituted, suddenly, by that vicariance. The list is that of the meanings of *subjicere, subjectus*. Philosophy is not always where it is usually foreseen. I learn more on the subject of the subject by playing ball than in Descartes' little room.

While Nausicaa plays ball with her companions on the beach, Ulysses, tossed about by the waves and the undertow, saved from the shipwreck, appears, naked, subject, beneath. Child of the blade, child of the passing of the ball.

This quasi-object that is a marker of the subject is an astonishing constructer of intersubjectivity. We know, through it, how and when we are subjects and when and how we are no longer subjects. "We": what does that mean? We are precisely the fluctuating moving back and forth of "I." The "I" in the game is a token exchanged. And this passing, this network of passes, these vicariances of subjects weave the collection. I am I now, a subject, that is to say, exposed to being thrown down, exposed to falling, to being placed beneath the compact mass of the others; then you take the relay, you are substituted for "I" and become it; later on, it is he who gives it to you, his work done, his danger finished, his part of the collective constructed. The "we" is made by the bursts and occultations of the "I." The "we" is made by passing the "I." By exchanging the "I." And by substitution and vicariance of the "I."

That immediately appears easy to think about. Everyone carries his stone, and the wall is built. Everyone carries his "I," and the "we" is built. This addition is idiotic and resembles a political speech. No. Everything happens as if, in a given group, the "I," like the "we," were not divisible. He has the ball, and we don't have it any more. What must be thought about, in order to calculate the "we," is, in fact, the passing of the ball. But it is the abandon of the "I." Can one's own "I" be given? There are objects to do so, quasi-objects, quasi-subjects; we don't know whether they are beings or relations, tatters of beings or end of relations. By them, the principle of individuation can be transmitted or can get stuck. There is something there, some movement, that resembles the abandon of sovereignty. The "we" is not a sum of "I"'s, but a novelty produced by legacies, concessions, withdrawals, resignations, of the "I." The "we" is less a set of "I"'s than the set of the sets of its transmissions. It appears brutally in drunkenness and ecstasy, both annihilations of the principle of individuation. This ecstasy is easily produced by the quasi-object whose body is slave or object. We remember how it turns around the quasi-object, how the body follows the ball and orients it. We remember the Ptolemaic revolution. It shows that we are capable of ecstasy, of difference from our equilibrium, that we can put our center outside ourselves. The quasi-object is found to have this decentering. From then on, he who holds the quasi-object has the center and governs ecstasy. The speed of passing accelerates him and causes him to exist. Participation is just that and has nothing to do with sharing, at least when it is thought of as a division of parts. Participation is the passing of the "I" by passing. It is the abandon of my individuality or my being in a quasi-object that is there only to be circulated. It is rigorously the transsubstantiation of being into relation. Being is abolished for the relation. Collective ecstasy is the abandon of the "I"'s on the tissue of relations. This moment is an extremely dangerous one. Everyone is on the edge of his or her inexistence. But the "I" as such is not suppressed. It still circulates, in and by the quasi-object. This thing can be forgotten. It is on the ground, and the one who picks it up and keeps it becomes the only subject, the master, the despot, the god.

Once again: on war, struggle, combat, and opposition. Murder is a principle. Crime is a principle. The all-out war of all against all never took place, is not taking place, and will never take place. One-on-one combat, lists, three-on-three struggles, Horatii and Curiatii, are appearance and spectacle, tragedy, comedy, theater. All against one is the eternal law. Three Curatii against one Horace, when appearance is torn like scenery and when the real must be reached. The result is always certain, and the war is asymmetrical. The parasites arrive in a crowd, and they take no risk. Sometimes, miraculously, the situation is reversed, with Horace the winner. It is spoken of then; it is the stuff that history is made of, and that makes us believe in the phenomenology of war. Horace was stronger than each of the other three, fatally wounded. The law never changes.

Here the process is even finer. The game is so deep that we must constantly come back to it. The combat of all against one is deferred by the flight/theft of the ball; vicariance and substitution constantly divert the path to the necessary result. They make our attention wander toward the beautiful combat of a spectacle where glorious uncertainty reigns, morale is safe, and people speak of nobility. And everyone rushes to the spectacle and bets on who will win and who will lose. It seems to be chance, since it's a game. Though it is only chains of necessity. The decline of sports today into prearranged games shows, as if it were necessary, where the principal attraction is and what it is really a question of. Everything always moves toward a war without risks, toward crime and theft, toward pillaging, looting, strongarming men and things. Use always comes from abuse and returns to it when the derivation disappears and no longer provides a constant change of rival.

Every theory of derivation consists in orienting our attention on rivalry; the word itself tells us so.

The furet, the ball, are tokens in a game, passed from one to another; they are probably jokers. The construction of the collective is done with jokers and an amazing act of building. Anything is built with anything. This logic is highly undetermined and is the most difficult to note.

Let us consider another joker, so undetermined that it is, as we know, a general equivalent. It circulates like a ball, money, a quasi-object. It marks the subject; it marks it effectively: in our societies, Cartesian meditations are soon written; I am rich; therefore I am. Money is integrally my being. The real doubt is poverty. Radical doubt to the extreme is misery. Descartes cheated; he should have gone out, a new Francis of Assisi, and gotten rid of his goods. Descartes cheated; he didn't throw his ducats into the stream. He never lost the world since he kept his money. The true, radical Cartesian is the cynic. Descartes never risked losing his "I," since he never risked his money. He never played his *malin génie* for high stakes—for the shirt off his back. He never was caught in the rain, in the mud, never asked the king passing by to stop blocking his sun. I have always doubted this doubt that does not go to the zero level of possession. A rich fool is rich; a poor fool is a fool. A rich "I" is rich; a poor "I" is an "I." We would then see who this man is.

The construction of the collective has been done with anyone and by means of anything. The furet is nothing, a ring, a button, a thing; the ball is a skin or an air bubble. I pass them or throw them to whomever they meet, someone who receives nothing or almost, it doesn't really matter.

The question still remains: what things are between whom? Anyone, you, me, him, that one, the other. And between them, these quasi-objects, maybe jokers. The stations are "they," circulation is done by "it," and we have written only a certain kind of logic.

In the same way, money is not much because it is everything; it is exchanged with the first passer-by, and another steals it from everyone, and another hoards it for no one.

These quasi-objects are blank, and the subjects are transparent. But interest increases with opacity and blackness.

The position of the parasite is to be between. That is why it must be said to be a being or a relation. But the attribute of the parasite, until now not mentioned, is its specificity.

It is not just anything that troubles a passing message. It is not just anyone who is invited to someone's table. A given larva develops only in a certain organism and is carried only by a certain vector.

Orgon must be devout to be parasited by Laurent and Tartuffe. Devout and something else besides for the adaptation to be perfect. The mix-up must marry the channel, must fit on its wavelength, must be easily superposed on the emission. Jean-François, Rameau's nephew, would not have had a chance in Mme Pernelle's son's house. I can make as much noise as I like; I shall not prevent my neighbor from seeing the sunrise. Fleas die on pebbles.

How is it that I love you; you, among a hundred thousand, me, and not another? Is it an illusion; is Don Juan's catalogue a wiser way of doing things?

We have reached the limits. Mammalian reproduction is an endoparasitic cycle. We parasite each other to speak, to eat, to organize injustice and legal extortion; for these projects everyone is good. We parasite each other to reproduce and multiply, but for that, these others must be both other and same, and they see each other naked. Not just anyone, not just anything, will do. A quantity of sperm, introduced in a box that is foreign yet adapted to it, thrives in it and is nourished by it; specificity begins. The fetus is a protean parasite, and remains so somewhat after birth. For how long? The evaluations vary. In the end, it is better to say forever. Weaning is only local. Man's child does not live by bread alone, or by milk, air, and heat; it needs language, information, and culture as well to form its environment, a milieu without which it would die. This milieu is human, properly human, produced by the small group: the parents, the family, the tribe, the clan, I don't know. If parasitism in general supposes that the host is a milieu or that the productions of the host constitute the environment, the niche necessary to the survival of the one placed there or who moves around there, we are all parasites of our language(s). It is only today that I understand my mother tongue, and why my tongue is my logicial mother. Sometimes those who have no mother throw themselves headlong into language.

Perhaps it is necessary to paint the event of the Pentecost as a group of newborns eagerly sucking the breasts that are the tongues of fire. My language is branched on my tongue. I seem to send and to give around; I receive my words from this niche; to speak is to feed. To speak is to suck the breast of the common logicial mother. The word is born of this mother, always a virgin, since she is always intact somewhere, since the language always exceeds my command of it. Here the parasite-noise is identical to the one who dines at the *table d'hôte*. I feed myself endlessly at the buffet of my language; I shall never be able to give it what it gave me. I am the noise of its complicated harmony, or its wail. I would die from not writing; I would die of not taking my feast of words with a few friends, from whom, somehow, I get my language. I shall never be weaned from it.

Not language in general, but my own. Specifically mine, that gives me daylight in the hubbub of foreign languages. I like its chamber music quality, the modesty that is almost deaf and dumb of its tonic accents, its somewhat nobiliary distinction, its secret Hellenicity, and its rare earths.* My mother (tongue), about to die, becomes a virgin once more; no one uses her local words any more; she is used for a thousand everyday uses; they all use her like an old rug or a whore. They try to rape their mother as she lies dying. I want her to be beautiful and alive as she was during the time that he who wanted beauty on earth spoke my mother tongue and fed on its modesty. It succeeded miraculously in being universally chaste.

Between Egypt and Canaan, during the days of famine and thin cows, wheat circulates on the donkeys in the caravans, and in the sacks of wheat, the money that Joseph got from his brothers, that Joseph returned, that circulates both ways and thus has no direction/meaning, and the cup circulates in Benjamin's bag, the cup of Joseph that marks Benjamin, the cup of the youngest brother that marks the youngest brother. Joseph was a victim, and Benjamin, thanks to Joseph, can again be a victim. He is marked with the sign of the cup. The long-sleeved tunic was stained with the goat's blood, and the cup was, at that time, empty of wine. Both of them marked by the absence of their blood and by the absence of their wine.

I shall never be able to be nourished by a language of money, a flat, tasteless language like a big bank note. No smell, no taste, shiny, viscous—lots of these are found. When language converges on money, it monotonizes its flow; it tends toward the whitest and flattest quasi-object. It

---

*Obviously, Serres is talking about the French language. —Trans.

extends its empire at the same time as money. It builds temporary, soft collectivities. Its power is parallel to its viscosity.

One does not simply eat the words of a language; one tastes them as well. Those who eat as quickly as possible find that a bit disgusting and repugnant. There are gourmands, however. One speaks as one eats; style and cooking go together—vulgar or refined. Words are exchanged as food is passed either like fast food, so as to move on to something more important, or in an atmosphere of ecstasy. It depends on us for certain quasi-objects to become subjects. Or rather: it is up to us for this transformation to take place.

Words, bread, and wine are between us, beings or relations. We appear to exchange them between us though we are connected at the same table or with the same language. They are breast-fed by the same mother. Parasitic exchange, crossed between the logicial and the material, can now be explained. At Pentecost, the new-born apostles, suckle the tongues of fire, divided and coming from a single base; at the Last Supper, everyone is a parasite at the master's table, drinking the wine, eating the bread, sharing and passing it. The mystery of transsubstantiation is there; it is clear, luminous, and transparent. Do we ever eat anything else together than the flesh of the word?

Our quasi-objects have increasing specificity. We eat the bread of our mores; we drink the wine of our culture; we speak only the words of our tongue—I am speaking, of course, of unfit people like me. And love, I ask you: what about love between two people? Here, then, is the specificity.

We are not individuals. We have already been divided; we are always threatened anew by being. Zeus, unhappy with our insolence, cut us in two; that is easily seen by looking at the navel, where the skin is brought together as if by tight purse-strings. We once had four legs and four arms, a round neck, two faces, four eyes that were strong and quick, and when we ran, we rolled on ourselves, limbs outstretched as eight spokes of a wheel so as to go very quickly. Zeus split us—he can do it again; in that case we would have to hop. Does the real individual have one foot, two feet, or four? Unlike Oedipus, I don't know how many feet a man has. Thus we were of three sorts: male, female, and androgynes, according to what we have—two dissimilar or two similar organs. As soon as the punishment of Zeus took place, the sad, severed halves ran to one another to intertwine, to unite, and to find their plenitude once more. Love is a chimera, the leftovers of the split-up parts. Thus spoke Aristophanes, the comedian, at the table of tragedy.*

Thus spoke comedy, the parasite of tragedy. Today everyone is

*Plato, *Symposium*, 189C–193D. —Trans.

invited by Agathon, the Good, crowned winner in the tragic contest—
everyone, including philosophy. Everyone drinks the wine of tragedy.
Everyone is the guest of the Good; we are all in the tragic hospitality or
the hostility of this morality. We all speak of love to pay our share of
the banquet. Love is the discourse of this reimbursement. Wine and
bread are transsubstantiated in this word, wholly due to tragedy. I speak
of love to acquit myself of my debts for the food given by the tragic.
If scales exists somewhere, love is in one pan, counterweighing the
tragic, seeking equilibrium.

Who are we, according to comedy? We are tesserae, tesserae of
hospitality, a quasi-object or rather a demi-quasi-object. A tablet, a
cube, or a piece of a bone that friends for bed, that companions for
food and drink, in short, that the host and his parasite, share by breaking. They break the tessera and produce a memorial. This is memorable,
says Plautus; you shall do this to remember me. The breaking of the
tessera is not a clean break; it is somewhat fractal, complicated in any
case, so random that it is individual, so serrated and notched that it is
unique. The tessera is an individual; it is chance; it is complex; it is a
memorial. Who am I? Unique, filled with lots of information, complicated, unexpected, thrown in the whirlpool of the aleatory, my body is
a memorial. The hosts and guests have made their farewells; they keep
the tessera, each having his fringed half. They travel; they die; they love;
perhaps they will never see each other again. They give the tessera to
their children, to their friends, to their grandnephews, to those they
want, to those they love. Through time and space, the one who has it in
his hand will recognize his exact other by this sign, this specific, adapted
interconnection. There is no other possible key for such a look, thanks
to stereospecificity.

We are tesserae and locks. Beings or recognition, like sema-
phores. Tokens, be they true or false. The false kind can adapt to everyone, whorish, fitting like an old shoe. My whole body is a memorial of
you. If I love you, I remember you.

Ἕκαστος οὖν ἡμῶν ἐστιν ἀνθρώπου σύμβολον ... * The word
tessera is a Latin word that never really stayed in the French language;
the Greek word is mine; every one of us is a symbol of man. Who am I,
once again? A symbol, but especially the symbol of the other.

The symbolic is there; it is divided and is not divided. What is
the symbol? A stereospecificity?

It is also a quasi-object. The quasi-object itself is a subject. The
subject can be a quasi-object.

Symposium, 191D. —Trans.

Sometimes the "we" is the passing, the signing, the drawing up of the "I."

On the Compiègne road, three blind, pitiful beggars yell to the passers-by. The clerk of the fable gives a bezant; he does not give them this bezant. They have it; they are blind; they don't have it. They feast the whole night through; they eat and drink; they sing. The quasi-object tends toward zero, tends toward absence, in a black collective. What passes among the three blind men can be, quite simply, a word without a referent. Reciprocally: without a referent, we are only blind men. We live only by relations.

Mad, quasi-mad, feigning madness, the host is well enough paid with an exorcism.

The Empty Table ─────────────────────
──────────────────────── *On Love*

They feast around Agathon on the day of his victory in tragedy. Good doesn't win every day: event, miracle. And still, he only triumphed on stage and behind the masks. Thus it was not true. Nor is it today. In the house of Good, at his table, they feast, they drink the good wine of the Good Lord. Who are they? Are they the inextinguishable gods?

A story is told that someone else recalls having heard told by a third, who . . . Mediations, relations—one can make believe one is lost in this fractal cascade. Some branching is immediately free or taken up again elsewhere; bifurcations follow one another; the teller is always supplanted. Let us evaluate the losses of the ball in this game of passes. The comparison between what is restituted of the message by Xenophon and by Plato immediately gives the victory, not to the host who celebrates it, but to the parasites. No, it was not tragedy; it was the horse race of the Panathenian games. The house was not the house of the winner, but that of his father; no it was not Agathon; it was Autolykus; no Pausanias wasn't there, but Critobulus was . . . Everything has changed; nothing is constant; the chain has been mutilated beyond all possible recognition of the message. Victory is in the hands of the powers of noise. We are no longer in mathematics: we are in the philosophy of history, or at least not far from there. We come to doubt the singularity and even the existence of the event, of which it is said that it is the referent of the texts. The only invariant is Socrates, but so disfigured that the only invariant is his name. Did some Socrates drink with a few friends? Victory to the parasites, those who eat and drink and who have hidden so well that we no longer know their names, their number, or

235

their presence, shadows, victory to the parasites on the chain that erase the very chain itself, victory to the parasites who erase their own footprints as they go by, victory to the parasites who have disappeared, named, appearing to substitute themselves for others, drinking and drunk, eating, eaten, snapping up the bread and snapped up by history.

History in general as it is written or told is a network of bifurcations where parasites move about. With their noise they prohibit us from hearing the noise of the parasites who are eating and the noise of the history they are making.

Parasites make history, a feast, a banquet, noise of chewing; parasites make us forget all that.

This noise does not always come from the heart or bowels of the earth. But sometimes it does.

The noise heard at the door temporarily stops the rats from eating the leftover ortolans. Why is it always the rats' point of view? Why don't we think of what happens to the host? He never sees that there are rats there. The door opens: no one is there. The table is immobile and the obscurity is quiet. Nothing has happened. The host closes the door and goes back to bed. The noise starts again, the noise of chewing, history. He gets up again. He opens the door suddenly. There will never be any rats.

The observer makes the observed disappear by bringing along his noisemakers. His sandals make the floorboards creak. He told his wife that he was going to see what was going on.

People always talk about the light that is indispensable for seeing and observing. Even Maxwell's demon needs this light.

People hardly ever talk about the noise attached like a string to the tongue, indispensable for speaking; people hardly ever talk about the signal attached to the sign. Noise of the mouth, of the teeth, of the lips, so close to the repulsive noise of an eater.

History as it is told makes a noise with its tongue. Science and logic make a noise of the logos. They can be considered to be null.

Whom do these noises make flee?

Quasi-blind, in tatters, pitiful, losing his limbs and his skin in patches and clumps, the leper moves forward with a rattle in his hand. Flee, good people; sickness is coming. The signal, ahead of the leper, makes a desert. No one. Sometimes, out of charity, the ladle, bread, a banquet. Behind him he leaves horrible pellicles.

Here and there, tongues can be heard that, by dint of their

noise, make the things about which they speak flee. Cowbells, hand bells, cattle bells. The signal of their signifier makes their referent flee.

Behind them they leave fragments. Pieces of texts and references. Tomorrow there will only be quotations. After Plato and Xenophon, the *Deipnosophistai* of Atheneus of Naucratis could be signed Bouvard and Pécuchet, copying, copying, copying as before.* Attaching detached fragments, leper.

This. Here this is. *Ecce homo.* I make history of it: I speak of it. It makes so much noise that it erases everything it says.

Intuition speaks silently or speaks softly enough so as never to scare things, to tame them a bit. Oil the door and silence one's steps to surprise the rats a bit before they leave. Perhaps film them among the bones and scraps. But only parasites have this genius for being invisible. I define the position of Gyges—that is to say, of Jupiter as Amphitryon, etc.—and history, alas, begins again.

The most objective history is the parasite, supplanting all the rest.

Cover noises with noises or pass silently?

Who bells whom? The cat? The rats, if they can. The cow? The farmers. And it is the parasite-noise of the parasite that eats.

Science has made a deafening noise since the bombings of Hiroshima and Nagasaki. It also leaves monstrous fragments behind. Who flees at the sound of these explosions? The world? Men?

The observer is perhaps the inobservable. He must, at least, be last on the chain of observables. If he is supplanted, he becomes observed. Thus he is in a position of a parasite. Not only because he takes the observation that he doesn't return, but also because he plays the last position. In the realm of the visible, of sight, and of evidence, either he is invisible, like Gyges or like a subject among objects, or he is the least visible. Don't let yourself be noticed; keep under the wind, for the realm of odors. Thus the parasite is the most silent of beings, and that is the paradox, since *parasite* also means noise. Small, protozoan, insect, it is invisible; it cannot be felt; it copies so as to disappear; it puts on a spotless white shirt; it keeps quiet; it listens. It observes. No. No, since the rats in the attic make the noise you know at the farmer's table. In

---

*The reference is to the last lines of Flaubert's *Bouvard et Pécuchet;* the novel's protagonists, at the end of the text, sit down to copy as they once did. —Trans.

fact, they make less noise than the door that creaks and the steps of the one who is ready to open it. In fact, the observer did not see the rats because he did not evaluate his own noise relative to theirs. The observer always makes less noise than the observed. He is thus unobservable by the observed. That is why he troubles and is never troubled, that is why he is an asymmetric operator. He supplants by essence and by function.

He is in the position of the subject.

The subject [*sujet*], thrown [*jeté*] down, as his name indicates, is the last of the series. If he is not the last, he is no longer the subject. It is not the one who makes no noise, but the one who makes the least noise.

Knowledge plays and has a run of luck.

Stories are related and told; we go further and further back. At the end of this end without end, we play with the illusion of attending the feast of immortality itself. Are they gods, the ones who eat and drink there, since we now know that they are not men?

Does the series of stories or relations copy these half-erased tracks sought by researchers looking for myths of origin? Pure series of light and shade, where the essential is never anything but the law of the series and never that toward which it leads.

Are they gods then? Certainly not. Perhaps allegories, prosopo-poeias, figures of speech or style. Perhaps they are Ideas: comedy, Aristophanes; philosophy, Socrates; medicine, etc. The genres/genera drink; the Ideas feast; they speak of love on the couches of the Good. A palace of abstractions.

Let us suppose that a Platonic Idea is there, in front of us, seated or lying down, it doesn't matter. We know that it plays the role of the attribute common to perceivable things that resemble it, that partici-pate in it, and get their name from it. All the beds in the world get their appearance from this common bed, this ideal bed, all men of the per-ceivable world from this ideal man, seated or lying on this bed, it doesn't matter. If the concept is realized, if a given, existing entity, even one outside the perceivable, is made from this Idea, be it man or bed, it is clear that it is juxtaposed, in another space, with the things whose Idea it is. Thus, in a third space, there must be a third man, seated or lying down, it doesn't matter, on a third bed, to take into account things and their Idea, which would then begin to participate in these very third, receiving their appearance and name from them. The third man is the attribute common to the set formed by the set of perceivable men plus the ideal man seated or lying down, it doesn't matter. And the operation begins again; as we expected, it is interminable. Philosophers do not detest these inexpensive infinites. I must say that this universal produces a difficulty: if I represent man in general, or comedy in general, seated or lying on the bed in general, this bed that would have all the characteristics, would immediately become individualized by the fact of that exclusion. It becomes unique. Thus Aristophanes, the comedian, is there on his bed, seated or lying down, it matters little. We'll have to start over. This figure is called the argument of the third man. The Idea becomes an image; it flees into the images of the hall of mirrors, a series of pure light and shade, where the essential remains the law of the series, and where one never finds what it leads to.

We shall never be at the foot of the bed of the gods. The story pushes what it tells ahead of it. Apollodorus gets it from Aristodemus, I don't know any more; someone else gets it from Phoenix—I don't find that astonishing. This sort of relation and of continual passing is constantly reborn from its ashes. Play with the idea that Phoenix is the son of Phillip, the clownish, parasitic Phillip of Xenophon's *Symposium,* who makes the others laugh by grotesquely imitating the dancers. The story always sends us back to another story. We do not know the argument of the third man; it appears only in the *Parmenides* (132a) but it is already there, alive, I mean spoken. I really think that it is always there in the philosophies that are horrified by the world. They all have a little strategic mechanics to reject the referent indefinitely ahead.

Either in history or in the philosopheme; either in the story told or in the rebegun reasoning.

Given a small simple system, a relation between two points or instants. Let us suppose for a moment that this relation functions badly, that there is noise in the channel, that there are parasites. That can happen, that can happen by chance, and perhaps that is what chance is.

Someone or something must intervene to reestablish the relation. Malebranche said that Descartes' God constantly had to regulate the clock of the world, which was always becoming out of order. Leibniz preferred a music box that was preestablished for all time, since God was resting. Hence the minimal evil and harmonic communication. Let us intervene to reestablish what is not preestablished. We do so to facilitate the relation, to optimize it, to simplify it. The intervention, however, complicates the system; it multiplies the branches of its graph. It enters into a bifurcation above; it makes a graft. The system, now more complex, probably gets more noise and its exposed to more parasites. This growth is fatal. We must intervene again; a third system is built. The new branchings are parasites. It never stops: that is the system; that is its history. The breakdown that happens to the one who is going to repair the breakdown. Evil fills space.

If there is a difficulty somewhere, create a commission. It will

meet in a plenary session to invent solutions. I already hear them dis-
puting with one another, even though I am only at the door. Who will
be president, who represents whom, etc. The arguments begin and really
never stop.

The argument of the third man feeds itself. Plato, remarkably,
tells stories of banquets where stories are told of other banquets. The
argument of the third man feeds itself at the table; it is parasitic. The
parasite is the third; it is indefinitely the third.

The day of Aphrodite's birth, the gods have a feast. No, it is not
Socrates who speaks; it is Diotima. No, it is Apollodorus, then Diotima,
the stranger from Mantinea, who came from far away, less from a spot
than from a number, where you can easily read the prophetess or
divination. The unfolding never stops, two bottoms, three, boxes in
boxes. Black.

We're finally here at the door of the feast of the gods. We have
arrived at the stable spot, the final referent. We shall finally see and
know. The banquet of the banquet of the banquet, the end of the series,
the point of accumulation.

No, we stay at the door. It opens a bit to leave a passage for
Poros. For Poros, a little god, completely drunk on nectar, on nectar,
for in those days men had not invented wine. But who is Poros, who
comes out of the black box? Alas! he is the passage itself, the path.
Poros is the name of the passage.

The initiation is dishonest. We have been cheated, completely
cheated. From the beginning, we have moved from discourse to discourse, either written or told; we have gone from box to box; each is
empty and contains the following; the explanation or the reading goes
from implication to implication; we are out of breath, waiting, in sus-
pense. Finally the black box is there, finally the true one, the true banquet, that of the gods, no longer that of ideas or of genres/genera, no
longer that of allegories, of figures of style or speech, of useless words,
but the banquet, where one really drinks the drink of immortality,
where good really wins, where love is finally love and no longer a
punishment, where wine is not drunk for illusions and hangovers, but
where ambrosia finally gives the invariability of what is. We have arrived.
The door opens. We don't go in. Someone leaves through the door. Who
is it? The door itself. They made fun of us. The only information that
comes out of the black box is that there is a channel through which
information passes. The only message that comes out of the path is that
there is a path by which messages pass. A thread comes out of the box.
The only thing that passes in the channel is the name of the channel.

I am a tired reader, out of breath; I've still read nothing after having read so much and run so much; I am in the position of Penia, misery. Starved, glued to the door. Beggar. I wait for bread; I wait for wine; I ask to be fed. Penia asks nothing else but the end of something to chew on. I require a bit of referent. Nothing. Penia gets knocked up. She is given only what costs nothing. They say, of course, that she had this idea herself. So they might well wish! If you meet a starving woman, get her pregnant; that might feed her. Cheater, robber, sponger. They keep everything and give nothing. I have been in misery for a long time, the misery of the poor world; it is not here that I might get a few crumbs. Those gods never let a drop fall.

Agathon the tragic is here. He is the Good, and he is not the Good. If he is the idea of the Good, I really think that the third good is necessary for us to conceive of Agathon and the Good together. The same goes for the god Eros: supposing he loves, a third Eros is necessary for us to conceive of what Eros participates in when he loves. We need a third comedy where Aristophanes and his comedy would participate. And so it goes, as much as one wishes. It is the argument of the third man. And then of the fourth man. The argument, like money, does not stop. It is the argument of the third banquet. Of the fourth, the fifth— there is no end to it. There must always be a third idea in which the couple formed by the object from this world and the idea of the object would participate. A series of banquets, thus a series of discourses or rather a series of stories, and the chain of Apollodorus, Aristodemus, etc., will necessarily find a Phoenix in the middle to be reborn indefinitely from its ashes. The story doesn't tell of the banquet, but of another story that tells, not yet of the banquet, but of another story that, again . . . It is the argument, no, the practice of the third story. And what is spoken of is what it is a question of: bifurcations and branchings. That is to say, parasites. The story indefinitely chases in front of itself what it speaks of. And I'm hungry.

Penia is knocked up; she gives birth to Love. Maybe we will finally know from this angle. Love also comes out of a black box, like Poros. The conjugated box of hunger and plenitude, of resources and poverty. Unviable fetus or viable child, birth or abortion, what do you say, you old midwife? Who is Love? Look at him well. He is a relation; he is the intermediary, $\mu\epsilon\tau\alpha\xi\acute{\upsilon}$, he is the passage again, the pass; he is what passes, quasi-object, quasi-subject, as I said before. He is the law of the series that we have followed since the beginning. Who is Love? He is the third man, the son of lack and of passage, pass and lack. We are going backwards again, cheated, tricked, robbed, mystified. What comes out of the box is the operational law that imposes the series of boxes.

Love is the third; it is third, between two. It is exactly the included third. Always between, between science and ignorance, neither
indigent nor wealthy, neither dead nor immortal, it is placed without
precision and with rigor in the laws of the logic of the fuzzy; it lives in
the fuzzy area of the threshold, homeless and near the door. It is the
third, the third man, excluded and included; it is the law of Platonism
and the law of this very book; it is; it is only the law of the story, of the
succession, of the series of stories. The old argument of the third man
was really that of the third indefinitely excluded, indefinitely included,
double frenzy.

Miserable, I went looking for food; they showed me the door.
Starved for love, I found love; it was only logic. Discourse, always
discourse. Faced with a veritable sea of beauty, I shall give birth only to
beautiful discourses. No referent, no bread, no wine, and no tenderness,
in this gallery of light and dark. Not a bit, not a drop, the desert of the
thing itself.

Attention! Alcibiades comes back, completely drunk. But who
is he then? I think I recognize him. Poros had left, reeling; he comes
back, my word!

The whole scene is reversed.

A moment, please, before returning to the entrance of Alcibiades.

Three ways to cure hiccoughs: interrupt breathing, gargle with
water for a while, tickle your nose until you sneeze.

The table is set; they speak of love, everyone in turn. It is Aristophanes' turn. But he has the hiccoughs and can't speak. A parasitic
noise that interrupts the series of discourses. It must be eliminated; these
sonorous spasms must be interrupted. To do that, his breathing must be
interrupted. It doesn't work? Make noise, says Eryximachus the doctor.
Either the continuous noise or gargling or a waterfall, canonic white
noise, in a cascade, or the bursting, catastrophic noise of the signal that
absorbs all the functions of our soul. And it finally works.

Plato says it as well as Horace or as La Fontaine with his two
rats. Agathon's parasites pay with words for the meal that the tragedian
pays for with his victory. They talk of love instead of bribes. The meal
is interrupted. By the discourse. Which is interrupted. By the hiccoughs.
Which is interrupted. By a sneeze. Noises.

It is not exactly like that. Or rather, it is true globally. Locally,
things are finer. Aristophanes, the comic, the great man, yields to Eryximachus, the doctor whose name contains, as we know, a burp. The
eructation of the old soldier. Everything that can be done with the

mouth is listed here: burping, hiccoughing, gargling, sneezing, breathing, discoursing (on love: kissing), eating, and drinking. They interrupt one another; they paralyze one another, a small mouth, around the mouth, of the large representation known as a banquet.

The burping doctor—the old soldier—has just cured the hiccoughing comic. And the latter is astonished: how could order, the good order of the body, have needed this hubbub? Must disorder be chased out by another disorder? Sneezing (or, respectively, gargling) chases away hiccoughs, reestablishes speech. A noise brings things back to order. Is this already the idea of order through noise? Aristophanes knew about clouds and chaos; he was a profound physicist.

He was a profound doctor. Reread the discourse of the burping struggle. Love is harmony. Medicine produces concord between the the elements, as do music and astronomy. Love and concord. What is health? Silence between the organs or the silence of the organs. No parasitic noise, that is harmony.

And yet, I sneeze, and now I've been cured.

We shall never know how a noise can be useful. How a parasite can be used. What noise makes the silence of the organs?

The mouth is the organ of the parasite. Its polyvalence is admirable: it is used for eating, speaking, yelling, singing, burping, hiccoughing, and gargling. Everything is there where it belongs, and nothing is forgotten.

Let us silently observe the increasing sequence of noises. The first little noises of the mouth parasite speech; slightly higher in intensity than the discourse, they chase it out: hiccough. Burping, sneezing, gargling, slightly higher than the hiccough, chase it away. They reestablish the discourse. A noise erases an order and reconstitutes another order. Noise destroys and noise can produce.

Here, with a besotted voice and the flute, Alcibiades brutally upsets what the hostess from Mantinea says; the outside door makes noise as if under the blows of a whole procession. First of all, let us observe the sequence of thresholds and doors: Socrates in ecstasy in the vestibule of the neighboring house; Poros, the path, leaving through the door of the gods' box; Love sleeps out, by the doors and in the streets; Alcibiades and Music make the door in the courtyard sound. All the apparitions and all the manifestations take place only in the fuzzy realm of the threshold. Of philosophy, of gods, of love, or of something else. Here appears . . . music, noise, din, and music. Noise destroys an order, the order of discourse; it also announces another order. Disorder is the end of order and sometimes its beginning. Noise turns around, like a revolving door. The beginning or the end of a system for the former; an entrance or exit for the latter. Exclusion, inclusion.

The logic of the parasite, on the side of the noise, remains coherent with the logic of the door by which enter the parasites who are going to drink or who have already drunk.

Poros leaves the box that we cannot enter, the box of the gods; we remain at the door, in the position of Penia. The reader, you or I, are in misery, in misery itself. But Alcibiades reenters, note well, reenters. He enters in Tragedy accompanied by Music—the allegory is too easy. Drunk, he has lost his principle of individualization. He enters, drunk like Poros, not on nectar, and he enters perhaps where Poros went out. The fact is that we have reached the point we wanted to reach. The door has returned to the new regime of noise; we finally attain the black box. In music.

The observer is finally amidst the observables. And Alcibiades speaks. He speaks of Socrates. He simply continues the series. Simple sneeze, his entrance; it reestablishes the series. Alcibiades praises Socrates, that is to say, love. Who is love? It is Socrates. And he is there. Finally the referent is there! Something or someone to chew on.

Deception. In Xenophon, Socrates or philosophy were already intermediaries, courtiers of love or procurers. Μεταξύ here, a while back, and μαστροπεία, now. Deception, it's even worse. Socrates resembles the Sileni, making noise with Pan's pipes and flutes, but above all, boxes that must be opened. The nightmare of the interminable series starts again; I have not stopped being misery.

But Alcibiades, who let me enter the feast, opens the box for me. And I am in it with him.

It is night. The trap worked well. Socrates has come to dinner. Finally the real feast. A new trap, he stays to sleep. Night falls; the lamp is put out, black box of a black box. The slaves have left and the door is closed, a closed box. All sleep, shadows. We have love in the flesh.

Finally.

What happens?

Nothing.

Disdain, derision, insult. He doesn't make love. And that is his glory, they say, his value and his marvelous status. They never did anything but speak, speak, speak of speaking, speak to say that they are going to speak, talky philosophy. No referent, no thing, no bread for Penia, no spread for the guests, no love for the lovers. Words to put you to sleep, wine to put you to sleep, words and wine to put the tragic and comic of existence to sleep. No bread for the poor, no love for the men, no wine for the feasts, nothing, always nothing, wind, nothing but wind.

They give you nothing; they keep everything for themselves; they will give nothing, not a drop, not a glass, not a single thing, words, nothing but words.

There was nothing to eat at this banquet. Old philosophy, *nouvelle cuisine.*

Up and awake, I put this discourse out the open window.

For once the explication worked. One fold [*pli*], two folds, three folds, the folds of folds, the law of folds, the theory of folds— when everything is unfolded, there is nothing inside, void and blank. The succession of empty black boxes was only the folds of a white sheet.

It was only prestidigitation, sleight-of-hand. How much time and life lost!

I'm capable, I'm prepared to tell this story. I was going up from Phalerum to the city when a man I knew recognized me and hailed me from far away. Hey! Wait for me.

Hey there! Wait for me! No, he didn't wait. We have all run behind him, climbed the hill, breathless, for over two thousand years. He didn't wait. He left nothing behind. When he had finally put everyone to sleep, he was a tranquil winner; he left to take care of himself in the gymnasium. As was his wont.

The furet moves around and around, the wooden furet, ladies and gentlemen.

Dialogue is an empty gallery where light and shadows play, where the noises of words reign, a little hell complicated with illusions and vanity.

Explication. I was a sailor; thus I know how to make complicated knots that are both beautiful and useful. Even a theory of knots, beautiful as well, has been produced in both pop topology and in the serious scientific variety. If you put them this way and the forces this way, they have a marvelous grasp. If you pull on each end, they untie almost by themselves; the bit of cord remains, smooth and flat. The knot is explained/unfolded [*s'explique*]; it comes undone; it is unknotted; it was nothing, nothing but folds, loops, and coils. When explained, the banquet shows the hungry its empty table.

The Devil ——————————————
————————————————— On Love

Alcibiades, completely drunk, crowned with ivy and violets and festooned with ribbons, enters the banquet, making a lot of noise. Noise, to-do, hubbubs, at the door of the room, besotted voices, the flute player, golden youth whoops it up. Alcibiades comes to drink at the guests' table; he interrupts the praises of Love; he is thus twice a parasite, by noise and by thirst. He is a parasite by his position in Athenian society.

Love has just been defined as an intermediary, μεταξύ. It is neither a god nor a mortal, neither rich nor poor; it occupies the middle spot between knowledge and ignorance. Love can be thought of as being among the fuzzy subsets. He is the included third. He is between. He sleeps in doorways, neither inside nor outside, neither excluded nor included, in the fuzzy realm of the threshold. The doorway with the door ajar. Poor, hard and dry, shoeless, his little naked feet in the snow, astute, crafty, sly, it could be Jean-Francois, Jean-François Rameau himself, a miserable parasite who is extremely intelligent, never outside, never inside, liminal, subliminal. What he wins he loses. He liquidates it.

Alcibiades, stumbling around, comes to sit down, to lie down next to Agathon. He runs, of course, directly to the host. He is in love with and jealous of him. Attention. Agathon is the host; he is the beloved; he is the Good. Let us think about three things at the same time: that Alcibiades runs toward the Good, in allegory; toward his love, toward discourse for example; and toward the one who offers drink to parasite him. One idea in three people or three ideas in one name. This is cause for reflection. Plato said it all, but he killed the parasite.

The ribbons come undone, as did the knots a while back, and

the pleasure-seeker is blinded a bit by them. Agathon orders him to be seated as the third at the table: take off his shoes! Alcibiades, suddenly sober: who is the third man? Am I the third; who is the third? The argument is there as well as the principle, in the clouds of the wine of Thasos and on the bed of the Good.

Here is the Trinity: philosophy, its object (I mean Socrates and the Good in person), plus this drunken young man between them. And if he is between, he is Love. Shoeless, for his shoes have just been taken off, coming from the threshold and from the door, between two winds, fuzzy-minded, ignorant and knowledgeable, demagogue and shameful, neither excluded nor included, invited by force and throwing in trouble and confusion, but still pursuing, beyond noise and through noise, the order of discourse. He is between; he is a parasite; he wants to get Socrates' relation to the Good from him.

He loves Agathon, he wants to be loved by Socrates, and he doesn't want Socrates to love Agathon. He want to divert his relation to the Good. He is really parasitic. He enters the chain of discourses, he praises Socrates, and thus, according to the rule of the *Symposium,* he praised Love and Socrates is Love. Suddenly, Socrates must move between Alcibiades and Agathon. He intercepts their love; he is between; he is a parasite. But Alcibiades, who loves Agathon, asks Agathon to come between him and Socrates, for each to be able to see and touch him, but the philosopher refuses for a reason touching on the order of discourse, as is usual. He can't stand it if Good is in the situation of Love. The possible combinations are all exhausted. Each of the three is the third to the two others.

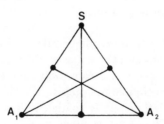

This third can be invited on the bed, to eat, to drink, to sing, or to praise. He is included. He can disturb the two others, and situated in the very middle, he prevents them from seeing or understanding each other: he intercepts all their relations. They have to pass by him to pass each other the cup, or something in general; they must pass by him for passing to occur. For the disruption to stop, he must be excluded. The saved and successful dialogue is this excluded third. We are there at last.

The question is no longer that of love. It is more general. Of the third: what he is and what he does. Once I was at the house of a host,

or of my father, my brother, or someone I loved. Once I received a tessera. So complex, so serrated, fractal, that it is a memorial. It is a double
recognition. On the side of knowledge: it is this one among others; the
tessera is recognition by specificity. There is only one piece in the world
that fits together perfectly with mine. Stereospecificity, which we have
known about since it mimicked the things hidden deep in our body by
their littleness, but also things less well hidden, yet still secret. On the
side of emotion, it is thanking. I carry the symbol on me and in me. You
carry the symbol on you and in you. Like a hyphen [*trait d'union*]. This
is mine, on me; it is in you, yours; tessera of exchange, a hyphen, a
"trait of union." The symbol is a quasi-object and a quasi-subject; undoubtedly you are and I am a symbol.

    Our bodies are memorials, by the wrinkles, the folds, the hol-
lows, and the forms, a sculpture made individual by time, what remains
of its style. So singularly serrated that it is a tessera. This symbol brings
us together, with its multiple mortises and tenons, unites us, throws us
together. This third disappears when two make one. The token is thrown
away. The successful dialogue is also this excluded third. If two equal
one, then three equal zero. Curious arithmetic of love. The symbol is
erased in front of its function; we knew this.

    There is no more asymmetry in this new space. The exchange is
assured; it is equilibrated. Must we speak of symbolic exchange? We can,
of course. But is it necessary? Not really, since a symbol is this bringing
together that is the condition of the exchange.

    The primitive value is the abuse value; the primary relation is
asymmetrical. There must be a symbol, a bringing together, for the exchange to take place or be possible.

    Somewhere Rudyard Kipling talks about two beings in love
separated by two oceans and three seas who, since their childhood, have
travelled in the same space of dreams and have moved forward by the
same steps in a fixed antiquity and prehistory. Their common specificity
is the map of their Utopia. It is spatial; it is a stereospecificity. It is
complex, serrated, fractal, it is a quasi-globe. Geography is full of
tesserae; *départements* with complicated boundaries interlink; the
Finistère plunges into the Iroise; but even more, at a great distance,
Africa, separated from the Americas, commemorates, in its form, its
former interlinking with them. The world such as it is is a puzzle, and
not only because of the man-made, arbitrary boundaries. Everything
happens as if our history—madness, murders, and chance—only reproduced, after all is said and done, the immobile movement of the most
deeply hidden tectonic plates.

    Kipling's two beings move in a space. The complex charting of their trip is the symbol of their union. The baroque globe of Tenderness is perhaps the universal psyche. More than three hundred years ago, even before Descartes, that happened by figures and movements.* People moved from place to place, from local singularities to local singularities of space. Was *L'Astrée* ever thought of differently? By displacements and condensations, that is to say, by movements and by figures. Is it necessary to overload the thing with energetics and topology and with a transcendental theory of nomination? Perhaps, but we must admit that it doesn't say much more than does Kipling, that is to say, than those pre-Cartesian charts, that is to say, than the tessera. The symbolic soul is an extent where singularities move and travel. And the symbol is a map.

After Alcibiades' praise of him, Socrates becomes ironic and plays on a word.† This game is a knot, a singularity, once again. You have beaten around the bush with all your circumlocutions. Alcibiades: περιβαλλόμενος. Your discourse of praise displaces our attention; you have another aim than the obvious one; you hide it. In fact, you want us, Agathon and me, to quarrel: διαβάλλειν. You beat around the bush to separate us; you are jealous of him and me; you keep turning around to have us quarrel so you can sit or lie down between the two of us: διαλάβη. To put yourself between. The last two alliterate, a little noise calling us. A fascination plays on that side, in a bundle [*faisceau*], in a sonorous knot. The first two play on meaning; they pull us toward the repeated word, their common verb. But suddenly, they play together with the συμβάλλειν of the symbol. Attention. You're turning round, Alcibiades (περί); you are looking for a place between us—you aim to have us quarrel (διά); you don't want us to be united (σύν). Συμβάλλειν, reunite; διαβάλλειν, separate. The *Symposium* ends badly; we are far from the marvelous tesserae of Aristophanes. The one between separates, it seems, more than he unites.

Here then is the game of the third; it is simple as ABC, and it is no longer a play on words; it may be a game of death. It turns around; it wanders; it waits. It looks out; it spies on. It is placed between; it intercepts; it forbids. Σύν or διά. It unites or it separates. One and the other, one or the other. It also works at exclusion and inclusion, just as it was the object, the passive party, sometimes the victim, of the two operations. Now it is their subject.

If it includes, it is the symbol. If it excludes, it is the dia-bol.

The appearance of the Devil, in person.

---

*Serres is alluding to Pascal's comment on Descartes (L.84/B.79). —Trans.
†*Symposium*, 222c. —Trans.

In white, silent and absent.

Plato doesn't say so; he can't say it—he hasn't formulated its concept. In the square of the game, in the logical or dialogical square of the dialogue, the place of the devil remains blank and vacant.

Noise, hubbub, din. A global din, general disorder hides this discovery like a cataract. At the time they get up to change places, to see who will be the Devil, to see who will make whom be the Devil, when Socrates had won the game, the bastard. The flood of noise erases the crime.

That, of course, happens near the door. No longer a besotted reveler, Poros or Alcibiades, but a whole band, a crowd. They enter, the text says, because someone was leaving. The input and the output, well-distinguished when the god Resource was going out or when the young man was coming in with his flute and his violets, are now mixed. The fuzziness of the threshold becomes the fuzziness of its function. It is no longer a valve; it is no longer a semiconductor; the two function together. We no longer know who enters or who leaves; everything enters and leaves, no longer a parasite, but a sequence, a band, Alcibiades or Poros in the plural; when a system admits a parasite, the parasite multiplies immediately, reproduces, makes a chain, a crowd, a number, an inundation. At the end of a few hours one single bacterium will have produced several million. Epidemic. The joyous band heads straight for the beds, toward the table. It occupies space; it goes right to the center.

A global din fills the room now; nothing was in order any more (οὐκέτι ἐν κόσμῳ οὐδενί). Noise has destroyed the system. This noise is perhaps the very figure of what was not said, or of the one who was not recognized, lying there, monstrously, on the bed. Victory to the powers of noise; victory to the parasites, to all the parasites. To those who will drink endless quantities of wine (πίνειν πάμπολυν οἶνον) or who will be obliged to do so; to those who will produce an indescribable clamor; to those who destroy the system they feed on, by multiplying. And finally, disorder reigns, by infection, by depletion of stocks, and by noise.

The Devil won the game. At the beginning of the discourses, they said that Love was the god between the gods; he was the Devil. Everyone had thought him symbolic; he was diabolical.

The dialogue said nothing. It disappears in the noise. Devoured by the parasites. Even the white is covered with the censor's ink.

The symbolic and the diabolical drink, looking at each other until one of them, beaten, falls asleep. They pass each other the third cup. They are three. They are two. They are one. It all depends.

Once more we must begin, and for the last time, beyond drunkenness and the night. Henceforth, the parasites are neutralized. Some of the guests have left the room, where the noises have abated; the others, drunk from having imbibed the whole night through, snore away, collapsed on the beds. The obscurity is long; here is the dawn; the cock crows to the Sun God.

A new noise, outside; the return of order of the Good, which will reign over the pseudo-cadavers of the drunken cave. The sleeping observer opens his eyes. The trio are still awake. Aristophanes, author of the symbol, has replaced Alcibiades, supporter of the Devil. The three drink more and more; they speak; they still speak. They pass the cup around clockwise. *Hoc memorabile est; ego tu sum, tu es ego; uni animi sumus.* With the passing of the quasi-object, we are the same, a symbol. Are we really?

No, no, still no. Philosophy with its cold-heartedness, with its military strategy, glory to Socrates who was courageous in combat, philosophy, with its black boxes, with its blank book, doesn't want that. It wants to distinguish; it wants to separate; it wants to be separate, distinguished; it wants to be a mistress and to be rare. Yes, Agathon, yes, Aristophanes, you are the same among yourselves; drink together and pass each other the cup; tragedy is comedy; comedy is tragedy; the included third; this is something else; the principle of individuation is abolished. These two make one, and they fall asleep. It is quite true that the theater is the theater, some sort of opiate to put you to sleep. I said that the comedy of Aristophanes is Good itself! We have all known that for a long time.

Socrates gets out unscathed. His beautiful individuation is different and evil. Ugly and evil. He runs to take care of his individuation at the gymnasium. To make it flexible, to clean it, to make it effective.

Does the Devil take care of anything else but the Devil? Know thyself, and never another.

The Worst Definition

Ulysses won the contest, making a simple arrow, the relation, irreversible, with no possible return, through the lined-up axes, the iron that separates.

End of the *Odyssey*, amidst the corpses.

The parasite doesn't stop. It doesn't stop eating or drinking or yelling or burping or making thousands of noises or filling space with its swarming and din. The parasite is an expansion; it runs and grows. It invades and occupies. It overflows, all of a sudden, from these pages. Inundation, swelling waters.

Noises, din, clamor, fury, tumult, and noncomprehension.

Asymmetry, violence, murder and carnage, arrow and axe.

Misery, hunger: poverty, begging at the doors; those who eat too much, drunk, those who never have anything but wind to chew on.

Sickness, epidemics, the plague.

Animal metamorphoses: bacteria, insects, rats, wolves, lions, and foxes; animals devoured by politics, flowers of the bouquet of love eaten by a hare, lovers separated by the Devil.

Inundation of hell, swelling up of history. Here is the Devil then; no, no, I wasn't expecting him. He's come; the book is done, as if it were burnt. I didn't know that it was irreparably a book of Evil [Mal]. The Evil of noise, of the song of hell, thundering; of hunger, illness, pain; dressed as animals and now undressed as a naked man; of Evil, quite simply. Meal, banquet, feast of the Devil.

It finally is separate from me. Thus the horrible insect slowly left my room, through the creaking door, one May morning, in Venice.

Something had begun.

Quiet, serene, no anxiety. The high seas.

December 1975–August 1979

Stories, Animals

Genesis — The Story of Joseph
The Acts of the Apostles — Pentecost
Homer — *The Odyssey*
Xenophon — *The Art of Hunting*
Plato — *Symposium*
La Fontaine — "Le Rat de ville et le rat de champs" (*Fables* I, 9)
"Le Satyre et le passant" (V, 7)
"Le Villageois et le serpent" (VI, 13)
"L'Huître et les plaideurs" (IX, 9)
"L'Homme et la couleuvre" (X, 1)
"Le Lion malade et le renard" (VI, 14)
"Simonide préservé par les dieux" (I, 14)
"La Tortue et les deux canards" (X, 2)
"La Grenouille et le rat" (IV, 11)
"Le Cheval s'étant voulu se venger du cerf" (IV, 13)
"Le Loup et le renard" (XI, 6)
"Le Jardinier et son seigneur" (IV, 4)
"La Cigale et la fourmi" (I, 1)
"Philémon et Baucis" (appendix to the *Fables*)
"Le Corbeau et le renard" (I, 2)
"Le Singe et le chat" (IX, 17)
"Le Loup et l'agneau" (I, 10)
Molière — *Le Tartuffe; ou, L'Imposteur*
Amphitryon
Rousseau — *Les Confessions*
Rousseau, juge de Jean-Jacques

THE JOHNS HOPKINS UNIVERSITY PRESS

The Parasite

This book was composed in Baskerville text and Palatino display type by Horne Associates, Inc., from a design by Cynthia Hotvedt. It was printed on S.D. Warren's 50-lb. Sebago Eggshell paper and bound in Kivar-5 by the Maple Press Company.